Staging
Alternative
Albertas

Experimental
Drama in
Edmonton

Staging Alternative Albertas: Experimental Drama in Edmonton

edited, and with introductions by
Patricia Demers and Rosalind Kerr

Playwrights Canada Press
Toronto • Canada

Playwrights Canada Press
54 Wolseley St., 2nd fl. Toronto, Ontario CANADA M5T 1A5
416-703-0013   fax 416-703-0059
orders@puc.ca • publisher@playwrightscanada.com • www.playwrightscanada.com

Playwrights Canada Press acknowledges the support of the taxpayers
of Canada through The Canada Council for the Arts and
the Ontario Arts Council.

Production manager/cover design: Jodi Armstrong.

National Library of Canada Cataloguing in Publication Data

Main entry under title:

Staging alternative Albertas : experimental drama in Edmonton

ISBN 0-88654-618-4

1. Canadian drama (English)—Alberta. 2. Canadian drama (English)—21st century.
I. Demers, Patricia, 1946- II. Kerr, Rosalind, 1941-

PS8315.5.A43S68 2002   C812'608'011   C2001-902119-4
PR9198.2.A42S68 2002

First edition: May 2002.
Printed and bound by AGMV Marquis at Quebec, Canada.

Surface Tension
Elyne Quan

Sacred Time
Brian Webb

Burnt Remains
Scott Sharplin

Love's Kitchen
Anna Marie Sewell

"As Long As the Sun Shines"
Christina Grant & Doug Dunn

My Perfect Heaven
Jonathan Christenson &
Joseph Robert Tremblay

Tales from the Hospital
Trevor Schmidt

La Maison Rouge
Manon Beaudoin

Songs in *Love's Kitchen*
words and music © Anna Marie Sewell and Cathy Sewell
"Where Do You Go?"
"He Only Wants"
"Heart of a Nation"

Cover photos (clockwise from top left):
• *"As Long As the Sun Shines"* – Moostoos, Chief of the Sucker Creek Band and brother of Keenooshayo. (Provincial Archives of Alberta)
• *My Perfect Heaven* – Joey Tremblay as Barefoot Boy, August, 1996. (Photo by Howard Silverman.)
• *Tales from the Hospital* – Linda Grass as Nurse in "Cross." Unconscious Collective 1998. (Photo courtesy Trevor Schmidt and the Unconscious Collective.)
• *La Maison Rouge* – The death of Blanche, featuring Denise Kenney as Rose and Anne Mansfield as La Mère, Vanessa Porteous as Blanche and John Ullyatt as Rostand. La Cité francophone production of La Maison Rouge, Edmonton, 1997. (Photo courtesy Ed Ellis.)

We dedicate this text to Andrew Currier

and

to the memory of Margaret Demers.

ACKNOWLEDGEMENTS

This collaboration about experiments in dramatic form has been itself an experiment. We have discovered that Drama and English "types" can work together. As well as thanking our playwrights for the privilege of presenting their work to a wider audience, we want to thank one another: our marathon hours of debate and rehash have taught us a lot about the reciprocity of textual analysis and stage realities. We would also like to thank the photographers who have allowed us to use their work. For helpful, enabling suggestions and expert assistance we are grateful to David Leonard of Alberta Historic Sites, Donna MacNeil of the Provincial Archives, Ruth McConnell of the Ethnology Program at the Provincial Museum of Alberta, Jim Miller of the University of Saskatchewan, Emily Springer of the Provincial Archives, and Al Willier of the Lesser Slave Lake Band Council. Kris Calhoun cracked several bureaucratic codes for us, Liz Grieve provided valuable editorial information, and Theresa Daniels was supremely patient with our numerous requests for format and program changes. Drama students Joelle Lemmen and David DeGagné supplied helpful background observations on the staging of *Sacred Time*. We also acknowledge with gratitude a grant from the Support for the Advancement of Scholarship Research Fund of the Faculty of Arts of the University of Alberta.

TABLE OF CONTENTS

INTRODUCTION

TEXT AND SPACE

These produced but previously unpublished one-act plays all explore Albertan space – as a geographical locale, a collage of mental habits, signs of identity. They open up physical, psychological and semiotic space. Representing eight different companies, the plays in this collection offer glimpses of a postmodern Alberta. The cultural logic of *Staging Alternative Albertas* stresses fragmentation and pastiche rather than unity and compositional poise. The deliberately fractured, splintered, jagged picture of Alberta, reconfigured with each kaleidoscopic shift, does not fit into neat frames or even into strict cartographic boundaries. For the space these plays summon into being with words and images is both a place and a gap, a specific location and an often haunted absence.

Braiding urban and rural locales, reflecting Aboriginal, Métis, Chinese, French and English linguistic backgrounds, and combining straight and gay sensibilities, these one-acts extend our understanding of dramaturgical form and the production of meaning. They enact traditions of alterity, reinvent and retell history, play with narrative and visual techniques. Undermining the smugness of economic stability, they also overturn stereotypes of rugged individualism and redneck bravado. Their composite but constantly shifting picture of Alberta is anything but placid and self-satisfied.

Elyne Quan's play explores the transnational space opened up by visual metaphors in the creation of a Chinese-Canadian female identity. Scott Sharplin's play uncovers the violent space of writing in textual and embodied forms. Christina Grant and Doug Dunn's historiographic pageant of the signing of Treaty 8 creates a hermeneutic space in which the audience strives to understand, to weigh and consider, the gains and losses of this event. Trevor Schmidt's quartet of tales implicates the reader or spectator in the sanitizing, eugenic space of biopower, as manifest in the dehumanizing tortures of a large mental institution. Brian Webb's performance piece combines dance, narrative, video and music to link the brutalizing spaces of an elk hunt and urban stalking. In the domestic space of a kitchen the Sewell sisters refashion family stories and songs to reclaim traditions of Aboriginal integration. Jonathan Christenson and Joey Tremblay weave poetry and music to ironize the predatoriness and alienation of queer space. Manon Beaudoin constructs the symbol of the house as a receptacle of the torment and secrets of gothic space.

Within this range of textual spaces there are also many shared features and motifs. A sign of either cohesion or alienation, music operates in several registers within the collection. In Grant and Dunn's *"As Long As the Sun Shines"* and the Sewells' *Love's Kitchen* it is a force to integrate, bind and prophesy. The mournful cello obbligato of Beaudoin's *La Maison Rouge* supplies what she aptly calls "the pulse of the story." By contrast, Christenson and Tremblay's *My Perfect Heaven* and Webb's *Sacred Time* underline the difference between their neo-primitive scenes and original, adapted scores. Ironic snippets from Rodgers and Hammerstein's "It's a grand night for singing" in *My Perfect Heaven* and percussive, passionate recreations of Miles Davis' "Witch's Brew" in *Sacred Time* stress the violence of the sexual hunt. The motif of feathers creates similar ironic distances – from the dreamy fantasies of the child Blanche and the abrupt end of her life in *La Maison Rouge*, the costumed detail of blue-black cock feathers which is recalled at the time of the most bloody and violating action in *Sacred Time,* and the dream of the Barefoot Boy who envisions himself soaring high in blue feathers amidst the abjection of *My Perfect Heaven*. Text itself and the act of writing convey their own powerful voltage in these plays. Sharplin's *Burnt Remains* not only debates the morality of preserving virulent Nazi hate literature but highlights the power of the Web to expose the hidden, denied, familial violence recorded in a sister's notebook. Texts exist in more than print form. As we realize from *Burnt Remains* and *Sacred Time,* they can be incised on and enacted through bodies; in *'As Long As the Sun Shines'* they can be summoned up through different recollections of and investments in the parchment of a treaty document; and in *La Maison Rouge* they can be carved and contained in the family house itself.

The spaces in this collection represent absence as much as presence; they figure the gaps and fissures separating people. Although the pictures in *Surface Tension* and songs in *Love's Kitchen* enable recognition, acceptance and a degree of harmony, this sense of personal or communal integration is the exception rather than the rule. The wrenching divides between brother and sister in *Burnt Remains*, patient and nurse in *Tales from the Hospital,* mother and son in *La Maison Rouge*, Barefoot Boy and his family in *My Perfect Heaven* and the hunter and the numinous in *Sacred Time* indicate that these distances can never be bridged. No easy meliorism or redemptive intervention is foreseen. Disgust, fear and envy, as enacted in overpowering violence, are not to be dislodged.

Moreover, the reader or viewer cannot stay detached, uninvolved, unaffected. Ironically, in creating divides and distances, these plays reach out and grab us by the moral lapels. We are implicated in the action. We cannot avoid asking ourselves questions about culpability in cultural regimes of deceit and hatred and abuse. Ultimately the selections in *Staging Alternative Albertas* engage us all in the space of debate.

Patricia Demers and Rosalind Kerr

SURFACE TENSION

by
Elyne Quan

INTRODUCTION TO *SURFACE TENSION*

"don't have an accent. don't dress funny. don't draw attention. don't speak Chinese in public. pretend you don't know it. don't get offended. don't get offended. don't use chopsticks. don't eat weird food. don't associate with other Chinese people. The ones who have accents. they're different. they're not the same as you. you're not like them. you're different. you're just like everyone else."

(Quan, Surface Tension)

Elyne Quan's *Surface Tension* is, as its title implies, an ironic exploration of surface appearances and the tensions created by the undue importance attached to them. In her particular case, it is about her concerns as a second-generation Chinese Canadian female growing up in the predominantly white Edmonton of the 1980s. Created specifically to address issues of Asian ancestry, Quan's piece was inspired by the anger she felt after an exchange visit to England:

> I realized that I had developed a comfortable and safe environment at home in Canada, that I was able to operate in relative ethnic neutrality because people knew me personally and knew of me by things other than my Chinese background. In Britain I was an unknown. My safety net was removed and people interacted with me as an Asian person. Saying I was from Canada when I was in Britain was never a satisfying enough answer for most people.
>
> I was hassled at customs. I was treated as if I was going to try to "infiltrate the country" (Hong Kong had not yet reverted back to mainland China rule and many Hong Kong citizens were trying to find ways out). I was treated as if I probably worked in a "Chinese Take-away" or a Laundromat. And for most of the time I was there I couldn't figure out what was wrong. I couldn't recognize what was happening to me. I didn't want it to be about race. But after a while, after talking to other Britons, other people of visible minorities who had experienced similar treatment, it became the only conclusion I could come to. And it made me angry.

The piece works by exposing the gaps between her obviously Chinese physical appearance and her just as obvious enculturation as an English Canadian. Rather than being a quest for rediscovering an essential Chineseness, it's about creating a transnational space where she can exist as both Chinese and Canadian.[1] Quan's quest for this more fluid sense of self is strikingly staged through her interactions with a series of images.

Using herself as the centrepiece, Quan appears for most of the show wearing a white paper dress on which various images can be projected as she tries out a variety of identities that she has either inhabited or fantasized about. The provisional quality of the paper cut-out dress, echoed in the paper screens and crumpled paper on the floor reinforced the sense that everything was being tried on. Quan begins by striking up the pose of a fashion model as she confides to us that she had always wanted to be taller and blonde, a revelation that leads her to confess that she developed such a desire as a small child when being a cute little blonde with curly hair was her ultimate goal. The shock effect of recognizing that she had chosen her ideas of beauty from western models is then made poignantly real by the actual photo of herself with permed hair in her grade-six school photo. Having revealed her difficulties in attaining this western ideal of feminine beauty, she now juxtaposes these with several equally mediatized images of Asian women, inhabiting each in turn as the image is projected on her dress.

Still not ready to speak as herself, Quan now speaks about a series of "friends" who experience multiple identity crises because of their mixed heritage. It is at this point that the endless overlays we have witnessed begin to crumble and the truth emerges. The last time she makes the "I · have · a · friend · who · wishes · she · was..." (10) statement, she offers four impossible adjectives: "- taller, - blond, - beautiful, - perfect" as possible completions. In contrast to the silent visual projection of these words, she finally admits out loud to the audience that what her friend wants is to be "different," someone other than herself.

For the rest of the piece, Quan's sense of "difference" will lead her to try to balance her dreams of herself with a more accurate one. At this point, we have been prepared for the climactic sequence when she gradually redresses herself in her grandmother's outfit and finds that the clothes are a perfect fit. The recorded sound of her mother's voice describing the garments and relating their history deepens our sense of this enactment of embracing and owning the past.

The Quan who checks herself out in the mirror, puts the paper dress back on the hanger, and exits the stage has found her synthesis of the two cultures.

Elyne Quan graduated from the University of Alberta with an Honours BA in Drama. A freelancer actor, writer and director, she has been a Co-Director for Concrete Theatre from 1996 to 2002. Recent performing credits include *Naomi's Road*, *Agenda*, and *The Garden of Forking Paths*. Directing credits include *Are We There Yet*? which won an Elizabeth Sterling Haynes award for Outstanding Production for Theatre for Young Audiences. She is currently at work on a new play entitled *One Block Radius* as well as several other performance pieces, including *Lig & Bittle*, co-written with Jared Matsunaga-Turnbull, a play for young people about size difference, friendship and acceptance, which will feature the writers as performers. Her most recent work with Concrete Theatre, *What*, the third segment in a piece entitled *Rice*, was created and performed by Quan with Mieko Ouchi and Jared Matsunaga-Turnbull. Each of three stories evokes an ancestral memory. Quan's *What* is a heart-rending account of fragmented family relationships.

Quan had done most of her work with Concrete Theatre, an Edmonton-based company of artists, that works in the community using popular theatre to promote change. The company mandate grows out of the belief that theatre is a "highly effective tool for building awareness, identifying important issues, developing communication and negotiation skills and creating an environment for change." Concrete Theatre works with community groups, encouraging them to explore personal experience, confront issues and analyze situations, and to help them communicate their discoveries to others through dramatic presentations.

NOTES

[1] Quan's interest in her own transnational position reveals the kinds of oppression connected with race and gender that many researchers are now exploring. See: *Transnationalism from Below*, eds. Michael Peter Smith and Luis Eduardo Guarnizo (New Brunswick, N.J.: Transaction Publishers, 1998); *Nations Unbound: Transnational Projects, Postcolonial Predicaments, and Deterritorialized Nation-States*, eds. Linda Basch, Nina Glick Schiller, and Cristina Szanton Blanc (Langhorne, PA: Gordon & Breach, 1994). The following definition of transnationalism indicates the approach these researchers are taking:

> a series of economic, sociocultural, and political practices and processes which transcend the confines of the territorially bounded jurisdiction on the nation-state and are an essential part of the normal lives of those involved (Guarnizo 1996:5). These ties are forged and sustained by immigrants through multi-stranded social relations that link together their societies of origin and settlement (Basch et al:7).

Surface Tension was originally produced by Concrete Theatre at Catalyst Theatre, Edmonton, Alberta, Canada in 1998 for *Triptych*, a collection of three performance installations created by three Asian Canadian women focusing on ancestry. The role of the woman was played by Elyne Quan. Installation design was provided by Melinda Sutton, sound design by Dave Owen, costume design by Elyne Quan and stage management provided by Wayne Paquette. Assistance was provided by The Canada Council for the Arts.

Concrete Theatre is an Edmonton-based social action theatre company that uses theatre to promote change. It has a mandate of presenting work from voices outside the mainstream.

SET
The set is a simple 6' x 8' flat platform with three one-metre wide strips of white paper hung equally spaced as the backdrop. The strips also act as screens for the images projected onto them. Scraps of paper litter the periphery of the playing space.

COSTUMES
The original white dress was constructed out of white rolled mulberry paper, crinkled and sewn by hand. It serves a dual purpose of shaping the space the woman occupies and being the screen which images are projected on. The Grandmother's outfit is a bright hand-sewn two-piece outfit with sleeves, frogs and a traditional wrap pant-waist.

SLIDES
The original production featured slides of the actor in different costumes projected onto herself. The Chinese characters mentioned in the script were projected primarily onto the strips of paper along the backdrop. Other slides or images are specified throughout the text.

SOUND
The sound cues for cymbal crashes are intended to sound like Beijing Opera cymbal crashes, not drum kit or marching band cymbal crashes. A variety of cymbal crashes, cymbal and wood block, or wood block, lends variation to the soundscape. The recorded segments (of the woman's and of the mother's voices) were recorded on tape for a live, imperfect sound.

SURFACE TENSION
by Elyne Quan

Music is playing as audience enters the space. Ideally it would be something from Rodgers and Hammerstein's Flower Drum Song *(i.e.* I Enjoy Being a Girl*). The stage has strips of paper of various sizes scattered upstage. There are three long screens along the back of the stage.*

WOMAN enters towards the end of the song, humming along to the last few bars of music. She is wearing an A-line, floor-length white paper dress.

She strikes a fashion model pose as song finishes. Holds pose through speech.

WOMAN
(*sigh*) I've always wanted to be taller.

I've wanted to be taller and… different. Sometimes blond. That would be something. I clearly remember that in grade one I wished I had blond curly hair so I could wear pale blue ribbons in it and be *really* cute. Not just kind of cute, but really cute. I was walking home from school for lunch. The sun was out and it was a beautiful day. I was looking down at the ground at my silhouette—specifically my head—and I remember wishing that I had curly blond hair. I would get noticed. Pale blue ribbons and pig tales. And a matching dress, frilly but not too frilly. And matching little blue shoes with white patent bows on them. Shoes can make or break an outfit, you know.

> *Breaks out of pose.*

Well as hard as I wished I never became blond. Go figure. And dye jobs in the early eighties weren't the science they are now. Curly blond hair for a little Chinese girl was a bit far fetched so I did the best I could. Perms! So I could actually have curly pigtails if I wanted them. Of course I was older by now so pigtails were out of the question.

> *Finds a large 8" x 10" school photo from grade 6 amongst the paper on stage. Crosses the stage presenting the photo to the audience.*

(*in a decidedly little girl Valley-esque manner*) Parted down the middle and curly and away from my face. Like the girl in Aha's "Take On Me" video.

> *Looks at the photo.*

Yeah. So I had bad hair all the way through my formative years. But hair isn't everything. For example:

She gestures to the first screen SL. Steps in front of one the screens where a
a slide of an image conscious Asian woman is projected. The woman is
young, hip, and wears designer clothing. For each of the images she adopts
a pose that is complimentary to the projected image but retains the image
on her dress.

It does reflect who you are. I know it's kind of bad but that's the way things
are. Like if you walked into a store with dirty or ripped clothes people
aren't going to run to serve you, right? Right? I don't like it either but that's
how things work. Besides, there's nothing wrong with wanting to dress
nice. No matter what your weird friends say. I'm not being judgmental.
They're weird! I'm sure they're all nice but, god, do they have to dress like
that? Fine whatever. Oh, can you pass me my shoes? My Nine West ones.
The black pair… mmm… maybe the brown… no the black. What do you
think? You're right. Thanks.

Steps out of image.

Compared with:

Slide changes to a two-person slide with a "Miss Saigon" motif – big,
strong Caucasian male carrying a gun and an Asian woman in a position
that says "protect me." The identity of the male should not be seen. Face
obscured or slide not extended to include his face.

He likes to be in charge. Isn't he cute? I let him do what he wants. Men
should be allowed to do what they think they want to do. Otherwise they
feel inferior and that's bad. Oh I have ways of getting what I want. I pout.
See? I'll demonstrate. (*pouts*) He usually caves in. And he still gets to feel
like he's in charge! He calls me his little China doll. Fragile and delicate.
I make sure I need rescuing all the time. Otherwise where's the fun and
adventure? Nobody wants to see me saving the day. Can you imagine me
with a big uzi strapped across my body beating off the bad guy? (*starts to*
giggle) Sorry, that just is so funny… tee hee hee…

Slide changes to a sex vixen. Heavy accent and straight from Playboy's
massage series, "The Secrets of Oriental Massage."

Oriental massage is my specialty. I can show you ways you never knew
existed. My Asian mysteries will mystify and amaze you and you will be
asking for more. I will walk on your back and serve your every need.

Slide changes to a girl from one of those cheesy low budget Kung Fu films.

You killed my family and burned my village. Now you must pay for it with
your life. HI YA! (*goes into a cheesy Kung Fu sequence that eventually ends with*
all the enemies defeated – a gong is sounded – big ceremonial bow at Centre)

Elyne Quan as WOMAN (Concrete Theatre at Catalyst Theatre, Edmonton, 1998).
Photo by Ian Jackson, courtesy of Concrete Theatre.

Slide of characters for "friend" comes up on the centre screen, overlapping her body. The movements are very still, very presentational and slow. Floating, arms up.

I · have · a · friend · who · thinks · that · everything · Chinese · is · bad · and · everything · Western, · well · American · is · good.

I · have · a · friend · that · will · only · date · white · guys · because · she · thinks · that · a · Chinese · guy · would · expect · her · to · be · subservient · and · weak.

I · have · a · friend · who · only · dates · Chinese · guys · because · she · thinks · that · they · understand · her · better · and · all · the · traditions. And · because · she · can · bring · him · home.

I · have · a · friend · who · thinks · that · if · she · told · her · parents · she · was · a · lesbian, · they · wouldn't · mind · as · long · as · her · partner · was · Chinese... and · a · doctor.

I · have · a · friend · who · doesn't · admit · that · she · is · Chinese. She · is · Canadian. Her · parents · just · happen · to · be · from · China.

I · have · a · friend · who · wishes · she · was...

She falls to the right. Slides are projected with the following words as she watches them change:

- *taller*

- *blond*

- *beautiful*

- *perfect*

She looks out at audience.

...different.

Slides pop up SC with the Chinese characters for "beauty." Recorded text. Slow, methodical movement. Movements indicate the woman is unhappy with her face as she looks in a mirror.

Sound cue – recorded text:

"don't have an accent. don't dress funny. don't draw attention. don't speak Chinese in public. pretend you don't know it. don't get offended. don't get offended. don't use chopsticks. don't eat weird food. don't associate with other Chinese people. the ones who have accents. they're different. they're

Elyne Quan as WOMAN with Chinese letters (Concrete Theatre, 1998).
Photo by Ian Jackson, courtesy of Concrete Theatre.

not the same as you. you're not like them. you're different. you're just like everyone else."

> *Cymbal crash. Slides out. Recorded text ends. The following speech is said over top of Tai Chi movement.*

Five foot one. One hundred and three pounds. Brown eyes. Black hair. Size six shoes. Sometimes five and a half depending on the manufacturer and style. Skin? Not bad. Not great either. Average fitness level. Could work out more. Single. Born and raised in this city. Right handed. University educated. Allergies? Yes. Pollen, mold, cat fur, dust. Mild asthma. Near-sighted. Thirty-four twenty six thirty six one seven zero eight seven three seven four seven three two five six four two.

> *Cymbal crash with wood block. Slides on SR & SL appear with the Chinese characters for "dream" and "mirror." Beijing Opera music is in the back-ground. Distinct opera gestures are made as text is spoken.*

In my dreams I'm not how I am now. I see myself differently. I feel... not the same as how I feel now, when I'm awake. I know I'm myself and not someone else, yet I'm not the same. Sometimes I am shocked when I wake and see myself in the mirror. I don't expect to see... me. For a moment I think I see the remnants of the person I am in my dreams... and then it fades away. And I'm left with... (*pause*)

In my dreams, I'm the star of the movie. And I'm comfortable in myself. I know what I look like without having to see my reflection and what I look like is not what I see here. (*beat*) Which makes me wonder... which one do you see?

> *Freeze. The fictional slides of the four women from earlier repeat on the screen SC then out.*

> *Cymbal crash.*

> *Slides appear SR & SL with the Chinese character for "small" on one and "girl" on the other. WOMAN picks up some bits of paper and a pair of scissors. She starts cutting out little paper dresses of different sizes to attach to a string with wooden clothes pins. She crinkles them up and flattens them out in order that they will look like the dress she is wearing. She then strings them up in front of the centre screen.*

> *Slides change to the character for "paper" on one and "clothes" on the other. A recording begins*. It is the WOMAN's mother. She starts to talk about the WOMAN's Grandmother's outfit. As the recording plays out the WOMAN finds a paper bundle tied with a rope. Inside is the Grandmother's traditional outfit. She unwraps the outfit. Methodically, she climbs out of the paper dress and leaves it on the floor. She then dresses*

Elyne Quan as WOMAN in Tai Chi sequence (Concrete Theatre, 1998).
Photo by Ian Jackson, courtesy of Concrete Theatre.

herself very carefully in the outfit, taking the time to make sure it is on perfectly and presenting the articles of clothing to the audience/mirror. Pants first, then the top. She finishes. She looks at herself. Closure. Beat.

Transcript for recorded text of Rosa Quan (Mother):

(*in Cantonese*) This outfit belonged to your Grandmother. When she was young, she made it. That's when she made it. For when she got married. (*in English*) When we get married. Before we made lots of new clothes. When they get married. And then so lots of different things. Ah, when a (*in Cantonese*) bride… (*in English*) the bride? When they arrive to the groom's house lots of relatives come to visit and count the new clothes. You know, how many… the more new clothes, that means the bride's family is richer. So, so it means a lot to the bride. So they make lots new clothes. This is I think is one of them. So that's why your grandmother keep it, you know, so well. And you can see it's so small that means your grandmother when she was young, she is, ah, very nice figure and very… I don't know how to explain it… she was a… very nice lady and good looking lady too. Beautiful. (*laughs*) And this, this already, when she was born is already called China but the style is still from Manchu so it's a piece, a nice piece of fabric but they still cut it to be make it a different style. You can see in the pants here, it is cut it to be different pieces and then sew it together makes… looks so wide… so big. But when they wear it they want it that way. That's why. But I think that's a very memory thing so that's why she want to keep one of those. Actually she got lots, before, but she just want to keep one or two for um what's it called… for souvenir? Something like that.

Oh, well, before we always hand make, you know, even those buttons. Sometimes when you make those buttons it takes longer than you make the whole clothes. Because it's have some in style. I don't know how it called. (*in Cantonese*) We call it flower buttons. Chinese people call it flower buttons because you have to wind the fabric. (*in English*) You know, use the same fabric to make… those different patterns for those buttons. So it looks very nice. So then the more you make it, that means the better clothes you make for it, 'kay? So you can see that, the sleeve? It's not in the middle. It's not long. But it's just like three-quarters, you know that's the style from before…

Carefully, she picks up the paper dress, puts it on a wooden hanger and hangs it from SC among the other little paper dresses. She looks at it one last time and walks to exit.

The end.

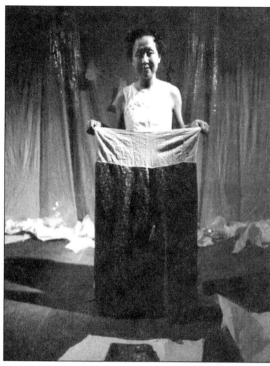

*Elyne Quan as WOMAN
examining Grandmother's costume
(Concrete Theatre, 1998).
Photo by Ian Jackson.*

*Elyne Quan as WOMAN
wearing Grandmother's costume
(Concrete Theatre, 1998).
Photo by Ian Jackson.*

BURNT REMAINS

by
Scott Sharplin

INTRODUCTION TO *BURNT REMAINS*

The way we talk about violence organizes the category for us: violence is thus something that operates by being unleashed, by breaking out, by bursting forth, by exploding. It is nervously bounded, but is always breaking boundaries, the boundaries that constrain it and the boundaries of others who are its victims. Violence is force, but force characterized variously by suddenness, uncertain warrant, the capacity to induce terror.[1]

When a software consultant arrives in a basement library with the job of scanning the books which have been carefully sheltered or hoarded by the octogenarian German librarian, uneasy discoveries about both the programmer and the librarian emerge. Through a series of clipped, deliberately ragged scenes often closing with ironic clangs, Scott Sharplin's play summons into being through words hidden and hate-filled pasts. *Burnt Remains* involves the viewer and reader in piecing together the fragments, making sense of the charred bits. It also implicates us in judging where the greater heinousness lies: with Schaeffner, the Nazi in the basement, cradling and defending in his *mitteleuropean* accent a text of hate literature, or with Ashbury, the yuppy programmer, whose confident talk and apparent work ethic permit him to bury and deny his past violent abuse and disfigurement of his own sister. Although the settings vary, the primary contrast between the overstuffed basement library and the bare studio where Ashbury's sister Jill, a performance artist, records her story to dance with fire and translate her scars, enables the play's exploration of writing itself. *Burnt Remains* uncovers different forms of the potentially violent space of writing, where the sign systems of pain are identified and laid bare. Whether imprinted on paper or incised on the body, these texts convey a sense of a haunted continuity branded in words, memories and acts of violence.

The contrast between the library which, as Schaeffner argues, enshrines "the value of *knowing* old things" and the artist's studio where Jill "reache[s] into memory and open[s] things up, like books" engages the audience to consider the value-ladenness and intricate connectivity of art. Schaeffner's collection of Nazi hate literature belongs to a "Humanities Project." Ashbury's Jewish fiancée, Rachel, who is fired as a tutor in a business run by Schaeffner's daughter, against whom Rachel has filed an unsuccessful charge of racial discrimination, is incensed by the anti-semitic text Ashbury has brought home from work and left casually in their apartment. Though Jill establishes contacts with Rachel and Schaeffner, adapting their stories for her performance, her own brother initially refuses to recognize her existence and then dismisses her as "crazy" and "insane." Jill's immolation drives home with horrific force the discomfort of the story her body's hieroglyphics narrate, when "people saw the writing and didn't like the things it said."

Fire supplies the resonant metaphor of *Burnt Remains*. The play is studded with remembered episodes of rescue from fire: Rachel's uncle was pulled from the fire in Belsen, and Schaeffner saved the single remaining copy of his prized anti-semitic text from the flames. Fire also symbolizes hate and offers the opportunity of obliteration. Ashbury wants to see the Nazi in the basement "go down in flames" at the same time as he burns Jill's notebook. Not only does Jill dance with and, climactically, offer herself up to fire as a truth-telling enactment of the branding and rape she suffered at the hands of her brother, the melting of her body signals, ironically, the longevity of her story. Although the words of her body appear to dissolve, they have been captured forever through Schaeffner's scanning of her notebooks onto the Web.

Burnt Remains is a memory play with a difference. Although it shares features of the remembered action and recollected pasts of such Canadian memory plays as James Reaney's The Donnellys trilogy, Timothy Findley's Can You See Me Yet? and Sharon Pollock's Doc and Blood Relations, Sharplin's play catapults the task of making sense of the contingent, discontinuous facts of the past into the world of cyberculture. Exploring horror in microcosmic and macrocosmic forms, Burnt Remains asks how "information" technology adjusts, represents and contextualizes the past. As well as experimenting with the convention-defying narratological techniques of the memory play, in which fiction and recollection, now and then, intersect and braid together, Sharplin's text complicates the issue of residual meaning. What sense can we make of the charred fragments of the story? Through a narrative design which mingles high-speed internet connections with the physical immediacy of performance art, this memory play invites us to assess the power of different media and their corresponding socially constituted categories of perception. While the Web can allow the computer scanner to blow the lid off the Humanities Project as hate literature, the medium can also expose the scanner's past itself, as recreated by his scarred sister. As Schaeffner taunts Ashbury, "the whole world can read the things you did…. It is written." The play's combination of technologically dispersed and physically emblematized data increases the feeling of unease and of shared moral culpability. The effect is comparable to the "taint of shame and outrage that eventually creeps into the audience,"[2] which one reviewer claims is the lasting impression of Philip Glass's operatic setting of Franz Kafka's In the Penal Colony, recently mounted by the Classic Stage Company in New York.

Playwright, director and journalist, Scott Sharplin is a graduate of the Honours English program at the University of Alberta, who subsequently studied at the National Theatre School. He has been writing plays for over a decade; his produced works include Touch, Peep Hole Stories, The Garden of Forking Paths, Signs of the APPLEcalypse, The Great Doughnut of Destiny and Notes from Underground. Since 1995 he has been creating and directing new and classic works, which revisit and occasionally rescript stories from Shakespeare, Borges and Dostoyevsky, among others, under the company name Sound & Fury Theatre. In 2000, Sound & Fury was incorporated as a not-for-profit theatre with the mandate "to challenge and excite audiences through the development of new work and the transformation of classic texts" in a medium of performative exploration of ideas of memory and imagination.

Burnt Remains was written in 1999, and received its first public reading through Workshop West's Springboards New Play Development Festival. On the subject of real-world models, Sharplin has remarked that for the character of the "Nazi in the basement," Schaeffner, he was "inspired, in a lateral-thinking sort of way," by the chapter on Elias Canetti in B. W. Powe's *The Solitary Outlaw*. Sharplin is clearly attracted to the figure of the subterranean dweller. His April 2001 adaptation of Dostoyevsky's *Notes from Underground* presented Misha as a "mass of contradictions," with speech patterns creating "a rhythm of strident declarations, possible objections (raised and dismissed), alternative interpretations (raised and dismissed), [and] self-justifications (raised and dismissed);" as a local reviewer observed, "Misha may be in a Fringe venue today, but he's auditioning for the big time."[3]

NOTES

[1] William Ian Miller, *Humiliation and Other Essays on Honor, Social Discomfort and Violence* (Ithaca: Cornell University Press, 1993), 60.
[2] Ben Brantley, "'In the Penal Colony': Kafka's Pen? A Branding Iron," *New York Times* (15 June 2001).
[3] Liz Nicholls, "Theatre-as-therapy explores tortured inner landscape," *Edmonton Journal* (12 April 2001), C5.

The first public reading of *Burnt Remains* occurred in Workshop West's Springboards New Play Development Festival in 2000. The reading was directed by Workshop West's Artistic Director, Ron Jenkins, with the following cast:

ASHBURY   James MacDonald
SCHAEFFNER   Dave Clarke
RACHEL   Mieko Ouchi
JILL   Daniela Vlaskalik

CHARACTERS

ASHBURY, late twenties, an optical software consultant.
RACHEL, mid-twenties, an English tutor. Ashbury's fiancée.
SCHAEFFNER, around eighty, a German librarian.
JILL, early twenties, a performance artist. Ashbury's sister. She has terrible burns on her face and body; she dresses to cover most of them (turtlenecks and gloves), but she can't hide her face.

SETTING

The set must be flexible as many different settings are depicted. However, two environments should dominate: the library, which is claustrophobic and overflowing with old books; and Jill's studio, which is bare except for a large white screen, behind which she will perform. How these set pieces connect, and how the other locations are presented, are left to the imagination of the designer.

LOCATION

Burnt Remains is set in an unnamed large Canadian city in the late 1990s. It does not reflect a geographical setting so much as it attempts to bring into focus a particular political and economic myopia which has preferenced technological growth at the expense of enrichment and learning. In this process, the idea of "culture" (or "multi-culture", that dubious talisman of Canadian self-esteem) shifts, becoming less a matter of personal memory and actualization, and more a measure of one's ability to keep up with the global community. This pressure obliterates pasts, even as it expands futures. *Burnt Remains* explores these tensions on a personal, not a regional, level; but I invite the audience to ask themselves if these tensions exist in their part of Canada; and if so, which side is winning.

BURNT REMAINS
by Scott Sharplin

Scene One

ASHBURY and SCHAEFFNER in the library. ASHBURY carries a laptop computer.

ASHBURY
I wouldn't lie to you, Mister Schaeffner.

SCHAEFFNER
Why was I not told of this?

ASHBURY
Simon would have sent you an e-mail about it.

SCHAEFFNER
And anyone did not think to come down the stairs and say to me in person?

ASHBURY
Well I'm here now.

SCHAEFFNER
Yes, to take away my books.

ASHBURY
I have to optically scan each page to transfer the data onto the internet. It's a very long and tedious process and I'd like to get started.

SCHAEFFNER
You want to destroy them.

ASHBURY
I want to make them accessible. All this old data doesn't do Trumpet any good down here. May I–?

SCHAEFFNER is blocking ASHBURY's path.

SCHAEFFNER
I have kept these books for fifty years for them.

ASHBURY
Yes, well, fifty years ago you were probably hot stuff but filing systems are a little different now. Life is change, Mister Schaeffner.

SCHAEFFNER
You take these books, you put the words on a screen.

ASHBURY
That's right.

SCHAEFFNER
So the whole world sees them.

ASHBURY
Yeah, the whole world.

SCHAEFFNER
And after that what do you do? What do you do with the books?

ASHBURY
The books?

SCHAEFFNER
What happens to the library?

ASHBURY
This is the library. The books are obsolete. Simon'll probably sell them. Or burn them, who cares?

SCHAEFFNER
And what happens to the librarian?

Scene Two

RACHEL in bed; the phone wakes her up.

RACHEL
What? Yes, hello? Hi! Laura! Hi! I'm not late, am I? Shit! I'm not – I'm in at ten? Oh… oh good, because, I thought, I, *brrring*, I – sorry–

Y– y–, well, sure, I – I, th– that's, yeah… yeah but I guess my… right, right… right, well couldn't y… well if you let me, let me make a… right…

Well I get a termination cheque, though, right?

Scene Three

ASHBURY waiting for bus. JILL at bus stop, writing in notebook.
ASHBURY talks on his cell phone.

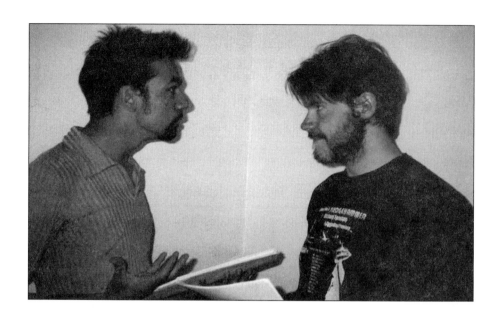

top, l to r: A.J. Richardson as ASHBURY and Matt Kloster as SCHAEFFNER
bottom, l to r: Lianna Shannon as RACHEL and Marie Jones as JILL
in Burnt Remains *reading (Sound & Fury Theatre, July 2001).*

ASHBURY

Well he's kind of sad, like, he's like some poor shmoe in a Dickens novel I guess. He loves his books, that's all. I just wish you'd told me before sending me down– y– (*Pause. JILL is staring at ASHBURY.*) Simon... hang on a minute. (*to JILL*) Can I help you?

JILL

Yes. I think so.

ASHBURY

Do I...?

JILL

Know me? I'm your sister.

ASHBURY

My...?

JILL

Jill.

Pause. They assess each other.

ASHBURY

Jill.

Scene Four

RACHEL on the phone.

RACHEL

Laura? H– hi. No, I just, I wanted to apologize, this morning, I just, there were some things that I wanted to say, that I don't think I said. All right?

Well I just wanted to say that I love it. I really, it feels right and I know I've been reaching them, that's all. I really enjoy working with them. Mr. Kurahashi in particular. And Luis, I, we *talked*, I mean the other day, we actually had an English conversation, he knew the words, he has to say some of them in Spanish first but then he *finds* them, it's so exciting to watch.

Well I need the money too. I need the job. My, my fiancé, we, we're engaged, and the wedding... thank you.... No, he's employed. He... he, ah... he's an optical software programmer...

Look, Laura, god, I just… I can't be fired, okay? I can barely say the word, I can't just look my future husband in the eye and, I mean what do you want me to do? Do you want me to beg?
(*hangs up*) Guess not.

SCENE FIVE

SCHAEFFNER on the phone.

SCHAEFFNER
I, ya, I– I am holding for Mister Solstein.

Ah, yes, Mister– it is, this is Gunter Schaeffner. I am the librarian. The Humanities Collection. Hello. I wish to say I am, I am angry because no one has told me my books were to be moved. For these things you need time, you need to prepare.

How long? The books, the library, I– it has, for Trumpet I have kept them there. For fifty years, I do this. They do not move, why, because they are in one place. So people can find them! So I know where they are. So you know where they are.

Mister Solstein, Simon, you are Simon Solstein. I know your father. He worked as clerk, for Trumpet, he was always coming and going. He was best at messages, I would say to him, "no one does the messages like Solstein!" And he would say back, "no one does the library like Schaeffner!"

You tell this man with the computers who comes that no one is to touch my books who does not know how to treat them. And no one is to take them away.

SCENE SIX

ASHBURY and RACHEL preparing for bed.

RACHEL
I read something today. In *Chatelaine*. "Thirteen Ways to Set Your Man on Fire."

ASHBURY
I got the new project today.

RACHEL
Number One was, you could greet him at home, wearing nothing but writing on your body, "All Yours." Or something.

ASHBURY
I have to talk to Simon again.

RACHEL
You think people do stuff like that?

ASHBURY
Like what?

RACHEL
What would you do if you came home and I had nothing on?

ASHBURY
Tell you you'd catch cold.

RACHEL
And writing? In... with chocolate sauce?

ASHBURY
There was this man. In the library.

RACHEL
A librarian?

ASHBURY
He wouldn't let me take the books.

RACHEL
Quoting is another one. From movies, though.

ASHBURY
Another what?

RACHEL
If you shout, like, "Show me the money" during sex. It's supposed to get you off.

ASHBURY
This guy thinks it's his mission from God.

RACHEL
One of them talked about the "swirl" a lot.

ASHBURY
Simon gives me the runaround. I mean, who is this guy?

RACHEL
Has anybody ever swirled you?

ASHBURY
What?

RACHEL
If I knew what it meant I could try it.

ASHBURY
That's all right.

RACHEL
It's not wrong to try new things.

ASHBURY
I don't know how you put up with it.

RACHEL
What?

ASHBURY
Dealing with people. Your job, all day long.

RACHEL
Have you ever done role-playing things in bed?

ASHBURY
And their accents. This guy, I, he was babbling.

RACHEL
They said you can do stuff besides, you know, (*makes a whip sound*).

ASHBURY
Could you–? I thought this time was here for us to talk.

RACHEL
Well? Aren't we talking?

ASHBURY
How our days went.

RACHEL
We are.

ASHBURY
That was your day? Reading *Chatelaine*? Didn't anything happen at work?

RACHEL
Didn't anything happen to you besides work?

ASHBURY

No.

RACHEL

You, maybe, I dunno, you saw some pretty woman at the bus stop, thought about how much you'd like to come home to your wife and–

ASHBURY

There was no one at the bus stop. And you're not my wife.

RACHEL

I might as well be, we've got all the traits of married couples.

ASHBURY

Can I go to sleep now?

RACHEL

See what I mean?

Scene Seven

JILL in bed. She wakes up aware that something is wrong. Her fear grows into a panic as she summons up the courage to open her eyes. When she does, she begins to scream and flail in terror. She pitches out of bed as though something were on her. Slowly she recovers. She looks around. She finds her notebook and begins to write furiously.

JILL

The worst... thing... ever.

Scene Eight

SCHAEFFNER and ASHBURY in the library. ASHBURY has a cart loaded with computer and scanning equipment.

SCHAEFFNER

What is this creature you bring in here now?

ASHBURY

Scanning equipment, Mister Schaeffner.

SCHAEFFNER

You get out. I talked to Mister Solstein, he told me no more with this madness. I have work to do here.

ASHBURY
He told you what?

SCHAEFFNER
Mister – your name is–?

ASHBURY plugs in his equipment.

ASHBURY
Ashbury.

SCHAEFFNER
Yes, he said Ashbury, no more will you see him.

ASHBURY
Is that what he said?

SCHAEFFNER
Mister Solstein, his father and I–

ASHBURY
(*giving SCHAEFFNER a memo*) Well, regardless of you and Mister Solstein's father, this is what I found on my desk this morning.

SCHAEFFNER
This–

ASHBURY
(*scanning shelves*) From Simon.

SCHAEFFNER
This means nothing.

ASHBURY
It means that I have to work down here. With your dust collection.

SCHAEFFNER
This is wrong.

ASHBURY
Are there any more lights you can turn on?

SCHAEFFNER
This is wrong, Simon said to me, he told me no. You speak to him. He told me no!

ASHBURY
A verbal agreement. Worth the paper it's printed on.

ASHBURY grabs a book off the shelves and heads for his computer.

SCHAEFFNER
Nein!

ASHBURY
Mister Schaeffner.

SCHAEFFNER
This is my library. My books! You understand? You do not touch, you will not touch my books without when I say so!

ASHBURY
I have to get to work.

SCHAEFFNER
Does this, your paper say I am not the librarian?

ASHBURY
It tells me to do my job.

SCHAEFFNER
But we follow my rules.

ASHBURY
Fine! You show me where to start.

Gives SCHAEFFNER the book. He re-shelves it.

SCHAEFFNER
Nothing starts in the middle.

ASHBURY
I'm sorry. Look, it really doesn't matter where I start. All the data gets sorted later. We'll do it your way.

SCHAEFFNER
There is a system.

ASHBURY
I'm sure it's great.

SCHAEFFNER
The start is here. Before the war.

SCHAEFFNER reluctantly hands ASHBURY a book.

ASHBURY
History books.

SCHAEFFNER
They are all history.

ASHBURY
Well, that's impressive.

SCHAEFFNER
You do not know what's in the books?

ASHBURY
I'm not much of a history buff.

He switches on the scanner light. SCHAEFFNER grabs his hand.

SCHAEFFNER
Listen. You work for Trumpet, for Mister Solstein, you should know this.
These books are the reason for Trumpet to exist.

ASHBURY
Trumpet is an information and commodities resource.

SCHAEFFNER
When I start here, when Trumpet was new, it was not this. It was *humanities*
resource. When Trumpet owns only one building, this building, it was all
these things, books, history and literature. Books with art, and music, and
dance. But you know what has happened? In the years, Trumpet gets
bigger, humanities becomes a *department*. Then it is one day a *section*. And
then one day I read, in newspaper Mister Solstein talks about Trumpet has
humanities, what did he say? An "ongoing humanities project."

ASHBURY
Yeah, that was last year.

SCHAEFFNER
This is what I am, now! In the basement. I am "ongoing project."

ASHBURY
Well, look. Between you and me and the wall, I think Simon can make some
dumb choices.

SCHAEFFNER
Between you and me and the wall, Simon is a greedy pig.

ASHBURY

That too. But listen. Once these books are online, Simon won't be able to touch them. If he wants to close down the whole humanities project it won't make a difference. Your books will last forever.

SCHAEFFNER

Not these books.

ASHBURY

This is the best thing that could happen to your books right now.

He turns on the fan for the scanner.

SCHAEFFNER

Not these books! These are my books! They will not last forever, when humanities is gone, when I am gone, they will be nothing! Don't put that there! (*grabs book*) You put them in a pot, now, make them into glue for your web?

ASHBURY

What?

SCHAEFFNER

Listen to me. This book has two stories. Inside is the story of before the war, the peasants in Germany, what they believed. That is one story. But there is another. You put this in your engine you will miss it.

ASHBURY

I won't miss anything.

SCHAEFFNER

This book was printed in Switzerland, there were two thousand copies only. The man who wrote it worked as sign maker in Berlin. He died after it was published, and it was, wife, his widow took to Italy. The books.

ASHBURY

Great.

SCHAEFFNER

Listen! This book is sold to young historian who is going to be married. He is to wed but he has debts, he gambles, and so he has to run away. He leaves his bride. What does he take? Only five books. This is one.

He takes a ship to Brazil. Here is stain from the seawater. For eight years the book sits on the shelf, the sun soaks in. He reads one section most, see, here the corners are worn thin. This chapter tells the story of Pentamerone, who loved the sleeping beauty.

When he dies the book is sold at auction. The man who buys it gives it to his daughter, there it sits until she is older and she gets it appraised. It is worth much. I buy it from her.

ASHBURY
Does Simon know all this?

SCHAEFFNER
I know it.

ASHBURY
I think I understand what you're saying, Mister Schaeffner. There's a sort of bibliographic aspect, too.

SCHAEFFNER
Two stories.

ASHBURY
I think you're right. I think it's important and I think I can take steps to ensure it's not lost. Maybe I can get Simon to include links to the bibliographic info, it wouldn't be too difficult. But you have to believe me, without this, they'd all be trash in a few years anyway. This is red carpet treatment.

SCHAEFFNER
Red carpet.

ASHBURY
Red carpet.

SCHAEFFNER surrenders the book to ASHBURY. ASHBURY nods, goes to the scanner, and cracks the book wide open, breaking the spine. SCHAEFFNER lets out a cry.

Sorry.

SCENE NINE

RACHEL is sleeping. JILL is standing, watching her. RACHEL wakes up aware that something is wrong. Her fear grows into a panic as she summons up the courage to open her eyes. When she sees JILL, she flails out of bed and onto her feet.

RACHEL
What do you want?

JILL
I'm sorry.

RACHEL
I'll scream. Who are you?

JILL
I should go.

RACHEL
How did you get in here?

JILL
I. The door.

RACHEL
This is private property.

JILL
I didn't know you were home.

RACHEL
My husband's a cop.

JILL
Your – your husband?

RACHEL
My fiancé.

JILL
He's a programmer.

RACHEL
How do you know that?

JILL
He told me.

RACHEL
Told you? When? Who are you?

JILL
At the bus stop. Yesterday. I wrote it down.

RACHEL
At the–

JILL
I'm Jill. His sister.

RACHEL
He doesn't have a sister.

JILL
He does. Or well he used to. I was her.

RACHEL
He would have mentioned you.

JILL
This is us, see. From before.

She gives RACHEL a photograph.

RACHEL
(*reads*) Christmas, 1978.

JILL
I never knew I kept that until just a little while ago. It was after I found it that I started to remember.

RACHEL
He – he would have mentioned you to me.

JILL
How long have you known him?

RACHEL
Long enough.

JILL
You're getting married?

RACHEL
Yes. Or, well, eventually. We haven't set a date.

JILL
Is this where he sleeps?

RACHEL
What? Yes. I'm not usually here, during the day, I mean. I work. I'm on vacation.

JILL
I'm a dancer.

RACHEL
Really.

JILL
A performance artist. Do you know what that is?

RACHEL
Yeah. I mean, well, not really. (*laughs*) Does anyone?

JILL
I dance shapes with fire.

RACHEL
Oh.

JILL
I translate. Or try to. My scars.

RACHEL
I think they're very distinguishing.

JILL
You do?

RACHEL
My aunt had scars like them, on her arms. They felt like satin.

JILL
You can touch mine.

RACHEL
That's all right.

JILL
What happened to her?

RACHEL
To? My aunt? She was burned, in the war. Part of my family was in Belsen, the concentration camp. My aunt and uncle. And the Nazis caught my uncle with some food for his family he wasn't supposed to have. They picked him up and threw him in a bonfire. And my aunt ran in and pulled him out. That's a true story.

JILL turns away and writes furiously in her notebook.

RACHEL
What are you doing?

JILL
Notes. For my show.

RACHEL
You have a show?

JILL
It's called "Burnt Remains."

RACHEL
I can't believe he never mentioned you.

JILL
We forgot about each other.

RACHEL
You had a fight?

JILL
I don't think he liked me. After.

RACHEL
After what?

JILL
He didn't like my…

RACHEL
Didn't like them?

JILL
I have more. Eighty per cent of me. You'll get to see most of it if you come to the show.

RACHEL
Can I ask you how you got them?

JILL
How? Yes. How I got them. It wasn't easy. You look at it backwards, from behind, you try to piece it together, like putting pages in order. You know that everything has a beginning, and that beginning is in the bedroom, and the bedroom is a dark place, a cringing place, because it's thick and is about to explode. Because I was trying to breathe. And all at once you felt a sense of cold, and you could think of how odd it was, because my down quilt was on top of me and I shouldn't be cold. Cold in a snowdrift. And this was the feel of it, for a moment, before I understood, before his hands on my body made me awake, and inside myself as I was burning. And somebody was screaming, up out of the bed, which was on fire, which he took me out of.

But I brought it with me. (*pause*) It's all in here. (*her notebook*) I've written it down. For the show. You should come. You might learn something.

SCENE TEN

SCHAEFFNER on the phone with Simon.

SCHAEFFNER
You have good memory, like your father. Mister Solstein the Clerk, he forgets nothing, he is an elephant! You tell him many long numbers to take upstairs, he will do it.

I want to tell you something, about your father when he was new at Trumpet. When I knew him from then. In the nineteen fifties, there was the Red Scare. The government was afraid of all the communists, and they think that all the Jews are the communists. And the government gave Trumpet its money, so when the government people came to the building, they did not want to see these sorts of people, yes?

It was only a week your father was working there, and the people from the government were coming that day. The president sees that Mister Solstein is here. He tells him he cannot be there. He tells him if he does not leave at once he will be fired. This! But Mister Solstein says he will not leave. He stands his ground. So I tell him, I take him to my library and tell him, here, you will work here, for the day, behind these books. It is so nobody will see him. This way he can stay.

He told me after that day that he would never forget my books. This is true.

Now this man you sent me…. He is not like your father or you, Simon. He does not know the value of knowing old things. The past. He forgets things.

SCENE ELEVEN

ASHBURY in the darkness, lit only by the scanning equipment.

ASHBURY
The scanner scans the page. It takes a picture. The picture is rendered digitally and transferred to the computer. Then the computer reads the page. It recognizes the shapes of different letters, fonts. It searches the picture for the shapes it knows. It builds the words and turns them into text. The text is saved as data, in HTML code, on the 'Net. Every computer reads it the same. Everyone can read the same book, at the same time. Everyone knows what it says.

SCENE TWELVE

JILL's studio. She lights a single, long flame, and places it in front of a projector light. The flicker of the flame is projected onto a screen. She steps behind the screen and begins to coax the flame's shadow until forms emerge from it (these are made by a film on the projector). The shadow characters act out a story while she (as a silhouette) acts as puppeteer.

JILL

Once there was a family. There was a husband and a wife and they were sent to prison. They got hungry. They got so hungry that the husband stole a loaf of bread. And when they caught him, they were going to hurt him, but they didn't. They didn't 'cause he cried and cried and cried and so they laughed at him. They called him names and left him all alone.

But then at night the husband snuck away. He was ashamed. He made Fire, and Fire said come. He jumped into Fire. His wife, she saw him jump and she ran out, she tried to grab him, pull him out but Fire had him so hot, he ate him up. Her arms turned red and Fire, he laughed and laughed and laughed. And that's what happened.

SCENE THIRTEEN

SCHAEFFNER and RACHEL sitting together in a waiting room. SCHAEFFNER is making notes to himself in a ledger.

RACHEL

Sind Sie hier lang gewesen?

SCHAEFFNER

Sorry?

RACHEL

Have you been here long? I'm sorry, my German is bad.

SCHAEFFNER

Your German?

RACHEL

I saw your book. Your writing. Oh, I didn't, no, I can't read it, I was just, I saw it was German. I can't *read* it. I can barely speak it.

SCHAEFFNER

What are you asking me?

RACHEL

I, oh, sorry. If you'd been here long.

SCHAEFFNER

Fifty years.

RACHEL

Y– oh, no, I meant – oh god! (*laughs*) I meant how long have you been *here*, waiting! You thought I meant– (*laughs*)

SCHAEFFNER

I wait for my daughter.

RACHEL

And I thought, how long have you been here, fifty years, wow, we try to work faster than that! (*laughs*) You say it differently in German, don't you? *Wie lang haben Sie hier gelebt?* [How long have you lived here?]

SCHAEFFNER

Fifty years.

RACHEL

I can imagine it would be confusing. English is the hardest language to learn.

SCHAEFFNER

Yes.

RACHEL

Is your daughter picking it up fast?

SCHAEFFNER

Picking?

RACHEL

English, I mean. I hope we're helping her along. I work here.

SCHAEFFNER

She works here.

RACHEL

She?

SCHAEFFNER

My daughter. She is staff director.

RACHEL

Really? Do I feel like an idiot! I had no idea.

SCHAEFFNER

Yes.

RACHEL
Your daughter is Laura Pecorini? That's great! I mean, I just never would've thought. I mean, because, I, well I guess I never knew her maiden name. And she has *no* accent.

SCHAEFFNER
She speaks many languages.

RACHEL
I must say, though, that it's all in parenting. It's very impressive for a family, I mean a first generation family, it's very important to encourage it at an early age.

SCHAEFFNER
Yes.

RACHEL
You must have encouraged her at an early age.

SCHAEFFNER
In our house, we had many books to read. All different languages. She would read till eyes were red.

RACHEL
And then you'd read to her?

SCHAEFFNER
Sometimes.

RACHEL
It's no wonder she is where she is today. You should be very proud of her.

SCHAEFFNER
I am waiting for her to come off from work.

RACHEL
She's a workaholic. Oh, that means, well it's not necessarily a bad thing. It just means–

SCHAEFFNER
Ja, ja, she works too hard.

RACHEL
But then I guess we all do, right?

> *She laughs, SCHAEFFNER responds by laughing politely. After a moment silence settles in. Pause.*

RACHEL
Could I ask you, Mister – I'm sorry, what is your–

SCHAEFFNER
Mister Schaeffner.

RACHEL
Mister, hi, I'm Rachel. Do you think that I could ask you a sort of favour, Mister Schaeffner?

SCHAEFFNER
Favour?

RACHEL
You can say no.

SCHAEFFNER
What favour?

RACHEL
This is going to sound tacky. I guess I'm sort of not in Laura's good books right now. It wasn't really anything major. You know how it is.

SCHAEFFNER
Her good books.

RACHEL
I was just wondering if you could maybe mention me. In passing. Sort of, just to put in a good word, like.

SCHAEFFNER
To put you in her good book.

RACHEL
No exaggerations. Even just that I was striking up a conversation. It's good to be social with the students.

SCHAEFFNER
I am not a student.

RACHEL
No, but if you were. Or if I thought you were. Just that I was willing to talk German. *Ich erinnere mich sehr schnell. Es benötigt bloß praxis.* [I remember quickly. All it takes is practice.]

SCHAEFFNER
I will tell her you were talking.

RACHEL
It would mean a lot to me.

SCHAEFFNER
What were we talking about, should I say?

RACHEL
What? Oh, I don't know, whatever. Germany.

SCHAEFFNER
I don't talk about Germany.

RACHEL
Oh. Well, then Canada, I guess.

SCHAEFFNER
You are from here?

RACHEL
Yes. Or, well from Montreal. My father's from Israel. Oh don't tell her we talked about me though.

SCHAEFFNER
Of course not.

RACHEL
Tell her we talked about the power of language, and I said what a thrill it is to watch somebody who's just on the edge of understanding something, watch them grasp and help them, show them where to put their arms out so they'll grab it. And you said yes, it made you think of Laura. Tell her that.

SCHAEFFNER
I tell her I talked to you.

RACHEL
Would you?

SCHAEFFNER
I promise.

RACHEL
Thank you. That would mean a lot to me. (*pause*) You have a wonderful daughter.

SCENE FOURTEEN

RACHEL and ASHBURY preparing for bed.

RACHEL
So tell me about your day.

ASHBURY
Rachel I need sleep.

RACHEL
I had a very unusual day.

ASHBURY
I have a report to make first thing tomorrow. Stand in front of Simon, tell him, no, I'm not on schedule, every time I grab a book I get a lecture, "zis book waz smuggled here by refugees–"

RACHEL
Do you know somebody named Jill?

ASHBURY
I know a lot of Jills.

RACHEL
Well this Jill's the one you spent Christmas 1978 with.

ASHBURY
Is this another *Chatelaine* game?

RACHEL gives him the photograph.

RACHEL
She's pretty, huh? She looks like you.

ASHBURY
Where'd you get this?

RACHEL
What difference does it make?

ASHBURY
Jill is, look, the things she says, the things she *tells* you–

RACHEL
No, I think what matters here is why you wouldn't tell me after, what, how long?

ASHBURY
I didn't not tell you.

RACHEL

How do you *omit* something like a sister–

ASHBURY

She's not my sister. (*pause*) She's crazy. Okay? She's my crazy sister, and I only call her that because she used to be that person, once. She doesn't know me. I mean she'll recognize that I'm her brother but she has no concept what that *means*, she just imposes something different every time. She's just crazy, she's "not right." And it's sad and it's tragic and there you are.

RACHEL

The burns.

ASHBURY

What?

RACHEL

Because of the, the... she went mad after–

ASHBURY

After what?

RACHEL

The *fire*.

ASHBURY

She told you about the fire.

RACHEL

Well, yes, well, first I saw, but look, this means–

ASHBURY

You saw her. She was here?

RACHEL

Well yes I saw her but the point here is not only did you not tell me you have a sister, you–

ASHBURY

Rachel.

RACHEL

You didn't tell me you had an *insane* sister?!

ASHBURY

She was here?

RACHEL
Yes, god, yes, she was just standing when I, god, why didn't you tell me?

ASHBURY
If she shows up again call me at work.

RACHEL
You, oh sure, *now* call you, if you'd – she could have hurt me or something.

ASHBURY
She won't hurt you.

RACHEL
I was *sleeping*, you know, and I wake up and there's this, this, this face...
look if you'd simply maybe mentioned to me that you have a scarred-up
nut-case char-broiled sister on the loose, I maybe could've been prepared!
Is all!

ASHBURY puts his head in his hands. Pause.

It's okay. Now I know. It's okay.

RACHEL rubs his shoulders.

It's just, when you don't tell me things it makes me wonder. It's called
doubt. I can't handle doubt.

ASHBURY
I can't handle her. Not now.

RACHEL
(*kissing his neck and back*) Well if you give me a handle I can help carry the
luggage. Okay?

ASHBURY
You're right. Okay.

They kiss.

What were you doing asleep here today?

SCENE FIFTEEN

*ASHBURY and SCHAEFFNER in the library. ASHBURY is scanning
pages, one at a time. SCHAEFFNER is sorting through books.*

SCHAEFFNER
This is chaos. You said you would keep these in order.

ASHBURY
I'm not a complete moron. I can read numbers.

SCHAEFFNER
You do not sort them by numbers.

ASHBURY
What do those numbers mean, then, on the spines?

SCHAEFFNER
Those numbers mean *nicht*. Keep them as I give them to you.

ASHBURY
Right.

SCHAEFFNER
(*examining a cover*) What have you done?

ASHBURY
What *have* I done?

SCHAEFFNER
This was not here before.

ASHBURY
That, what?

SCHAEFFNER
This! Scratching!

ASHBURY
I don't see a scratch.

SCHAEFFNER
Because you cannot see the *book,* is why you do not see the scratch!

ASHBURY
(*takes the book, examines*) There are fifty scratches on this book. Is one more scratch, at this point in its little lifetime–?

SCHAEFFNER
Give it to me. (*takes it back*) These are not scratches. They are *schmutzbissen.*

ASHBURY
(*laughs*) What?

SCHAEFFNER
But this, this is scratch. Scratch with your name on it.

ASHBURY
What the hell is *schmutzbissen*?

SCHAEFFNER
Dust bites.

ASHBURY
Dust mites?

SCHAEFFNER
Dust bites. Attacks from dust.

ASHBURY
Dust doesn't do that to books.

SCHAEFFNER
Really.

ASHBURY
Librarians might.

SCHAEFFNER
You like to speak of things you do not know.

ASHBURY
And you just like to speak.

SCHAEFFNER
Look at this. How old is this book?

ASHBURY flips the book open.

You will not find a publication date.

ASHBURY
Well, then it's probably pretty old.

SCHAEFFNER
Published eighteen-hundred fifty-nine.

ASHBURY
Yeah, that's impressive.

SCHAEFFNER
(*shows him a battered book*) And how old is this one?

ASHBURY
Even older?

SCHAEFFNER

No. It is two years old. This is what happens to books by those who cannot take care of them.

ASHBURY

Okay, so why is the number on the two-year-old book smaller than the number on the six-million-year-old one?

SCHAEFFNER

I do not store them by age. The damaged, they go on the bottom. Where it's cooler.

ASHBURY

All right, lemme ask you this. I get this vague feeling that you like to look after your books. Call that a wild guess. And that's good, I admire it, because I'll bet it makes you a better librarian. I mean sure, it makes you so deluded that you shelve everything in a completely illogical fashion so as to escape the trained swarms of killer attack dust, but in the long run you'll have a higher success rate and down the road they'll thank you. And they do. We do. Thank you. Thank you, really, all your – thank you.

SCHAEFFNER

You don't deserve to thank me.

ASHBURY

Well Simon thanks you.

SCHAEFFNER

Simon does not deserve to work for Trumpet.

ASHBURY

What? And, so, what, I do? Are you the new CEO? No, you're the librarian, and you can get off your high horse because that makes you lower than janitor, here at Trumpet, Mister Schaeffner. Because at least we still need janitors.

> *Pause. Goes back to scanning. SCHAEFFNER crosses to a shelf and retrieves a very battered book.*

SCHAEFFNER

You see this? You see this? Look at this and then I will not talk.

ASHBURY

I see it.

SCHAEFFNER

This is the most valuable book in my library. It was printed in Germany, in nineteen-thirty. What is the worst thing to ever happen to you, Mister Ashbury?

ASHBURY
What?

SCHAEFFNER
Have you breaken your leg? Or you were very sick as a boy, *ja*? *Grippe*? In hospital?

ASHBURY
Why?

SCHAEFFNER
This book has been through more than you. One of a kind, no other copy. In Germany it is in bookshop, before the war. The Nazis find the brother of bookstore owner in black market. They follow him to shop and burn it to the ground. Is one of only books the owner could pull from fire. All others black, they crumble. *Feuerblasen.*

ASHBURY
Give it to me and I'll make it live forever.

SCHAEFFNER
No. You will never touch this book.

ASHBURY
I have to "touch" every–

SCHAEFFNER
I cannot keep you from all these. But I keep you from one and your job is useless, it will never be over. So you stop now if you like, you will never be done what they tell you to do because you will never touch this book.

ASHBURY
And who are you to tell me–

SCHAEFFNER
I am the librarian.

He sits down with his hands across the book and looks at ASHBURY.

SCENE SIXTEEN

JILL at bus stop, writing in notebook. SCHAEFFNER walks by, wearing his coat, and holding the burnt book. Also a hot dog, which he tries to eat while holding the book gingerly. He stops and stares at her. When she looks up, he looks away, and tries to eat his hot dog. She stares at him. He looks at her, she looks away. Finally their eyes meet.

SCHAEFFNER
You should not hold your book like that.

JILL
What?

SCHAEFFNER
It hurts the spine.

JILL
It's not a book. I write in it.

SCHAEFFNER
Then it is a book.

JILL
Oh. (*pause*) Don't get catsup on yours. (*laughs*)

SCHAEFFNER
I have to go.

JILL
You work where my brother works.

SCHAEFFNER
Excuse me.

JILL
Tell him I said hi.

SCHAEFFNER
I will do that.

He exits.

SCENE SEVENTEEN

RACHEL on the phone. Several beats.

RACHEL
H– hi! Hi, is this – oh great! I thought you'd forgotten me. Rachel Lewis, my name is Rach… L-E-W-I-S. I work at Lyndon Languages. Do you need the address? Laura Pecorini. P-E-C-O-R-I-N-I.

Well I got fired this week, without warning. I mean literally without, she just called me, t-two days ago, I was scheduled, and she told me to not bother coming in. Just like that.

Well I mean she said, she said things about, you know, "I don't seem interested in promoting discoveries in my students." She said it was off the, the evaluation forms, but I-I've seen them, I've talked with my own students, they say–

No, she's been very an-antagonistic for a while. Just with me. I heard, you know, the walls are thin, I went by to go to the resource room to get books and she, I heard her, in her office, once, I heard her say... well she was talking about racial issues. Is all I'll say.

How should I know if it was about me? All I heard, I heard her say that some... people, of some ethnic persuasion, can't teach languages very well. That people of that, that group, they, they're too "insular." That was her word. No, she called the group, the... my... do I have to say it?

SCENE EIGHTEEN

> *JILL's studio. She lights the flame on the screen, as before, and dances characters onto the screen, as before.*

JILL
Once there was a family. There was a good brother and a bad brother. The good brother was in trouble, they were after him, and so he came running to the bad brother and said "Help me, help me, I've got books they want to burn, help me to get out of here, I'm your brother!" But the bad brother wouldn't help him. He called him names. He told them where the good brother was hiding.

But then at night the bad brother heard a fire. He ran out and he saw that it's his brother, it's his own brother after he turned him in, they burned him and all his, everything he owned, the books. Fire took it all, except for one. The bad brother took the book and cried and cried and cried. And that's what happened.

SCENE NINETEEN

> *The library, night. SCHAEFFNER sleeps in a chair, with his arms still wrapped around his damaged book. The door opens and ASHBURY enters quietly. He goes to turn on the light but thinks better of it. He moves to his scanning equipment and begins switching things on. He doesn't notice SCHAEFFNER. He is about to switch on the scanner when the cell phone rings. He moves to the door and answers it.*

ASHBURY
(*lowering his voice*) Ashbury.

Hi, sweetie. How you feeling? Well I'm at work, I'm working late. Because I'm behind schedule. Well I didn't know I'd be behind schedule until I fell behind schedule.

I told you I'm at work. Why, because it's late, that's why I'm whispering. Everything's shut down. There's nobody here. Well I just, I don't know, I just am. Because it's quiet. (*holds the cell phone out*) You see, it's quiet. When it's quiet I'm quiet.

(*at normal volume*) All right, there, you happy? What can I do for you? Well why did you call? Well, I'm sorry. I didn't know how late – you can't expect me – no, look – well I'm sorry. I'll let you know.

Oh, for… Rach forget about her, all right? She's harmless, it's not like she's gonna come after you with a chainsaw or something. You'll be fine. All right? Forget about her.

> Goes back to turning on scanning equipment. SCHAEFFNER stirs but doesn't wake up.

Anyway I thought you were giving classes Thursday nights. Well who's teaching the classes? Are you all right lately? You take a lot of time off work, I thought, I dunno – you're not pregnant or anything are you? N-no that – that was sort of a joke.

> Turns on the fan. SCHAEFFNER stirs some more.

Hey Rach, what's the worst thing that's ever happened to you? Yeah but I mean like did you have your tonsils out, or hurt your head or something? Wh–? No, no, god, no I'm not implying anything. No, it was just something ol' Baron Munchausen asked me today.

> He takes out a cigarette and lights it.

Baron – the, y'know, the librarian-shaped fossil they keep down here. The coot Simon pays to make my life hell. I told you about him already.

> He fumbles the lighter when putting it away. It falls to the floor and he kicks it over towards SCHAEFFNER. He bends over after it.

Well then I guess *you* can't expect *me* to remember everything *you* tell me either. Nothing, all I'm saying is… we both… we…

> ASHBURY has followed his lighter to SCHAEFFNER's feet. He looks up slowly and then backs away.

(*whispering*) Hon I gotta go. I have to work. Later. Yeah. Okay. Bye.

Hangs up. Looks at SCHAEFFNER. SCHAEFFNER does not wake up. Slowly ASHBURY smiles, shakes his head. He steps forward and inspects the librarian. Very slowly, he reaches out and removes the book from SCHAEFFNER's grip. He steals back to the scanning equipment and inspects the book under the light of the scanner. He beams over at SCHAEFFNER.

You can't stop progress, Mister Schaeffner.

He opens the book, and a handful of sheets fall out of it and scatter around the scanning equipment.

Shit.

SCENE TWENTY

RACHEL is in a coffee shop, drinking a frothy, latte-like confection. She's trying to write in a notebook. Not having much luck. JILL enters with a coffee. Stops in front of RACHEL's table.

JILL
What is that? (*indicating RACHEL's coffee*)

RACHEL
What? (*looks up*) Oh god.

JILL
I saw your coffee, it looks good.

RACHEL
What are you doing here?

JILL
Same as you.

RACHEL
Are you following me? Don't follow me.

JILL
I, no. I saw you come in. I was there.

RACHEL
What, so, oh, this is, is what, a coincidence?

JILL
I was in the corner writing, there. See you're closer to the door, you would have seen me come in. (*beat*) Or are you following me?

RACHEL
No! What? I – look – I'm sorry. This is just a little weird.

JILL
I come here a lot.

RACHEL
No you don't. *I* come here a lot. I would have seen you.

JILL
You didn't know me before. Who I was.

RACHEL
Well, you still sort of make an *impression*. (*pause*) I'm sorry.

JILL
He told you I'm crazy, didn't he.

RACHEL
Oh god.

JILL
He says that a lot. Because it means he can forget about me.

RACHEL
I don't want to be having this conversation right now, okay?

JILL
What are you doing?

RACHEL
What? I'm working, I – I'm – busy, working.

JILL
Writing?

RACHEL
Yes. A sort of presentation I have to make and it's very important.

JILL
I should leave you alone then.

RACHEL
Okay.

JILL
But I want you to know I'm not crazy.

RACHEL
I believe you.

JILL
You just assume I'm crazy 'cause I look crazy. 'Cause you look at my face
and you think anyone who looks like that, who's had that happen to her,
I would be crazy if it happened to me like that, *looked* like that. I would look
in the mirror and I would go mad.

RACHEL
That's not what I think.

JILL
Look. Look at this. I want you to see this. (*gives her a news clipping*) This is
from today. It's a preview of my show tomorrow.

RACHEL
That's great.

JILL
That's to prove to you I didn't make that up. See my brother thinks that if
you don't look normal then you can't do anything. That's why he thinks I'm
crazy.

RACHEL
That, that's not right. He doesn't believe that.

JILL
You don't know him very well.

RACHEL
I've known him forever, I've known him for five years. We're going to get
married someday.

JILL
After I left home I forgot about him. It was on purpose I think. I forgot
about everyone for a long time. But for the show I began to remember.
I wrote it all down.

RACHEL
What?

JILL
They even said it in the article, read.

RACHEL
(*reads*) "In search of an emotional spark for her production, Ashbury–"

JILL
(*under*) They mean me.

RACHEL
(*reads*) "–turned to her past, and to her harsh and often traumatic childhood relationships with her immediate family."

JILL
They quote me later on too.

RACHEL
What the hell is this?

JILL
No picture, though.

RACHEL
What "harsh and often traumatic relationships–"

JILL
Sometimes you have to talk big, you know, for the press.

RACHEL
What is this show of yours?

JILL
I told you.

RACHEL
What is it *about*?

JILL
I told you. I just reached into my memory and opened things up, like books.

RACHEL
Things, what things? About who?

JILL
All of them. The faces, like the places, you have to look at it backwards, from behind. His face is the clearest though, in all the whole house, soft like a pillow, I remember the bedroom. That's what door he opened. When you think of it, it shouldn't make you short of breath like that but it does. The feel of it, remembering, like hands on my body like I'm burning. Inside me where it's burning. When I'm screaming. But I can't scream. I couldn't breathe. He could breathe though and he breathed me he breathed into me he set me on fire. (*Pause. She takes the clipping back.*) I didn't tell them all that though. That's just for you.

SCENE TWENTY-ONE

ASHBURY at home. He is trying to repair the damage he did to the book – however, he can't even figure out what order the loose pages go in.

ASHBURY
(*imitates SCHAEFFNER*) Now zis book iz very old, it vaz published before zey invented fucking page numbers.

He tries to decipher the German grammar. Something catches his eye. He reads.

Juden.

He wheels his chair over to his PC. He types in a sentence from the book and clicks on the screen. Pause. He reads.

Jesus.

He picks up the phone, dials. Pause. As he's waiting, he types and translates some more text.

(*into phone*) Hello, Simon, it's Ashbury. Listen, I was just sorting through the books in the library, and I... y-yes, well I'm sorry I'm calling so late. But there was this book that the librarian... I know you have. (*reads the screen*) Jesus. (*into phone*) I know, and I appreciate that, but I really think you want to hear this.

No, sir. No, I'm still up for the job. That's not necessary, sir. Y-you're right, and I have always prided myself on my ability to solve my own... yes. It's just this one book–

Right. Right. I'll do that. Next time you hear from me, it'll be to say, project's done. Yes. I'm sorry. Yes. Thank you, sir. Good night.

Hangs up.

Looks like it's you and me, Herr Schaeffner.

SCENE TWENTY-TWO

SCHAEFFNER in the library. He is drinking heavily. He sits beside the computer console and writes in a notebook.

SCHAEFFNER
The library. Section One. Numbers one to three, for history before the First World War. Double numbers are assigned to books in worst shape. Section

Two, four to six, the First War and between. Here placement is for language first, then country second. Section Three, seven to nine, World War Two. Country first, language second.

Important note: books greater in height than thirty centimetres are separate. It is important to mark card with red marks when I... when *librarian...* files these books.

Scene Twenty-three

ASHBURY and RACHEL in bed. RACHEL wakes up in a panic – lurches out of bed, panting and frightened.

ASHBURY
What happened?

RACHEL
I dreamt... I had a bad dream.

ASHBURY
About what?

RACHEL
I, it, the worst. What you said. The worst thing ever.

ASHBURY
I... well, what was it?

RACHEL
I, I don't know. I don't remember.

ASHBURY
You don't remember the worst thing that ever happened to you?

RACHEL
You know dreams.

ASHBURY
Oh.

Pause.

RACHEL
You were there.

SCENE TWENTY-FOUR

ASHBURY arrives at the library. SCHAEFFNER is waiting for him.

SCHAEFFNER
Where is it?

ASHBURY
Good morning.

SCHAEFFNER
What have you done with it?

ASHBURY
It's a great day out there, isn't it? Birds are singing. "T.G.I.F."

SCHAEFFNER
I will call Solstein, I will tell him you are – you have robbed–

ASHBURY
Let's keep Solstein out of this. (*turns on his equipment*) I want to talk with you about our professional relationship, Mister Schaeffner.

SCHAEFFNER
What?

ASHBURY
I feel that it's deteriorated. I'd like to fix that.

SCHAEFFNER
You have stolen the book from me. It was you.

ASHBURY
You see, that's a perfect example of what I mean. A word like "stolen–"

SCHAEFFNER
(*overlapping*) Ja, stolen, out of my, my hands, you stole–

ASHBURY
(*overlapping*) It's not professional, is what I'm saying – there's a language, etiquette–

SCHAEFFNER
(*overlapping*) I am sleeping, like a, like a *child* and you come–

ASHBURY
HEY! ENOUGH! (*beat*) You want your book back, shut up and listen. You are the nosiest librarian in history, you know that?

SCHAEFFNER
Why are you doing this?

ASHBURY
I'll tell you why. (*he turns on the light for the scanner*) I have a job, here at
Trumpet. And when you work for Trumpet, you're expected to complete
the jobs you're given. And unless you're employed for the purposes of
nostalgia, you're supposed to do your job quickly.

SCHAEFFNER
So it's for kissing ass, you took my book.

ASHBURY
No, I am – why am I not getting through to you? This is *my* job. Simon told
me to come down here and *take* the books–

SCHAEFFNER
Did he, out of my arms, did he say, when I sleep–?

ASHBURY
(*overlapping*) No he wasn't specific, see, he just wants me to do it.
Everybody wants me to do it. And I want to do it.

SCHAEFFNER
I know.

ASHBURY
And I'm even willing to be flexible, I came down *here* – I used your, your,
whatever, your *system* – I'm trying to tell you that I just want to do my job.
All right? Just like you. And if we cannot work out some equitable way to
get both our jobs done then what – what kind of men are we?

SCHAEFFNER
What kind of men?

ASHBURY
So here's my deal to you, Mister Schaeffner. If you will let me work here,
unimpeded, with no interference or running commentary from you… and
no sit-ins… then you get your book back.

SCHAEFFNER
You are mad.

ASHBURY
In the same condition as it left the fold. I'll even give you fifty bucks to have
it restored.

SCHAEFFNER
Madman. You have stolen Trumpet's property.

ASHBURY
Yeah?

SCHAEFFNER
You are trying to – what is the word? Blackmail?

ASHBURY
That is a word.

SCHAEFFNER
Ja, and I will tell Solstein and you will lose your job.

ASHBURY
Really?

SCHAEFFNER
That is the deal.

ASHBURY
Is it?

SCHAEFFNER
Ja.

ASHBURY
And what are you gonna tell him?

SCHAEFFNER
(*goes to exit*) You can read it in e-mail.

ASHBURY
You gonna tell him I stole a book?

SCHAEFFNER
Yes.

ASHBURY
You gonna tell him which book?

SCHAEFFNER
What?

ASHBURY
Which? Which book I stole?

SCHAEFFNER
It – it does not matter–

ASHBURY
Oh I think it does. It does because I stole the most valuable book in the library. Remember? That's what you said.

SCHAEFFNER
It is.

ASHBURY
Well, then you'd better tell him that. I mean it's bound to have some weight. You don't want it to sound like I stole your *Reader's Digest*, right?

SCHAEFFNER
I will tell him what is important.

ASHBURY
And the book is important. So you'll tell him and he'll ask you, what's this book about?

SCHAEFFNER
What are you doing?

ASHBURY
And you'll tell him.

SCHAEFFNER
What–

ASHBURY
You'll tell him, right? What's in the book?

Pause.

SCHAEFFNER
You do not know.

ASHBURY
I don't?

SCHAEFFNER
No.

ASHBURY
You sure you didn't tell me?

SCHAEFFNER

Yes.

ASHBURY

Because you sometimes run off at the mouth a little bit, you know–

SCHAEFFNER

You do not read German.

ASHBURY

No, but my computer does. You see last night I fed the book into a Babelfish translator. Do you know what that is?

SCHAEFFNER

No.

ASHBURY

Well it's fairly primitive but it gave me a pretty good idea of why your little German book is so important to you. I liked the part where it lists thirteen things you can do to get rid of *Juden* in your neighbourhood.

SCHAEFFNER

That is not right. It does not say that.

ASHBURY

No?

SCHAEFFNER

These books are for *history*–

ASHBURY

Well then let's go tell Simon Solstein what kind of history it is you subscribe to, Schaeffner. We can go tell him right now. Of if you cooperate and let me do my job, starting now, then Simon won't find out a thing, because your history book will disappear. Just like all the *Juden*. And that's my final offer.

Pause.

Oh, and I'm allowed to smoke in here, too.

SCENE TWENTY-FIVE

RACHEL is making a presentation to a panel. She is very nervous.

RACHEL

Good morning. My name is Rachel Lewis, I was an employee at Lyndon Languages. I taught English as a Second Language to immigrants, and

I loved my job and I think I was getting pretty good at it but then I was fired. By the senior staff director, that's Laura Pecorini.

W-well my complaint? I don't know if I should call it a complaint, I think it's a *concern*. And all I'm concerned about is... well, whether people who apply to work at Lyndon in the future, and if they're the same – of the same ethnic background as myself... well I think they have a right to know about Ms. Pecorini's attitudes.

I-I-I can't say, I mean who, really, who can say, who's in a position to judge anyone else, who's "racist?" Right? J-just because she's said some things? Because she feels the need to criticize or, or condemn something that's a *part* of who I *am*?

Did I–? When I–? No, I-I don't know, I don't remember. When they ask you for your race on application forms, I just put "white." It's not because I feel white, it's just safer.

Well, she found out because – because, I, I was talking with her father. In the waiting room, while he was waiting for her, this was just before I was fired, and, and I happened to mention to him that – or I said that it was Yom Kippur soon, or something, I forget what, but it slipped out I was Jewish. To her father. And her father, who I might add just looked like a sweet old German man, well he started to fume and just swear like a madman, and I was mortified, my face was burning, because what are you supposed to *do*–

I can't. No, look, don't ask me to repeat the things he said. I try not to remember things like that. But I remember his expression. And, and Laura's, Ms Pecorini's – she was just laughing. With her eyes, she was laughing. She didn't care.

She – what? No, she was there. We were in her office. Well what did I say? No, we, we were there, I remember she was, or in the waiting room because it was just, just after I got my notice, and I was there to, to, to ask her...

Look, I just – I just want my job back.

<u>SCENE TWENTY-SIX</u>

> *The library. SCHAEFFNER is here, alone. Drinking. He goes over to the scanning equipment and contemplates its destruction. However, before he can do anything to it, JILL appears at the door.*

JILL
Excuse me.

SCHAEFFNER
What do you want?

JILL
I was looking for my brother. They said he'd be here.

SCHAEFFNER
Now everyone is invited.

JILL
I saw you, on the street.

SCHAEFFNER
Ja, I remember you. I do not forget a face.

JILL
He's not here.

SCHAEFFNER
He has been called away. Maybe by Solstein! Who knows?

JILL
Well could you give this to him? It's a flyer.

SCHAEFFNER
Maybe I should trade it to him. Make him a deal. (*laughs*)

JILL
I'm gonna go.

SCHAEFFNER
Is this important to him?

JILL
What?

SCHAEFFNER
You should not leave important things in stranger's hands.

JILL
It's for my show and I want him to come.

SCHAEFFNER
Show? What show?

JILL
Read it. I'm doing a show. You're even in it, sort of.

SCHAEFFNER
I am not in your show.

JILL
Well I wrote things down about you. What I thought.

SCHAEFFNER
What things?

JILL
It's just a story, sort of. It came into my head when I saw you. Here. (*she finds the spot in her notebook and shows it to him*) See what the show is, is I mix these stories that I write with my own memories of things.

SCHAEFFNER
(*reading*) "Old man with book."

JILL
That's you. You had this old book in your hands and I–

SCHAEFFNER
(*He grabs JILL's arm. She drops the notebook and retreats.*) Yes? Have you seen it? Do you know where it is?

JILL
Oh god.

SCHAEFFNER
What has he told you? About me, what did you write down? You should not believe what he tells you.

JILL
It's not like this, you're not like that, don't be red, I'm just, I'm visiting.

SCHAEFFNER
I'm sorry.

JILL
There are just things that I'm trying to see that I'm trying to, but you're not one of them, you weren't there you're not now the thing that's roaring–

SCHAEFFNER
It's alright. I'm sorry. It's alright. I didn't mean to frighten you.

JILL
Please hand me my book now.

SCHAEFFNER
What?

JILL
It's at your feet, please pick it up and give it to me. I'm going.

SCHAEFFNER
I didn't mean–

JILL
It's okay I'm just going.

SCHAEFFNER
I, yes, I. Here.

> *He picks up the notebook, brushes it off, turns it around. JILL reaches out for it but something on the open page has caught his eye. He frowns as he reads it. After a moment, JILL steps forward and snatches it.*

JILL
Thank you.

SCHAEFFNER
Is that about him?

JILL
Good-bye.

SCHAEFFNER
You and him? Was that him? (*JILL is gone. He calls out.*) Was that him?

<u>**SCENE TWENTY-SEVEN**</u>

> *At home.*

ASHBURY
What's going on?

RACHEL
What's going on?

ASHBURY
You called me, I came. (*beat*) It's the middle of the day. (*beat*) Rachel.

RACHEL
What is this? (*She holds up the book.*)

ASHBURY
It's for work.

RACHEL
For work, this is work, this is what you call work? (*She throws the book at him.*)

ASHBURY
Careful.

RACHEL
I, bullshit, this is not from work. I have never seen you, in four years, you've never brought home something like – like–

ASHBURY
Look, I told you, I told you all about the, the, the library, the–

RACHEL
And you just felt perfectly comfortable *leaving* it lying around the house–

ASHBURY
I didn't know you could read German.

RACHEL
I didn't read German. I read the translation sheets you left beside it. (*swears in Yiddish*)

ASHBURY
All right, I'm sorry. Really. I'm, I wasn't thinking. I forgot. You never–

RACHEL
You *forgot* that I was *Jewish*?

ASHBURY
I'm sorry.

RACHEL
You forgot that my family was at Belsen?

ASHBURY
Your family was never in fucking Belsen.

RACHEL
Oh–

ASHBURY
When I met you you'd never heard of Belsen.

RACHEL
Fuck you.

ASHBURY
You want me to explain this? (*the book*)

RACHEL
No.

ASHBURY
Because I have an explanation.

RACHEL
Is that like an excuse?

ASHBURY
I just, you automatically *assume*–

RACHEL
Do you have an excuse for that book?

ASHBURY
Do I, no, I don't have an excuse, there is no excuse. This book should be demolished.

RACHEL
Well then do it!

ASHBURY
Look, it's complicated.

RACHEL
It's a conspiracy. You and them.

ASHBURY
Rachel, look, look, please. This is just a tool.

RACHEL
A what?

ASHBURY
A tool. A means to an end, look, the contents don't matter.

RACHEL
So that's why you *translated* it, to show to your Aryan buddies at work?

ASHBURY
My–?

RACHEL
Yeah, so where was your family during the war?

ASHBURY
You're right! You've found me out, Rachel, I'm a Nazi. You've been sleeping with Hitler for the last four years.

RACHEL
(*crying*) You think that's fucking funny?

ASHBURY
No. (*Pause. ASHBURY kisses his two forefingers and draws an invisible circle on the floor*) Remember this?

RACHEL
No.

ASHBURY
I'm declaring a Truth Zone.

RACHEL
Don't do that.

ASHBURY
I want to. Have I ever lied to you in a Truth Zone?

RACHEL
How should–

ASHBURY
Have I?

RACHEL
No.

ASHBURY
Then here it is. I'm on your side. I screwed up bringing that home but it is not mine, I don't subscribe to anything it says and I would never wish anything like that on anyone. I don't believe in hurting anybody. Especially you.

Pause.

Okay?

RACHEL
What about her?

ASHBURY
Who?

RACHEL
Your sister. Would you ever hurt her?

ASHBURY
Why are you asking me that?

RACHEL
Because you're still in the circle.

<u>SCENE TWENTY-EIGHT</u>

JILL in her studio. She stands in front of the screen and watches the projector as it creates another story out of the flame.

JILL
Once there was a family. There was a mother and a father and a sister and a brother and everyone was happy except the sister. The sister was different and everybody laughed and laughed and laughed. And she had no friends so she had to make friends up, and one of the friends she made up was Fire.

She and Fire would play all day down in the vacant lot, alone. They'd sometimes play a game where they would see how high they both could jump.

But one day someone came. Her brother came and saw them playing and he hit her and he called her names and then he said – he said that she'd been bad and wasn't, couldn't play with Fire or she'd be punished. So she said g'bye to Fire. And Fire was sad. He cried and cried and cried.

But then at night he came into her room.

ASHBURY steps into the room behind the screen. For a moment he is just a silhouette. JILL turns and sees him and leaps backwards, petrified.

ASHBURY
Jill? Jill?

JILL
Yes?

Comes out from behind the screen.

ASHBURY
We have to talk some. (*pause*) Do you know who I am?

JILL
Uh-huh.

<u>Scene Twenty-nine</u>

RACHEL and ASHBURY at home. RACHEL is getting dressed up to go out.

RACHEL
I read something today. In *Chatelaine*. There are ways you can tell when someone's lying.

ASHBURY
What are you doing?

RACHEL
Their eyes, for instance. Their eyes always do things. (*beat*) What time is it?

ASHBURY
Why?

RACHEL
Why, we don't want to be late, is why.

ASHBURY
Late for what?

RACHEL
For the show.

ASHBURY
What show?

RACHEL
Or if they get defensive. That's another way.

ASHBURY
There isn't a show. I told you–

RACHEL
What people say, it's just never the whole story.

ASHBURY
And even if there were a show–

RACHEL
If there were a show you wouldn't miss it for the world. You wanna disappoint your sister? Your long-lost–

ASHBURY
(*under*) Rachel.

RACHEL
–Looney tunes sister? This might be the start of her rise to stardom.

ASHBURY
Good for her.

RACHEL
She invited us specifically.

ASHBURY
Two days ago you were scared to even look at her.

RACHEL
I'm not scared. You're scared of listening to her.

ASHBURY
I'm not, look, I just don't think we should go out tonight. We've had, it's been a difficult day.

RACHEL
What do you mean?

ASHBURY
What do I–? Nothing, it's been – we had a fight.

RACHEL
No we didn't.

ASHBURY
About the book?

RACHEL
That wasn't a fight.

ASHBURY
What was it?

RACHEL
Well it doesn't mean that we should miss–

ASHBURY
It means I'm tired, I'd rather sleep–

RACHEL
Sleep, that's perfect, all you ever do is work and sleep. Are you aware that there are other things going on in the world? That people have lives?

ASHBURY
You're not being rational.

RACHEL
I want to see what she has to say. All right? About you.

ASHBURY
Well I don't.

RACHEL
Because it's the truth?

ASHBURY
Jesus, Rach, how hard is it to just, just *trust* me?

RACHEL
It used to be easy.

ASHBURY
Well, then–

RACHEL
But maybe I was stupid. *Chatelaine* says there's always lying somewhere in relationships.

ASHBURY
You believe *Chatelaine* but you don't believe me.

RACHEL
We're going to the show.

ASHBURY
Rachel!

The phone rings.

RACHEL
Don't answer it. We're out.

ASHBURY
Rachel. If we, listen, if we *go*, if we *participate*–

RACHEL
(*overlapping*) I don't want them to sell out or something.

ASHBURY
(*overlapping*) We're confirming, her, her fantasies, her, everything, we give it weight–

RACHEL
(*overlapping*) If they're just fantasies then what difference does it make–

ASHBURY
(*overlapping*) Because they're *lies*, you know what it's like, you tell a lie and then it *grows*–

RACHEL
(*overlapping*) No, I don't know what it's like, I want to know–

ASHBURY
(*overlapping*) Oh, so, what, you've never told a lie?

RACHEL
No I have never told a lie.

ASHBURY
I– (*Beat. The phone is still ringing.*) Fuck.

RACHEL
Don't answer it.

ASHBURY
Wait. (*answers the phone*) Ashbury.

RACHEL
I'm going.

ASHBURY
No, she's out. She's at a show.

RACHEL
Who is it? Hey.

ASHBURY
I see. All right. I'll tell her. Thanks. (*hangs up*)

RACHEL
Well?

ASHBURY
That was someone from the Office of Human Rights. They said your appeal was turned down.

RACHEL
Oh. (*beat*) I got fired. (*beat*) Just today. Or, well, Tuesday.

ASHBURY
Huh. (*beat*) Well, I guess the show's on me, tonight, then.

SCENE THIRTY

> *Backstage. JILL is warming up. She practices a movement over and over
> again: she starts prone, rises up arching her back, and then leaps away
> with a gesture of terror. SCHAEFFNER enters unseen.*

SCHAEFFNER
That is very beautiful.

JILL
You're not supposed to be back here.

SCHAEFFNER
I am sorry.

JILL
I'm warming up.

SCHAEFFNER
I cannot stay for the show, you see.

JILL
Do I know you?

SCHAEFFNER
We met today. In the library.

JILL
Well. Thanks for coming, anyway.

SCHAEFFNER
Is this your first performance?

JILL
Yeah.

SCHAEFFNER
Are you nervous?

JILL
No. Yes.

SCHAEFFNER
I wish you the best of luck.

JILL
Why can't you stay?

SCHAEFFNER
I am an old man. I need to rest. Would you – sign this?

> *He holds out the flyer she gave him earlier.*

JILL
Oh. Okay. Uh…

SCHAEFFNER
I have no pen.

> *JILL digs her notebook out of her bag, and pulls the pen out of that. She signs his flyer.*

SCHAEFFNER
Thank you. Do you think I could see your notebook?

JILL
What?

SCHAEFFNER
For a moment. To see in the mind of an artist.

JILL
It's personal.

SCHAEFFNER
I am very discreet.

JILL
I mean it's mine. It's my life, in there. You can't.

SCHAEFFNER
I promise to return it.

JILL
I remember you.

SCHAEFFNER
I will not damage it.

JILL
You're the one.

SCHAEFFNER
I keep books well, it is my trade.

JILL
You, you're the face, from then, the face out of time. In my room.

SCHAEFFNER
Please.

He advances on her. She backs away.

JILL
You're with him, all of them, the faces that flicker. That forget. I don't want you here, I didn't ask you to speak. I want you to go.

SCHAEFFNER
I will go. But I need one thing.

JILL
Help.

SCHAEFFNER
Do not scream.

JILL
Help!

SCHAEFFNER grabs her and covers her mouth.

SCHAEFFNER
Shut! Be quiet please. I do not want to hurt you.

He looks at the notebook, which is over by JILL's bag. He looks at JILL.

Your skin feels soft. You think it is dry, like paper. But it is not. It is like satin.

<u>SCENE THIRTY-ONE</u>

In the darkness, an announcer's VOICE:

VOICE
Ladies and gentlemen, we are sorry to inform you that tonight's perform-ance of "Burnt Remains" has been cancelled due to sudden illness. The box office will be happy to exchange your tickets to another night's perform-ance. Once again, we apologize for the inconvenience.

SCENE THIRTY-TWO

ASHBURY and RACHEL outside the theatre.

RACHEL
Should we go back and check on her?

ASHBURY
She's not really sick. She's flipped out again.

RACHEL
So she never tells the truth, is that the deal?

ASHBURY
Pretty much.

RACHEL
What if you're wrong?

ASHBURY
Go ahead then.

RACHEL
You're her brother.

ASHBURY
Look, if you were right about me and her, then I'd be the last person she'd want to see. So go alone. But then if *I'm* right, who knows what she'll do to you?

Pause.

RACHEL
Do you love me?

ASHBURY
Rachel.

RACHEL
Wait. (*She kisses her fingers and draws a circle on the sidewalk, around ASHBURY.*) Do you love me?

ASHBURY
Yes.

RACHEL
Then stop fucking with me.

ASHBURY
What do you want me to say? Tell me what to say and I'll say it.

RACHEL
Why'd you never mention her?

ASHBURY
After the fire they locked her up. She was crazy. And nobody wants a crazy sister, it's not – you don't go *telling* people.

RACHEL
Not even your wife?

ASHBURY
You're not my wife.

RACHEL
So you just forgot her?

ASHBURY
I was scared of her.

RACHEL
Scared.

ASHBURY
Yes.

RACHEL
Scared of what she'd say.

ASHBURY
No. Crazy people.

RACHEL
People might believe her.

ASHBURY
No.

RACHEL
Did you do it?

ASHBURY
What?

RACHEL
Her. Did you burn your little sister?

Pause.

ASHBURY
Come on, let's get a cab.

RACHEL
If you step out of that circle I'll leave you.

Pause.

ASHBURY
All right, then.

Grabs RACHEL and pulls her up against him.

RACHEL
Let go.

ASHBURY
What's the matter?

RACHEL
Let me go.

ASHBURY
No, I think we could both use a little truth session–

RACHEL
(*under*) Let me go don't touch me!

Pulls away. Pause.

ASHBURY
When I was five I fell off the monkey bars onto my face, on the gravel. That was the worst thing that ever happened to me. I remember the pain, striking the tarmac, and I remember crying and reaching out, and the blurry figures in the distance. I could feel them looking at me and I knew it was because my face was gone, I only had half a face, it's been stripped off and replaced with gravel. That's what I thought. But there isn't even a scar. I was five, and I remember it like that. When Jill was burnt I was twelve. I just know that I woke up, I felt the heat, thinking – or imagining a white flash, like the whole world on fire. Feeling satin. Wishing for it. Wishing, white, so I, dirty, I... *why can't I remember?*

And that's all the truth I have left.

SCENE THIRTY-THREE

The library.

SCHAEFFNER
Good morning.

ASHBURY
It's Saturday.

SCHAEFFNER
Did you bring it?

ASHBURY
Why did you call me?

SCHAEFFNER
You want to finish the job, you should finish the job. Why stop for the weekend?

ASHBURY
Is that all?

SCHAEFFNER
How was the show?

ASHBURY
What show?

SCHAEFFNER
You know what show. (*He tosses down a crumpled-up flyer.*) I was sad I could not stay.

ASHBURY
What's going on?

SCHAEFFNER
You brought the book, yes?

ASHBURY
Yes, I brought the book, but you're not getting it or anything until you–

SCHAEFFNER
Good. I want to read you something.

ASHBURY
Don't waste any more of my time.

SCHAEFFNER
Oh this is not a waste. (*He brings out JILL's notebook and reads.*) "Her brother came and saw them playing and got mad. He hit her and he laughed at her and then he said – he said that she'd been bad and couldn't play with fire and would have to be punished."

ASHBURY
Where did you get that?

SCHAEFFNER
(*reads*) "But then at night he came into her room."

ASHBURY
Where the fuck did you get that, what's going on here?

SCHAEFFNER
You want me to continue?

ASHBURY
If you hurt her–

SCHAEFFNER
What I did to her is not the issue.

ASHBURY
Give that to me.

SCHAEFFNER
We are making a deal now, yes?

ASHBURY
That's not yours, give it back to me.

SCHAEFFNER
I think I will not. I think I will call Solstein and the police and maybe the whole world and tell them what is in here.

ASHBURY
Whatever it says in there, whatever is written–

SCHAEFFNER
They do not have to know. It will all be forgotten.

ASHBURY
What do you want?

SCHAEFFNER
You give me the book. You tell Solstein nothing. And you will take your things and leave my library now and forever. That is my final offer.

ASHBURY
I have a job–

SCHAEFFNER
Not for long.

ASHBURY
I have, my, my, my wife–

SCHAEFFNER
You have made me do this.

ASHBURY
I won't be manipulated by lies.

SCHAEFFNER
Yes, you will.

Pause.

ASHBURY
God damn it.

He takes out the damaged book and offers it to SCHAEFFNER. They exchange the book for the notebook.

SCHAEFFNER
Now you will leave here.

ASHBURY
(*weighs the notebook in his hand*) Fine.

SCHAEFFNER
You will tell Solstein you have finished with the library.

ASHBURY
Whatever.

SCHAEFFNER
And of this book you will tell him nothing.

ASHBURY
Oh I'll tell him alright.

SCHAEFFNER
What?

ASHBURY
I'll tell him everything. (*about the notebook*) Did you read all of this?

SCHAEFFNER
You cannot. We had a deal.

ASHBURY
I'll tell him about the Nazi in the basement. That his "Ongoing Humanities Project" is spewing hate literature all over the Web.

SCHAEFFNER
You will not.

ASHBURY
Yes, I will. See I don't care if these books ever get scanned or not, but I think by now I really want to see you go down in flames, Mister Schaeffner.

SCHAEFFNER
He will fire me.

ASHBURY
You never know. They've ignored you down here for fifty years, they might ignore you till you die.

SCHAEFFNER
Simon is a Jew.

ASHBURY
He's a busy man.

SCHAEFFNER
You are a terrible person.

ASHBURY
Figure that out by yourself, did you?

SCHAEFFNER
It is there, on the page. You can toss me away but you will not get rid of those things.

ASHBURY
I told you, it's bullshit.

SCHAEFFNER
Then why did you want it back?

Pause. ASHBURY takes out his lighter and burns the notebook.

ASHBURY
Now it doesn't matter.

SCHAEFFNER
The whole world.

ASHBURY
What?

SCHAEFFNER
The whole world will know.

ASHBURY
Not now, they won't.

SCHAEFFNER
It is too late. I have already done it. Put it there. On the Web.

ASHBURY
You did what?

SCHAEFFNER
All night long.

ASHBURY
You can't… you don't have the faintest idea what you're talking about.

SCHAEFFNER
I do. I watch you scan the books. You taught me.

ASHBURY
You wouldn't get past the first prompt.

SCHAEFFNER
I have done. It is out there. Now the whole world can read the things you did. (*beat*) It is like you say, it does not matter now if it is true or not. It is written.

<u>Scene Thirty-four</u>

> *JILL's studio. The flame is lit and JILL dances behind the screen. This scene is done entirely in silhouette.*

JILL
Once there was a girl who had things written on her body. People saw the writing and didn't like the things it said. It made them scared. They looked the other way.

She pours gasoline on herself.

They pretended that she wasn't a person at all, that she was made of wax. She was a silent wax statue. And the words were written in the wax, so if the wax got hot the words would go away.

She steps to the centre of the screen so she is in line with the projection of the flame.

So they lit her on fire.

She lights herself on fire.

The end.

"As Long as the Sun Shines"

by
**Christina Grant
and Doug Dunn**

INTRODUCTION TO *"AS LONG AS THE SUN SHINES"*

The Crown's understanding of the symbolism used by the First Nations at the time the treaties were negotiated is reflected by the words written in the purported documents of these treaties: "As long as the sun shines, the river flows and the grass grows." From the Elders' perspective, the symbols used by each of the treaty parties were meant to symbolize the commitment of each of the parties to maintaining, nurturing and protecting the relationship of peace, friendship and alliance agreed to between the nations who were party to the treaties.[1]

Christina Grant and Doug Dunn's *"As Long as the Sun Shines"* is a dramatic re-enactment of the signing of Treaty No. 8 on June 21, 1899, at Lesser Slave Lake.[2] This historiographic pageant, shuttling back and forth between then and now, uses a late-twentieth-century narrator to introduce a series of tableaux which dramatize anxieties in late-nineteenth-century Cree and White communities about the signing of documents that effectively transformed Native history in the Athabasca, Mackenzie and Peace River Districts. In revisiting the circumstances surrounding the creation of Treaty No. 8, the tableaux explore issues of understanding for both Natives and Whites and, admirably, with an unwillingness to take sides. What is remarkable is the sense of loss; the questions and misgivings voiced by the Cree Chief Keenoosayo, his brother Moostoos, and Mahekun Kisowaso about their disappearing resources, their freedom to use the land as always, and the need for a treaty which privileges White law resonate forcefully in our ears today, when the history of residential schools and land claim settlements indicate how differently promises have been interpreted.

The narrator's scene-setting establishes both the urgency of the situation and room for error in 1899 as part of the complexities of understanding what actually happened; this device opens up the play's hermeneutic space. "Understand" is a prominent verb throughout the text. Violent clashes between White prospectors in the Klondyke and Native hunters and trappers threatened to destroy peace as well as trade and settlement. Grant and Dunn's scenes skillfully alternate between Native and White perspectives. In the two opening tableaux family scenes convey atmospheres of high anxiety. Domestic exchanges between Neesochesis and his daughter, between this Headman and band members, and between wives relay frustrations about Whites killing "our people" in the rush for gold and about the differences separating traders' values and those of trappers and hunters. Commerce for the traders' clothes, guns and sugar depletes the Native supply of furs. The subsequent family scene involving Chief Commissioner Laird, a widower, whose overwork in preparing for the expedition to the north prompts the fretful concern of his maiden sister and young daughter, introduces its own misgivings. Laird wonders aloud about the trustworthiness of the members of his own party, while the appearance of entrepreneur Richard Secord underscores the threat to the Métis, many of whom will sell their scrip (certificates to land) for a pittance rather than travel to Edmonton to redeem them, and to the treaty Indians who will have received cash payments. Such worries were well-founded; as the *Edmonton Bulletin* reported of the signing, "every trader has his canvas spread and his wares exposed to catch the dollars from the Indian as he gets paid."[3]

The three scenes at Lesser Slave Lake, before and during the signing, literally intensify the divides between two camps of understanding. While Laird misses the humour of the Native negotiators, they for their part are quick to question the motives of the treaty-creators and to press for provisions about education of their children and medicine especially for the elderly. The fifth and final scene emphasizes the continuing dialectic between two schools of discourse: the pervasive tone of "Euro-authority" and the wary, interrogating caution of Keenoosayo, who asks, prophetically, about the longevity of the terms, instruction of children "as long as the sun shines and water runs" and non-interference with religious beliefs. Illustrating the Cree principles of "Tâpwêwin" (speaking with precision and accuracy), "Wîtaskêwin" (agreeing to live together in peace) and "Tipahamâtowin" (treating each other commensurately),[4] Keenoosayo proclaims that "we *are* all brothers here." However, he does not admit that the Queen, the Great Mother, owns the land, only that he and his people are willing to share. What Father Lacombe applauds as a wholesale endorsement of the White terms of the treaty is, in reality, a different concept of a relationship to the land given by the Creator and its bounty. The epilogue of Treaty No. 8 promises "as remembered and understood by our Elders" filters the document and circumstances of 1899 through the assumptions about historical treaties enunciated in such documents as the 1996 *Report of the Royal Commission on Aboriginal Peoples* and repeated statements by Elders, who reacted with incredulity "that anyone, much less the Crown, could seriously believe that First Nations would ever have agreed to 'extinguish' their God-given rights."[5]

"As Long as the Sun Shines" refuses to make easy judgements of blame or condemnation; rather it invites the audience to continue the debate whether or not both parties in the treaty fully understood the facts and implications of their actions. As a combination of history and writing, the real and discourse, this dramatic re-enactment remains historiographic in the sense Michel de Certeau has described, by connecting facts and fiction, "working as if the two were being joined."[6] This hybrid text, in which "tipis shake with argument" and disagreements erupt between commissioners and entrepreneurs, also underlines the epistemological tensions between the White language of law and Native ways, between gardens, houses and fences and moving camps, between a concept of land ownership and a recognition of the land as the Creator's, between a desire to listen, talk to and accommodate the commissioners and a fear of being "bound like fish in nets."

Athabasca-based playwrights and journalists, Christina Grant and Doug Dunn, were commissioned by the Treaty No. 8 Centennial Committee of the Lesser Slave Lake Indian Regional Council to produce a play re-enacting the signing of Treaty 8 between the Cree Chief and Headmen of Lesser Slave Lake and Her Majesty's Commissioners. Grant and Dunn met with Elders and Native and White historians to gather facts and anecdotes that would comprise the script. With a cast of twenty, including seven descendants (or people who were there at the time) of the original signatories (both Native and White), and as the conclusion of the week-long Conference to Further the Understanding of Treaty No. 8 and the Distribution of Scrip in 1899 and of celebrations featuring pow wows, round dances and Elders' sessions, it was performed on June 21, 1999, in the hamlet of Grouard, a mile from where the treaty was actually signed, since that location was too wet and low to accommodate a large open air stage, grandstands and thousands of people. Among the audience were thirty-eight chiefs from bands within the Treaty No. 8 region, the then federal minister of Indian Affairs and Northern Development, Jane Stewart, and more than two thousand Natives, Métis and Whites. In spring 1999 earlier versions of the play had been presented in schools across northern Alberta.

NOTES

¹ Harold Cardinal and Walter Hildebrandt, *Treaty Elders of Saskatchewan; Our Dream is That Our Peoples Will One Day Be Clearly Recognized as Nations* (Calgary: University of Calgary Press, 2000), 54-55.

² Treaty No. 8, concluded between David Laird, Indian Commissioner for Manitoba and the Northwest Territories, and Cree, Beaver, Chipewyan and other Indian Chiefs and Headmen, was designed in its own words "to open for settlement, immigration, trade, travel, mining, lumbering, and such other purposes as to Her Majesty may seem meet, a tract of country" including all of northern Alberta, parts of Saskatchewan, British Columbia, and the Northwest Territories (see Figure 6). By the terms of the Treaty and in its block capitals, "the said Indians DO HEREBY CEDE, RELEASE, SURRENDER AND YIELD UP to the Government of the Dominion of Canada, for Her Majesty the Queen and Her successors for ever all their rights, titles and privileges whatsoever, to the lands included within the [stated] limits." The document makes provisions for "the said Indians... to pursue their usual vocations of hunting, trapping and fishing throughout the tract surrendered, subject to such regulations as may from time to time be made by the Government," for life on or off reserves, and for the payment of "the salaries of such teachers to instruct the children of said Indians as to Her Majesty's Government of Canada may seem advisable." The gift which seals the deal "in extinguishment of all their past claims" is the presentation of the treaty medal (Figure 5) and payment of thirty-two dollars to each Chief, twenty-two to each Headman and twelve to "every other Indian of whatever age," along with small annual payments thereafter and the receipt of either farm implements or ammunition and twine "for making nets annually." In addition to giving up all rights and submitting to further appropriations "required for public works, buildings, railways, or roads of whatsoever nature," the Chiefs were bound to "HEREBY SOLEMNLY PROMISE and engage to strictly observe this Treaty, and also to conduct and behave themselves as good and loyal subjects of Her Majesty the Queen." The signing of the Cree Chief KeeNooShayOo on June 21 was followed by similar events, called "adhesions," at Peace River Landing on July 1, Dunvegan on July 6, Vermillion on July 8, Fort Chipewyan on July 13, Smith's Landing on July 17, Fond du Lac on July 25, Fort McMurray on August 4, Wapiscow Lake on August 14, as well as signings the following summer involving Beaver, Cree, Slave, Yellow Knife, Dog Rib and Chipewyan at Sturgeon Lake, Fort St. John, Hay River and Fort Resolution. The complete text of Treaty No. 8 and its adhesions is available in *Indian Treaties and Surrenders*, 3 vols (Ottawa: King's Printer, 1912; rpt. Saskatoon: Fifth House, 1993), III: 290-301. Charles Mair's *Through the Mackenzie Basin* (1908) is an account by one of the original signatories; it is available in the Western Canada Reprint series, introductions by David W. Leonard and Brian Calliou (Edmonton: University of Alberta Press, 1999).

For a discussion of the historical context of Treaty No. 8, see Arthur J. Ray, Jim Miller and Frank J. Tough, *Bounty and Benevolence: A History of Saskatchewan Treaties* (Montreal and Kingston: McGill-Queen's University

Press, 2000), 148-169. As for the promise of non-interference in traditional ways of life, these authors conclude that "the oral histories of Treaty 8 people make it clear that the descendants of those who agreed to the treaty believe that this promise was not kept" (169).

[3] As quoted by Graham Thomson, "Quest for a Treaty's True Spirit," *Edmonton Journal* (13 June 1999), F1.

[4] Cardinal and Hildebrandt, *Treaty Elders*, 48, 53.

[5] Cardinal and Hildebrandt, *Treaty Elders*, 58.

[6] Michel de Certeau, *The Writing of History*, trans. Tom Conley (New York: Columbia University Press, 1988), xxvi.

On the morning of June 21, 1999, a cast from Edmonton, Slave Lake, Athabasca and parts between performed the 1+ hour drama with an audience of 2,500 people at Grouard, with the following cast:

Narrator	Shannon Cunningham
Neesochesis, headman	Ron Walker
Isabel, Neesochesis' wife	Jo-Ann Bellerose
Isabel Jr., Neesochesis' daughter	Maryel Sparks Cardinal
Mahekun Kisowaso (Wolf is Angry)	Stan Isadore
Kisikawo Pisim, Mahekun Kisowaso's wife	Michelle MacIsaac
Eunice, Laird's sister	Ann Hadaway
Inspector Snyder, NWMP	Kim Henry
Richard Secord, land speculator	Richard Secord
Dorothy, Laird's young daughter	Alicia Karl
Chief Commissioner David Laird	Richard Tosczak
Major James Walker	Lorne Larson
Father Lacombe	Jay Smith
Keenoosayo, leader of Woodland Cree	Cliff Fimrite
Moostoos, Keenoosayo's brother	Tim Willier
Weecheewaysis, headman	Shannon Armitage
Felix Giroux, headman	Dwain Davis
The Captain (Cree headman, Sturgeon Lake)	Dan Cardinal
Bishop Grouard	Father Arté Guimond
Native Elder	Edna Rain

Nonspeaking roles: Metis, Native and White bystanders in Treaty negotiation scenes. Especially Native elders & women. Also, RCMP members at the Treaty signing (bearing flag, etc.)

Directed by Doug Dunn and Christina Grant
Co-Directed by Bertha Twin and Bill Stewart
Casting by Bill Stewart
Costume consultant: Bill Stewart

"AS LONG AS THE SUN SHINES"
DRAMATIC RE-ENACTMENT OF THE SIGNING OF TREATY NO. 8
by Christina Grant and Doug Dunn

SCENE ONE – NATIVE FAMILY

> *In this scene: NEESOCHESIS, ISABEL JR., MAHEKUN, ISABEL and KISIKAWO. The setting: Aboriginal family group dialogue with three separate components. Set about one week before arrival of the treaty commission, which has been delayed. NEESOCHESIS is seated on a tree stump before his tipi, whittling. As narration ends, ISABEL enters, rolling a hoop with a stick; she is clearly frustrated.*

NARRATOR

One hundred years ago, the world was changing fast for the Indians of northwest Canada. Ancestors of the Cree, Dogrib, Chipweyan, Beaver and Slavey had lived off the land for at least 8,000 years. Then came the fur trade. That was the first Natives saw of the white man. Missionaries followed. Methodists came into the north country in 1842, and Oblate Catholics and Anglicans shortly after. These campaigns all kicked off a chain of events that brings us to the story of Treaty No. 8. The Indians and Metis—who were called half-breeds back then—went through a lot of hard times after white people came on the scene. The hot market in furs had made animals scarce, and diseases like smallpox almost wiped out some bands; they had no immunity, and no doctors. Natives 100 years ago still hunted, trapped and fished, but had become dependent on traders to survive. Hard times or not, the Indians, half-breeds and traders all got along. Natives had their own social structures and laws, and many found a way to blend Christianity with their own spiritual beliefs. But pioneers were coming, and then the prospectors of the Klondike gold rush. If everybody was to keep getting along, some agreement to share the land had to happen.

A year before the signing, the government sent a message to priests and police officers across the north: "Explain the treaty to the natives," they were told. "Tell them what they'll get, and that it would be wise to agree."

So, 100 years ago, everyone here was talking about the Commissioners on their way from Edmonton. It was the tradition of Native people to look seven generations ahead in their decisions. If the Commissioners thought this would be a quick and easy job, they were in for a shock.

We don't know exactly what happened at the signing of Treaty Number Eight. Native people have passed down stories, and notes by journalists and members of the Commission party are all just different writers' impressions. We do know there was a lot of room for error, and translation between Cree and English was far from perfect.

Today we live and sometimes struggle with the results of that meeting on the shore of Lesser Slave Lake. We need to understand what happened.

Cue for ISABEL JR. to enter.

Our drama begins with two Cree families camped at the west end of the lake. It's early June, 1899, and they—like many others from the region—have been waiting for the Commission party to arrive. The visitors are more than a week late, and everyone is getting a little tense.

ISABEL JR. attempts a play manoeuvre, growing increasingly frustrated. Narration ends. She suddenly sits down in anger, seemingly over the object. NEESOCHESIS laughs gently and motions towards the game.

NEESOCHESIS
The fish does not jump to the hook at the first throw of the line, my young Isabel.

ISABEL JR.
(*outburst*) It will never go for me!

NEESOCHESIS
(*thoughtful, concerned*) This game is not what truly bothers you.

ISABEL JR.
When are we going home, ne-papa?

NEESOCHESIS
(*sighs, reaches over and touches his daughter's shoulder*) You miss our camp.

ISABEL JR.
We have been here too long. I want to go back.

NEESOCHESIS
Do you not enjoy your play with your cousins and these new friends?

ISABEL JR.
The play is good. But many of the adults are quarrelling… and there are bad stories.

NEESOCHESIS
Bad stories?

ISABEL JR.
My cousins tell me of white men poisoning dogs and killing horses!

NEESOCHESIS
Ah yes; the gold seekers in the mountains. But they are far away.

Actors prepare at Grouard, June 1999. (Ethnology Program, Provincial Museum of Alberta)

ISABEL JR.
The stories say they are killing our people only for being in their way! And they steal our caches, and our canoes… and whatever else they want.

NEESOCHESIS
You are right. The white men's ways are different from ours; there are many things we do not understand about each other.

ISABEL JR.
I am afraid, ne-papa. There are so many new white men. The traders, they are our friends. But more white people come, and I can't tell who to trust. How many more will come ne-papa? How many more?

> *NEESOCHESIS shakes his head, but before he can respond, MAHEKUN bursts onto the scene.*

MAHEKUN
Neesochesis!

NEESOCHESIS
(*to daughter*) I think you better go my girl; it seems I have matters with Mahekun. (*ISABEL JR. runs off backstage, behind the tipi. NEESOCHESIS motions for MAHEKUN to sit, saying "api, api…."*)

MAHEKUN
I have met the Captain from Sturgeon Lake. You remember Louison? He has been taken by the spirit of Whitego!

NEESOCHESIS
Tell me of this, Mahekun.

MAHEKUN
(*intense, agitated*) Louison got sick at Bald Hill. He told his brothers he would kill them and their children if they did not kill him first. Whitego!

NEESOCHESIS
(*pause, considers the information, nods*) And did they kill him?

MAHEKUN
The people begged Pay-i-uu to protect them, and he struck Louison with an axe.

NEESOCHESIS
(*quietly*) It is our way. It could not be helped.

MAHEKUN
(*anger mounting*) Yes, It is our way. But the Captain says Napesis and Pay i-uu, with Chuck a Chuck who is witness, are being taken to Edmonton to face white man's justice.

NEESOCHESIS

(*momentarily alarmed, then resigned*) Ah, moon e yaw wuk's law. (*attempts to calm his friend*) Mahekun, we have met with the priests, who are our friends. They spoke of the treaty. We must obey white law now, no longer our own.

MAHEKUN

(*angry*) The white man's laws do not fit in our world. What should they have done; wait for the mounted police and let Louison kill everyone?

NEESOCHESIS

They would tell us to tie him, bind him, do what we must. But not to kill. That is the job of the white man now.

MAHEKUN

(*peak of anger; standing*) No! This is our life, our way.

NEESOCHESIS

There are many things that will change soon, Mahekun. It will be hard for us to accept. (*motions him to sit again, he does, reluctantly*) But we've met with the Fathers, and they say the treaty will make a strong bond of peace between the nations and avoid bloodshed. They say it is best that we sign. Still, I too fear what might come for our people.

> ISABEL, KISIKAWO and ISABEL JR. emerge slowly from behind the tipi stage left, loaded with baskets of berries; they stand back and chat quietly, noting but not engaging the men.

MAHEKUN

(*incensed, but calming down*) I am not afraid. And we do not need this treaty. The white man can come and we will trade with him – if he does not harm us we will treat him the same. It has always been this way.

NEESOCHESIS

More white men are coming; many small streams become a river, Mahekun. They too need land to live. But we will talk further with our people before we sign this treaty.

MAHEKUN

(*intense*) We have talked too much. When the commissioners arrive, send them back with nothing in their hands. Reject the treaty. Let the white men find other land to take. (*suddenly rises and leaves*)

> NEESOCHESIS follows. The women and ISABEL JR. move forward, shaking their heads, motioning towards the departing men. They carry a blanket, baskets and a collection of herbs and roots.

ISABEL

(*NEESOCHESIS' wife; speaking while moving*) It is the treaty they speak of; it has caused so much trouble in the land. All the tipis here shake with argument.

KISIKAWO

(*ISABEL's friend and wife of MAHEKUN*) This is a difficult time. It is said the treaty is a good agreement between peoples... perhaps so. The men will decide, and sign the paper or not, and we will get what the white men promise or not. But if your husband Neesochesis and others sign, will it mean more food? (*The three arrive downstage, set down the blanket and begin sorting.*)

ISABEL

(*speaks in Cree, then*) You remember, Kisikawo, it is not so bad now as it was ten years ago. (*in Cree: true/ta-phew*) But I see the animals grow scarcer each season. The treaty may do many things, but I cannot see how marks on a paper can change that.

KISIKAWO

Last winter, my children's bellies were sore; they were hungry for many days. Our fish and our berries are not enough; we need the meat from our hunting.

ISABEL JR.

Ne-papa says the hunting is not so good.

ISABEL

It's true, my Isabel. Moose and deer are hard to find. The traders and the white men are hunting too for food. Ne-papa followed a moose for five days before the kill. (*sadly*) This is not as it used to be.

KISIKAWO

And the furs for trading... the beaver and the marten... and even the lynx... they are disappearing. Our men must go further and further.

ISABEL

There are many changes brought by the white man. We have his clothes, his guns, his tea and sugar. But always for these we must give furs. Twenty beaver pelts will buy a rifle. Soon, there will be no more beaver. Soon, there will be no more rifles.

KISIKAWO

The traders will do anything to get their furs. The moon e yaw wuk trappers and their poison... it is a sorrowful time for the animals in the forest.

ISABEL

(*stops sorting to gesture, the others pause too*) My husband tells me of animals taking this poison and crawling away to die; (*disgust*) the meat and the fur rot in the bushes. And Weecheewaysis, his best hunting dog ate poisoned flesh and died. (*KISIKAWO and ISABEL JR. react, mirroring her revulsion.*)

KISIKAWO

(*gesturing while the other two resume sorting*) Traders do not live like us, following the animals, moving our camps. They cannot understand; they have their gardens and their houses with fences. And they say more white people want to come and make villages.

ISABEL

Everything around us is changing.

KISIKAWO

And there is such sickness, Isabel. My husband is a strong hunter, a good hunter. But his mother, she is old and weak. She has white man's disease. I have heard of tribes full of white man's disease that our medicine cannot heal.

ISABEL JR.

Some of my friends in this camp are thin and cannot play. What's wrong, ne-mama?

ISABEL

They have the sickness; it is all around us. I fear it too.

KISIKAWO

If your husband Neesochesis signs this treaty, will all this end?

ISABEL

I do not know. But he says it is a treaty of peace, fairness and honesty. He says it will help whatever is to happen in the future. It is a treaty of friendship and good relations. And so, I believe Neesochesis will sign.

Narration takes over as the women finish sorting, pack and leave.

Scene Two – Hotel Room, Edmonton

In this scene: David LAIRD, EUNICE, DOROTHY, Inspector SNYDER, Richard SECORD. The setting: The day before departure of the treaty commission, which has been delayed due to weather and a shortage of supplies. LAIRD is seated at a table covered with lace cloth, reviewing piles of papers in preparation for the commission setting out the next day. His sister EUNICE is sitting nearby, sewing. LAIRD sighs from intense concentration, takes his glasses off and rubs his eyes.

NARRATOR
Meanwhile, back in Edmonton, the government people are getting ready
to head north. Many businessmen and bankers are with them. They're
hoping to make some money when half-breeds cash in their scrip. Scrip
is a piece of paper that either promises a piece of land, or can be used like
money to buy land. The treaty offers reserves (and promises) to Indians.
Scrip is the compensation offered to half breeds – or any Indian who doesn't
want treaty. The word is, though, that just as at other treaty signings, the
Natives will consider scrip notes worthless. In a hotel room in Edmonton,
Chief Commissioner David Laird is burning the midnight oil. He's been
invested with the task of representing Her Majesty Queen Victoria and the
Government of Canada, and he's feeling the weight of that tonight.

EUNICE
You are working too hard, David. Let me make you some tea.

LAIRD
(*settles back, appreciative*) I think not. But what would I do without my dear
sister to take care of me.

EUNICE
Much more than is good for you, of course. However I suppose that is why
you've been entrusted with so many important tasks.

LAIRD
I like to do what I can, you know that Eunice. And I'm afraid I was the most
experienced fellow they could find. I do know Indians.

EUNICE
(*agreeably*) You do know Indians. But this assignment worries me, David.

LAIRD
It has been a while since we signed a treaty.

EUNICE
More than 20 years.

LAIRD
And much has happened…. But we need this treaty, Eunice. The Athabasca
country and land of the Peace River are rich with fur, timber, minerals…
and there is talk about oil. It's the last area to be opened up for settlement,
and that, my dear, cannot go ahead without "making peace with the
natives."

EUNICE
Avoiding bloodshed on both sides… so important. But David, my fears
cannot be dismissed. Even you must admit we do not know the tempera-
ment of these northern Indians. We have only scattered reports, and some

The Expedition, consisting of thirteen wagons and fifty men, leaves for the North on 29 May 1899. (Provincial Archives of Alberta)

of those alarming indeed; Indians attacking men set for the Klondike…
skirmishes… deaths! (*LAIRD shakes his head, feeling she's overreacting.*) I know
often it is the Klondikers' fault, still… deaths.

LAIRD
The Klondikers have only gold on their minds. Where there have been
graves, they've made their own. In any case, I shall have the Mounted
Police under Inspector Snyder ensuring the safety of myself and our
company.

EUNICE
(*urgent and loud*) But what do you know of the Indians' numbers? What do
you know of the danger?

LAIRD
Eunice, my dear, lovable worried sister, calm yourself. They need me
to treat with these Indians. There will be no trouble. They're a peaceful
people… when not unduly provoked. At the very least we shall return with
no X's on the papers. But even that is unlikely; the missionaries and police
have been telling the natives about our very generous offer—and that it's
the wisest course of action—for the past half year. It is my belief they shall
sign happily. It is a good offer… and in any case, the only offer. Settlers are
coming in. Everyone wants to ensure peace.

LAIRD
(*notices his daughter at edge of room*) Dottie!

DOROTHY
Papa?!

LAIRD
Did we wake you? Come. (*He motions her to him. She skips sleepily over and he
pulls her into his lap.*)

DOROTHY
Papa, I don't want you to go.

LAIRD
(*exchanges look with EUNICE and puts full attention on DOROTHY*) I know.
But I will come home to you as quickly as I can. I have made other trips,
you know how it is.

DOROTHY
(*emphatically, gazing at him*) No, Papa. Stay here with me. (*looks down*) I am
afraid you won't come back.

LAIRD

(*hugs her tightly, teasing*) Ah, you have the same worry bones as your Auntie Eunice. (*serious*) My sweet Dottie. We will miss each other. (*pause*) I'll bring you back something. What would you like… maybe some moccasins?

DOROTHY shakes her head "no" and looks down. LAIRD lifts her off his lap and gently presses her away from him, his hands on her shoulders.

LAIRD

I will bring you a present. But mostly I will bring myself back, safe and sound… (*lighter tone*) for you to torment with your play. (*hug and kiss on the forehead*) Go now, and get some sleep.

DOROTHY

Good night Papa. Good night Auntie Eunice.

EUNICE

Good night love.

They hug briefly, DOROTHY leaves sadly. LAIRD muses and collects himself

EUNICE

That little one is why you must take the greatest care. You are all she has. (*pause*) David, you do not know for certain what will happen.

LAIRD

That is correct, I don't know for certain. But we have heard these Indians are a noble lot. Their chiefs and headmen are wise and thoughtful men. They will choose to sign, mark my words. They will choose to sign.

EUNICE

(*sigh of resignation*) Well my dear brother, I shall have faith in the situation as you do and pray for your safe return.

Loud knocking on door; LAIRD and EUNICE are startled.

LAIRD

Rather late caller. (*opens door*) Inspector Snyder.

SNYDER

(*tips hat to EUNICE*) Ma'am. (*to LAIRD*) Apologies for the hour, Sir. But in light of our early departure in the morning, I thought it best to check in with you.

LAIRD

No trouble, inspector. I was going over some figures myself just now. Eunice my dear, to bed now. You'll see me off in the morning.

EUNICE

(*smiles to both men*) I shall. Good night, David. (*nods to SNYDER*) Inspector Snyder (*He tips his hat as she leaves.*)

LAIRD

(*motions to SNYDER*) Please, sit down. A spot of brandy, Inspector?

SNYDER

No thank you, sir. I shall be brief. About the arrangements. The rest of the supplies have finally arrived from Winnipeg.

LAIRD

An unfortunate delay.

SNYDER

The flour is loaded and the bacon and tea will be delivered in the morning. We are now fully equipped. Our wagons will number 13 and we have 50 men in all. Also, a number of land dealers, bankers and interested parties intend on coming along.

LAIRD

Quite a party. Tell me inspector, do we trust the full contingent of those travelling with us? More than $300,000 in the chest. Very tempting.

SNYDER

True, sir. But I have assembled the best of the best of my men, you can be assured of that. And, as you know from previous experience, many of those businessmen with us expect to profit from the natives and half-breeds who will sell their scrip.

LAIRD

Unfortunately you are right. Not the best for the Indians, but a sad reality. I hope the missionaries and your fellow redcoats will have convinced the Indians to take scrip for land. The scrip being offered is non-negotiable. But I fear they'll want to remove this clause from the deal. It is a shame. The treaty will give Indians reserves, but land scrip is the only way the half breeds may secure ground for themselves.

SNYDER

That's a fact, Sir. They should all take land as offered. I'm happy that Father Lacombe is coming along. He'll warn the half-breeds against selling their scrip right away to land dealers for a pittance. (*pause*) But what any of our northern Indians will do, at this point, is pure speculation. We'll see when we get there. (*stands, stretches*) I will take my leave now, Sir. I know we are both very tired; and we have a considerable journey ahead.

LAIRD

That we do, Inspector. But I have every confidence in you and your men, and Mr. Henry Round is a most competent transportation director. Oh… what of our physician?

SNYDER

Yes, Dr. Christopher West. He seems to be a most agreeable fellow, and highly recommended, though rather young.

LAIRD

Well, sometimes youthful enthusiasm can substitute for experience, especially on such an arduous expedition. (*with gravity*) I fear that our Dr. West will encounter many sad cases along the way. Reports indicate considerable disease and illness among them, and most of the natives won't have seen a medical doctor in some time. Many will no doubt avail themselves of the opportunity.

SNYDER

I'm sure you are quite right, Sir. Until morning then, sleep well, Mr. Laird.

LAIRD

You as well, Inspector. Until morning.

> *They shake hands. As SNYDER is about to leave, they are surprised by Richard SECORD popping his head in the door.*

SECORD

Evening, gentlemen! Just passing by and saw the light. Big day tomorrow.

SNYDER

(*exchanges dour look with LAIRD*) Mr. Richard Secord. Ready to go I'm sure – I noticed your wagons right up front looking mighty fine.

SECORD

Quite an adventure ahead.

LAIRD

(*wry*) Yes, we know. Inspector Snyder and I were just discussing the rather large group of businessmen—such as yourself—coming along. I'll warn you, Sir, that we have taken every precaution to keep the half-breeds from selling their scrip.

SECORD

(*taken aback, slightly humoured*) Now Mr. Laird, these people are perfectly able to think for themselves. They have their own ideas about all of this, and if they wish to sell, the least we can do is to make it easy for them. We're providing a service.

SNYDER
There's nothing we can do about you coming along, Mr. Secord. But we'll be watching.

SECORD
Don't worry about us, gentlemen. We'll offer a fair price, and everyone will be happy. I suggest you direct your attention to the liquor sellers and the like. It is they who stand to do harm to the Natives. (*tips his hat*) 'Till morning. (*departs*)

LAIRD
(*to SNYDER*) Service or not, I'm not happy with these entrepreneurs.

SNYDER
We'll keep them all in order, Sir. Good night then.

LAIRD
Good night to you, Inspector Snyder.

> *SNYDER leaves. LAIRD closes door, turns and muses for a moment, straightens a few papers and walks out of the scene.*

NARRATOR
They did get off the next day. In the rain. 160 kilometers of ruts and mud to the Athabasca landing. There they loaded everything onto two scows and a York boat and Trackers hauled them upriver to Lesser Slave Lake. The trip was supposed to take 10 days. It took 21. Nothing could have looked better to that commission party than the tipi village that appeared like a vision when they rounded Shaw's point.

SCENE THREE – FIRST MEETING, THE LAKE

> *In this scene: KEENOOSAYO, MOOSTOOS, LAIRD, WALKER, LACOMBE and SNYDER. Also, others as crowd, if available. The setting: It is June 19, a sunny afternoon on the shore of Lesser Slave Lake. The treaty party has just arrived by boat SR. LAIRD, WALKER, LACOMBE and SNYDER come forward to meet KEENOOSAYO and MOOSTOOS SL, who are apart from anyone else, waiting and watching the entourage's approach.*

LAIRD
(*speaks with authoritative air, though respectful*) Greetings. I am chief commissioner David Laird. (*extends hand*)

KEENOOSAYO
(*nods, shakes hand*) I am Keenoosayo, here to greet you on behalf of our people. This is Moostoos, my brother.

Moostoos, Chief of the Sucker Creek Band and brother of Keenooshayo.
(Provincial Archives of Alberta)

LAIRD
Tobacco for you. (*gives a pouch to each Indian; they accept*)

MOOSTOOS
(*nods in the direction they came*) Your journey was long and difficult.

LAIRD
(*nodding in agreement*) Very. (*wry but careful humour*) With all the rain our trackers gained a new respect for mud, pulling our heavy boats up the Athabasca. I truly admire the half-breeds who do this work every day. (*looking around and beyond KEENOOSAYO*) There are many people here; we are pleased.

KEENOOSAYO
More than 200 to meet and discuss this treaty. Also, The Captain from Sturgeon Lake is here, although only 22 men are with him. There is much unease.

LAIRD
I understand. But I'm certain we can show in our address tomorrow that signing treaty is a wise decision. I trust everyone is prepared to sign… provided of course our arguments please you. (*pause*)

KEENOOSAYO
My people have asked me to speak for them. We must be free to use this land as we always have, or we cannot agree with the terms of the treaty.

LAIRD
(*bringing KEENOOSAYO forward, gesturing and pointing*) Do you see that tree, Keenoosayo? After treaty, if we want that tree and it is on land that is reserved for you, we must buy it from you. This land will be as it was for your use.

> *KEENOOSAYO is not convinced, though remains, as always, respectful.*
> *KEENOOSAYO and MOOSTOOS exchange looks but do not respond.*

(*responds quickly to their reticence*) After this meeting you can go to the Hudson's Bay fort, where our provisions are stored, and rations will be issued to you of flour, bacon, tea and tobacco, so that you can have a good meal and a good time. This is a free gift, given to you whether you make treaty or not. It is a present the Queen is glad to make to you. I am now done, and shall be glad to hear what you have to say.

> *KEENOOSAYO nods to acknowledge, but gives no clear indication of his*
> *response. A few moments of awkward silence, broken by…*

LACOMBE

(*stepping forward, effusive*) Greetings, Keenoosayo and Moostoos! I am Father Lacombe of the St. Albert mission. It has been more than 30 years since I travelled into your land. (*gesturing broadly*) I find it as beautiful today as it was then. You are indeed blessed to make this God's country your home.

KEENOOSAYO and MOOSTOOS nod, without expression.

LAIRD

And allow me to introduce Major James Walker, Commissioner for half-breed scrip. (*They shake.*) And Inspector Snyder, Northwest Mounted Police. (*They shake.*) Tell me, Keenoosayo; Mr. James Ross of our party, has he not been with you a number of days?

KEENOOSAYO

He arrived seven days ago, overland from Edmonton. Our people have asked him many questions about the treaty, and he has been generous with his answers, (*hint of humour*) and his gifts.

LAIRD

(*misses the humour*) Splendid; as we had hoped, given our misfortunes. We appreciate your patience in awaiting our arrival.

MOOSTOOS

The treaty is important now. Conditions will only get worse.

WALKER

You are quite right, Moostoos. And we hope we can all come to an agreement that will be good for your people, the government of Canada and the Queen.

KEENOOSAYO

It is our hope as well, David Laird. But we have many great concerns.

LAIRD

We have heard. But believe us, Keenoosayo, when we say your people may continue to hunt and trap and move about as you always have under treaty.

KEENOOSAYO

It must be so. The Indian loves his way of living and his free life. When I understand you thoroughly I shall know better what I shall do. Up to the present I have never seen the time when I could not work for the Queen, and also make my own living. I will consider carefully what you have said.

MOOSTOOS

We will speak with you again tomorrow, with all our people.

LAIRD
Until tomorrow, then.

> *KEENOOSAYO and MOOSTOOS gesture, turn and leave. LAIRD and the others move off, stage left, quietly discussing what has been said.*

NARRATOR
So, Laird discovered he didn't exactly have things sewn up. Keenoosayo and the headmen were as prepared for these negotiations as he was. It looked like this was going to be a very long couple of days for everyone.

> *It's evening, and KEENOOSAYO and his headmen are meeting in a circle, the way they always do, to talk about the treaty, and the future. There is a lot to think about.*

SCENE FOUR – NATIVE MEN GATHER

> *In this scene: KEENOOSAYO, MOOSTOOS, NEESOCHESIS, WEECHEEWAYSIS, FELIX GIROUX, THE CAPTAIN. Entering later: MAHEKUN, followed by KISIKAWO. The setting: KEENOOSAYO and his headmen—plus THE CAPTAIN—are gathered in a circle on the grass to discuss the treaty signing the following day. The mood is serious and contemplative, lightened now and then by some jests. They all feel the seriousness of what is about to happen, yet maintain dignity and humour throughout. They pour tea, THE CAPTAIN and MOOSTOOS fill their pipes and smoke as the conversation unfolds. Seating order from stage right: WEECHEEWAYSIS, NEESOCHESIS, THE CAPTAIN, KEENOOSAYO and FELIX GIROUX.*

WEECHEEWAYSIS
Keenoosayo, it troubles me that they press so hard for treaty now. Why did they not talk when you asked for a treaty nine years ago? Our people were starving, far worse than today.

KEENOOSAYO
It was important then for us, but they had no need. Today it is different.

THE CAPTAIN
I am old and miserable now. I want to accept the treaty. You may think I am foolish for speaking as I do now. Think as you like. When I was young I was an able man and made my living on my own. But now I am old and weak. (*in Cree:*) I speak for all my people.

MOOSTOOS
We hear what you are saying, old one. And we understand.

Keenooshayo states his case at Lesser Slave Lake, June 1899. Photograph was likely taken by a North West Mounted policeman for Charles Mair, who included it in his Through the Mackenzie Basin: An Account of the Signing of Treaty No. 8 and the Script Commission *(1908).*

FELIX GIROUX

(*smiling*) I hear it is because you have had too many wives, that you are now tired. (*laughs with others*)

WEECHEEWAYSIS

It is true, though. We too have the old and tired and it is difficult to care for them. We should speak of this tomorrow with the commissioners.

KEENOOSAYO

The commissioners have said we should turn to farming and raising cattle. How can the old till the ground to feed themselves? We are hunters and trappers and fishermen. I do not like some of what this treaty says.

Interrupted by the soft approach of MAHEKUN.

FELIX GIROUX

It is late Mahekun. Did your wife tell you to sleep under a tree again tonight? (*He and the others laugh wholeheartedly.*)

MAHEKUN

(*laughs with them, then speaks*) No, I gave her a present today. (*somber*) I have come to speak to our leaders about the treaty. Some of the young men here have been talking together and we wish to tell you how we feel. (*He offers tobacco to WEECHEEWAYSIS who is closest.*)

WEECHEEWAYSIS

(*glances to the others, finds assent*) Thank you, brother. (*in Cree:*) Sit and share with us.

MAHEKUN

You know it is with great respect that we speak. You, our leaders, are wise and know many things, but we are against this treaty. We do not want more and more white men in our land. If what they say is true, that we will be able to hunt and fish and live the way we always have, then why do we need this treaty at all?

FELIX GIROUX

It is with a heavy heart that we consider all before we sign, my young friend. There are many good things about the treaty the priests and Mounted Police say. But you are not alone wondering about hunting, fishing, trapping, our way of life, and their laws. And we must think of other matters, of education, medicines.

MAHEKUN

What of these? If we keep the white man out we will have no need of these things. It is they who brought the disease and hardships.

KEENOOSAYO

It seems to me that we have no choice. More and more will come, whether we wish it or not. (*He is interrupted by the approach of KISIKAWO, who is carrying a snack of fish for the men.*) What is this?

FELIX GIROUX

You are a tricky fellow, Mahekun. Send a pretty girl with good food to bargain with. You are learning from the whites and their presents. (*laughter by all*)

They begin to eat and the scene fades with NARRATOR taking over.

SCENE FIVE – THE SIGNING

In this scene: Seated on ground SL across from table: KEENOOSAYO, MOOSTOOS, NEESOCHESIS, THE CAPTAIN, WEECHEEWAYSIS, FELIX GIROUX. At table: LAIRD, WALKER, SNYDER standing to side. On chairs to their left, LACOMBE and GROUARD, standing to their left and between the commissioners and the Indians, RCMP members bearing flag. Standing behind and apart from the headmen is MAHEKUN. Scrip Commissioner WALKER to the side. SECORD observing. (As available: Native and Metis men various ages, women, especially Native Elders, White traders). The Setting (action happens behind narration): RCMP bring in the table, Union Jack and seating. Tone of Euro-authority pervades. Assembled behind or around as signing ceremony gets underway are Metis, White traders, Native people. Ceremonial start: RCMP lead procession into "tent" and sit down. KEENOOSAYO and headmen enter, and sit on ground. Commissioners sii on low stools behind table. LACOMBE and GROUARD sit.

NARRATOR

It's show time. David Laird needs the Indians to sign, and to sign today. Lesser Slave Lake is only the first stop; he has to keep moving and collect endorsements, called "Adhesions," across the Peace River and Athabasca Country before the end of the summer.

Laird had been given broad discretionary powers. That meant he could make promises on the spot, even though the terms of the treaty had been decided ahead of time. Laird probably believed the government would honour whatever he promised that was NOT on the written treaty, once he made his case back in Ottawa.

LAIRD

(*unrolls Commission from the Queen, stands forward to deliver firm, confident speech to all about terms and value of treaty*) Red brothers! We have come here today, sent by the Great Mother to treat with you, and this is the paper she has given to us, and is her Commission to us signed with her Seal, to show we have authority to treat with you. I have to say, on behalf of the Queen and the government of Canada, that we have come to make you an offer. We have made treaties in former years with all the Indians of the prairie, and from there to Lake Superior. As white people are coming into your country, we have thought it well to tell you what is required of you. The Queen wants all the whites, half-breeds, and Indians to be at peace with one another, and to shake hands when they meet. The Queen's laws must be obeyed all over the country, both by the whites and the Indians. It is not alone that we wish to prevent Indians from molesting the whites. It is also to prevent the whites from molesting or doing harm to the Indians. The Queen's soldiers are just as much for the protection of the Indians as for the white man.

KEENOOSAYO
(to LAIRD) You say we are brothers. I cannot understand how we are so. I live differently from you. I can only understand that Indians will benefit in a very small degree from your offer. You have told us you come in the Queen's name. We surely have also a right to say a little as far as that goes.

WEECHEEWAYSIS
I stand behind this man's back. (pointing to KEENOOSAYO) I want to tell the commissioners that there are two ways, the long and the short. I want to take the way that will last longest.

NEESOCHESIS
I follow these two brothers, Moostoos and Keenoosayo. When I understand better I shall be able to say more.

FELIX GIROUX
(to LAIRD) This treaty will be good for you; but what of us? Things I have heard tell me our people will be bound like fish in nets. We have our ways of living; we do not wish to change!

LAIRD
We understand stories have been told you, that if you made a treaty with us you would become servants and slaves; but we wish you to understand that such is not the case, but that you will be just as free after signing a treaty as you are now. The treaty is a free offer; take it or not, just as you please. If you refuse it there is no harm done; we will not be bad friends on that account…. Now, as to the terms. (motions for KEENOOSAYO to sit) If you agree to take treaty, everyone this year gets a present of $12. And so a family of 5 gets $60, a family of 8, $96. And for every year after, $5 each person forever. (fades as narration takes over)

NARRATOR
(narrates over mimed speech continuing behind) That $5 is worth about $100 today. There was a long list of terms in this contract between The Great Mother the Queen and the Indians. The treaty offered one square mile—640

The Treaty No. 8 Medal. The Native leaders who signed Treaty No. 8 received sterling silver commemorative medals, showing on one side the treaty commissioner and a chief shaking hands, and on the obverse Queen Victoria's profile. This medal was given to Alexandre Laviolette, the first Chipewyan Chief in Fort Chipewyan. (Ethnology Program, Provincial Museum of Alberta, H86.49.1)

acres—to each family of 5. Now it's here that a change was made to the standard treaty. This agreement didn't insist on all the reserve being in one spot. Indians under Treaty No. 8 could take their land "in severalty." That meant in different places. They couldn't just pick any land though. It had to be "subject to approval of the government." The Crown didn't want Indians staking out ground that might interfere with the rights of, or lands desired by, white settlers.

The whole concept of land ownership was a problem for Native people. Regardless of the words Laird used, they never understood they were giving up the land. In their minds, it was owned by the Creator. This is how Elders explain it today: "We don't own the land, the land owns us." The Natives were being asked to take up farming. The problem was, these people didn't know the first thing about it, and there was nobody around to teach them.

It's a good thing Laird had more appealing things to offer.

LAIRD
(*resuming full voice*) …If you do not wish to grow grain or raise cattle, the government will furnish you with ammunition for your hunt, and the twine to catch fish. The government will also provide you with schools to teach your children to read and write, and do other things like white men and their children. Schools will be established where there is a sufficient number of children. The government will give the chiefs axes and tools to make houses to live in and be comfortable.

NARRATOR
(*taking over again*) Of course, the giving wasn't all in one direction. In return for the favours, Indians had to make some promises. They wouldn't inter-fere with or molest any miner, traveller or settler, but be good friends with everyone. And if a white man were to molest them or shoot their dogs or horses, they would not retaliate, but report it to the police… who would see that justice was done.

Keenoosayo and the headmen are divided. They love their people, and know their hearts. The natives didn't ask for this treaty. But their leaders have great vision, and want peace between the nations. As Keenoosayo makes his decision, he knows that things will probably get worse before they get better. He is looking seven generations ahead.

KEENOOSAYO
(*to his people, stepping forward*) They say they represent the Queen, the Great Mother. They say she owns this land, but is willing to share. We too are willing to share. Canada (*said in Cree*) means clean land. But our land can only be kept clean if our relations with other nations are clean and good. This treaty will protect all of us; help us keep Canada (*Cree*) free of bad will and bloodshed. We must be generous and kind in our thinking and in our

acts. The Queen expects the next generations to share in the benefits and blessings our Creator has given to us. This is a treaty of peace, fairness and honesty. It is a treaty of friendship and good relations. We are all brothers here. We will come to know each other, and be friends.

Visible, elated, supportive reaction from LACOMBE.

MOOSTOOS
I feel I must speak… (*stands*) What the commissioners offer we will have to take. We all see it. I believe we can keep hunting and fishing, and let these white people come and use the land, in their way, beside us. I am not happy with all of the bargain. But the terms they offer are not less than they were for the Blackfoot and plains people. I have sat with Father Grouard and others; I listen to what they say, and they believe we should take treaty. This way we can get along. If they keep their promises, I want to sign. (*nodding of heads and vocal agreement*)

MAHEKUN
(*calling out from his position at edge*) Mr. Laird, does our nation fight your wars under treaty?

LAIRD
Signing treaty will not mean you will have to battle for the Queen. There will be no forced military service for the Indians.

FELIX GIROUX
(*calling out*) You take money from traders for the government. Will we have to give you money too?

LAIRD
What you speak of is taxation. Indians will never have to pay taxes. This I promise.

KEENOOSAYO
(*to all*) We have had many days to think about the treaty. We need to look into our hearts and decide. As your chosen leader, I ask all who agree with the terms to stand, so I shall know if I will sign.

LACOMBE
(*rises, jumps in with fervent speech; starts in Cree with "please, your attention, my friends… then, in English*) Knowing you as I do, your manners, your customs and language, I have been officially attached to the Commission as advisor. Today is a great day for you, a day of long remembrance, and your children hereafter will learn from your lips the events of today. I consented to come here today because I thought it was a good thing for you to take the treaty. Were it not in your interest I would not take part in it. Your forest and river life will not be changed by the treaty. And you will have your annuities, as well, year by year, as long as the sun shines and the earth remains. Therefore I finish my speaking by saying (*with a flourish*) Accept!

FELIX GIROUX
(*rises quickly, in humour*) It is a long day we are asked to endure. I, Felix Giroux will club anyone who does not stand now! (*gestures in mock threat to crowd; others pull him back, with laughter*)

KEENOOSAYO
(*to his people, gathering their attention again*) Of all the terms of the treaty, we fear most for our hunting, fishing, trapping… our way of life. It is wise to be wary. However, I have considered carefully the terms commissioner David Laird has brought. The treaty promises to give ammunition and twine to those who ask. It would not be reasonable to offer us these things if it is the intention of the government to change the laws for fishing and hunting, to restrict us in these things. And so my fears on this matter are not so strong. I ask you to consider this…

> Suddenly KEENOOSAYO sees gestures of dissent among the other headmen and his people, and without further comment sits down.

LAIRD
(*alarmed, trying to assuage*) Indians have been told that if they make a treaty they will not be allowed to hunt and fish as they do now. This is not true. Indians who take treaty will be just as free to hunt and fish all over as they now are. Please understand. The Queen owns the country, but is willing to acknowledge the Indians' claims, and offers them terms as an off-set to all of them.

KEENOOSAYO
(*pause, with gravity, beginning directly to LAIRD*) Are the terms good forever? As long as the sun shines, the grass grows and the river flows? Because there are orphans we must consider, so that there will be nothing to be thrown up to us by our people afterwards. We want a written treaty, one copy to be given to us, so we shall know what we sign for. Are you willing to give means to instruct children as long as the sun shines and water runs, so that our children will grow up ever increasing in knowledge?

LAIRD
It is the policy of the government to provide in every part of the country, as far a circumstances permit, for the education of Indian children.

KEENOOSAYO
In the matter of schools, there must be no interference with our religious beliefs. Will this be a part of the treaty? We wish it so.

LAIRD
(*pauses, confers with James WALKER*) We assure you that the law, which is as strong as treaty, provides for non-interference with the religion of the Indians.

MOOSTOOS

(*to LAIRD*) Often before now I have said I would carefully consider what you might say. You have called us brothers. (*jesting*) Truly I am the younger, you the elder brother. Being the younger, if the younger ask the elder for something, he would grant his request the same as our mother the Queen. (*serious*) I am glad to hear what you have to say. Our country is getting broken up. I see the white man coming in, and I want to be friends. I see what he does, but it is best that we should be friends. I will sign this treaty!

Crowd and headmen reaction: general shout of approval by headmen.

LAIRD and party, stand and nod and vigorously shake hands with each other. LACOMBE rushes to congratulate KEENOOSAYO and headmen on a wise decision. SNYDER moves offstage to get money chest.

LAIRD

(*to KEENOOSAYO and headmen*) We are glad you understand the treaty is forever. If the Indians do as they are asked, we shall certainly keep all our promises.

He congratulates KEENOOSAYO, puts medal over his head, gives him the flag. KEENOOSAYO touches pen to sign and LAIRD gives him cash. Then he moves off and MOOSTOOS comes to touch pen and get cash. Others follow.

NARRATOR

(*begins when KEENOOSAYO gets the flag*) Back on that day, nobody could foresee all the difficulties that lay ahead. There's a feeling of optimism and hope. It's party time... especially when Laird cracks open the money chest. (*short pause*) As expected, most full blood Indians took treaty, and most half-breeds took scrip. But there was some crossover. Elders say that in the line-ups there was as much confusion as excitement.... "Which are you going to take?" they asked each other as they got closer to the table. They had heard so much in the speeches. And it was all happening so fast.

MAHEKUN is downstage left, brooding. LACOMBE and GROUARD move over to him to console. THE CAPTAIN, FELIX GIROUX and NEESOCHESIS stay upstage centre. When last one signs, MAHEKUN pushes the priests away, walks slowly to LAIRD. Headmen slowly move toward LAIRD. FELIX GIROUX stops SNYDER from confronting MAHEKUN. MOOSTOOS stops short of LAIRD; LAIRD offers the cash, THE CAPTAIN speaks to MOOSTOOS in Cree, telling him to accept the money. MOOSTOOS snatches it from LAIRD's hand and storms off. Those remaining on stage exit. Narration begins right after MAHEKUN exits and while others are moving off stage.

NARRATOR
The mixed blood people in the north had a very separate culture from
Indians. My great grandfather Sam Cunningham was a leading member
of the Metis community at Lesser Slave Lake. He acted as an interpreter
during the signing, and he knew what happened afterwards. Some used
their scrip money to buy supplies to help start a new life further north. And
a few did use it for land, although a lot of the ground in the Treaty No. 8
area wasn't much good for farming. By the end of the summer, 48 people
had chosen land scrip, and just less than 2000 took money scrip – for a
fraction of what it was worth.

There were definitely some bad news stories. It was hard to resist all the
goodies spread out by merchants who came along with the commission
party. A lot of people spent their cash on things they didn't need, like
alcohol. A reporter from the Edmonton Bulletin said scrip money "lasted as
long as a snowball in a stove."

LACOMBE enters, sits at the desk and opens letter.

When Indians and some missionaries finally saw the deal in black and
white, they were upset. Many promises Laird made just weren't there. And
over the years, some things didn't turn out as they had imagined. Education
became residential schools run by churches; thousands of Indian and Metis
kids grew up without their families. They did learn how to read and write,
but paid a high price for literacy and other skills like gardening and home-
making. There was widespread loss of traditional spirituality, language and
culture.

*NARRATOR exits stage. LACOMBE stands, comes forward to downstage
centre, reads letter aloud. Pauses, exits as Native Elder comes forward to
stand in the same spot, passing him/her without eye contact.*

LACOMBE
A letter from my colleague Father Falher. Father Falher tells me he has
written the Bishop, and sends me a copy.

"Dear Bishop Breynat:
In 1899 had we not prepared the Lesser Slave Lake people to accept treaty
with the government, if Bishop Grouard had not advised the chiefs to sign
treaty, telling them there was nothing which was not to their advantage, the
treaty would still be waiting to be signed today. When Bishop Grouard sent
me to Wabasca (at the request of Mr. Laird) to prepare the people and calm
them (they were more or less in a state of revolt), I carried with me the
Government promises. And I was very surprised when later on I was
shown the document supposedly signed by the Indian Chiefs at Grouard
and thereabouts. So many important things are missing. But we do
remember these things, and we suffer."

The document of Treaty No. 8. This printed version, black and red on white parchment (75 x 49.5 cm), was sent to all Chiefs who had signed in 1899. (Boreal Institute for Northern Studies, University of Alberta)

Conclusion – The Promises

> *Native Elder narrates list of promises. Afterward, she/he stays onstage but moves to centre upstage.*

Treaty No. 8 Promises… As remembered and understood by our Elders:

1. Schools, education, teachers
2. Doctors
3. Hospital/medicines free
4. Indians retain minerals and water rights
5. Sub-surface rights retained
6. Exempt from taxation
7. Land acquired by Queen was only 6″ surface rights
8. Hunting, fishing, trapping and gathering rights retained
9. Land purchased for farm did not include forests
10. Rations provided for the destitute
11. Policing
12. Legal representation
13. Exemption from participation in war
14. No Indian shall hang from rope
15. Ammunition and twine supplied
16. Right to barter
17. Canvas for tents
18. Cattle/horses provided
19. Farm and haying equipment/instructors
20. Gardening tools/shed
21. In case of hunger, all gates shall be opened
22. Promised vast tracts of land for reserves
23. Land in severalty if so desired
24. Protection of fish and animals
25. Non-interference of religious beliefs
26. Non-interference with our mode of livelihood
27. Wildlife was for Indians; Whites were bringing their own cows, pigs, chickens etc.
28. Promise not to be confined to reserves
29. Majority of Elders don't recall hearing of land surrender
30. Promise of suits for chiefs and headmen
31. Promise to receive treaty money forever
32. Treaty right to trap anywhere within Treaty No. 8 area
33. Treaty right to hunt anywhere within Treaty No. 8 area
34. Treaty right to fish anywhere within Treaty No. 8 area
35. Friendship and peace treaty
36. Government will not let Indians starve
37. No harm to come to the Indians
38. Policing by chief and headmen on own traditional lands
39. As long as the sun shines, the grass grows and the river flows, these promises were made.

FINALE – SONG AND PROCESSION

Dene drums begin, and we hear the start of keyboard/guitar song tune. Singer enters and begins Oti Nekan song. Native and Metis children emerge in a slow procession from behind tipi (upstage), crossing stage to line the ramps on both sides, forming the outer edges of a large half circle. The children are costumed to depict various occupations (doctor, hockey player, etc.).

As actors emerge to join in the song they will fill the centre part of the half circle. On the second chorus, four actors join the singer from all four stage entry points, and sing along with her. Chorus repeats and other actors come from all entry points and join singing. Crew joins them, all in a steady, building flow. Audience is encouraged to join in as the song finishes.

Oti Nekan
By Shannon Cunningham, 1999

We have waited for this time for so long
A time when dusky night fades towards the dawn
We stumbled, we have fallen, but always survived
Fighting with all our hearts to keep our dreams alive

There has always been hope
There has always been life
Struggling through the darkness towards the light

Oti Nekan, we will be one
Oti Nekan, we will be one
Oti Nekan, we will be one
One people, my brother, my friend

Confusion, collision, simply because we could not see
How very few are the differences between you and me
We will honour the promise, the spirit and the life we chose
For as long as the sun shines, the grass grows and the water flows

Oti Nekan, we will be one… (*etc., repeat to fade*)

The end.

Moostoos, Chief of the Sucker Creek Band and brother of Keenooshayo.
(Provincial Archives of Alberta)

Joey Tremblay as Barefoot Boy, August, 1996.
(Photo by Howard Silverman.)

Linda Grass as Nurse in "Cross."
Unconscious Collective 1998.
(Photo courtesy Trevor Schmidt and the Unconscious Collective.)

The death of Blanche, featuring Denise Kenney as Rose and Anne Mansfield as La Mère,
Vanessa Porteous as Blanche and John Ullyatt as Rostand.
La Cité francophone production of La Maison Rouge, *Edmonton, 1997.*
(Photo courtesy Ed Ellis.)

TALES FROM THE HOSPITAL

by
Trevor Schmidt

INTRODUCTION TO *TALES FROM THE HOSPITAL*

"You get too attached. They aren't worth worrying over. They're here because no one else wants them. Surely you can see that. You certainly don't have to put so much investment in them. We're here to look after them, but clinically. This is a place of business."

(Schmidt, *Tales from the Hospital*)

The production of Trevor Schmidt's *Tales from the Hospital* in May 1998 served as a timely reminder for Edmonton audiences that the painful effects of the Alberta sterilization act that was enforced between 1927 and 1973 could not be easily forgotten.[1] For many years, stories of what had gone on in the institutions where the "unfit" had been placed had operated at the level of cautionary folk tales passed down from generation to generation.

It was only in the 1990s that actual victims began to come forth to demand compensation.[2] During the year that *Tales* was written, many such cases were still being reported in the newspapers.[3] Thus audiences who came to see the show already had an actual historical context in which to locate it. Moreover, despite the fact that Schmidt did not specify any actual sites, they could easily make connections between the play's setting which the nurse Blanche Mains describes as having rows and rows of windows "that stare like empty eyes/dead/and sometimes the dead stand in them/their hands against the bars" ("Cross") and the notorious hospitals at Red Deer and Ponoka where sterilizations and other medical experiments had been routinely carried out.

Schmidt's fictional characters stand in for recognizable inhabitants of such institutions starting with the young beautiful but slow farm girl who delivers the first monologue. Her tale of hospital life includes her cataloguing a series of operations that have been performed on her, although she remains blissfully unaware of her sterilization.[4] The next monologue delivered by the vicious head nurse whose clinical behaviour borders on the pathological, describes her drowning of an old man in the bath. She is followed by her polar opposite, the outcast nurse, now laundry woman, who slaves in the boiler room to provide clean linen for her charges. The fourth and final monologue is offered by another nameless patient, in this case, an angelic-looking religious hysteric driven insane by her incarceration.

Schmidt wrote and designed the play in such a way that audience members were required to participate in a tour of the hospital and listen to each tale separately. The venue, the largest room in the dark and cavernous Arts Barns, not a welcoming space to begin with, was made less so by the control exerted over audiences who could only enter when invited. Being allowed to see only one site at a time, and having to move from one dim space to another by observing subtle lighting cues created a situation in which spectators lose control over where or with whom they can sit, or whether they will even find seats. Thus spectators were put in the position of having to put the various pieces together with the result that they could only make sense of the apparently random patterning once the final monologue had been delivered.

Using this manner of presentation was enormously powerful, since it drew attention to the inability of the separate individuals to make sense of their experiences, while at the same time offering each of them as testimonial sites of institutional abuses.

One of the important patterning devices which greatly enhanced the overall meaning of the piece was the striking effect created by the different ways in which the various characters wore and handled the hospital linen. Since hospitals are meant to be places of cleanliness, the condition of the linens in each monologue carries implications of the power relations at stake. For example, the first patient remained unusually still, except for her interactions with a very long piece of white sheet—the only tangible object left to her to relate to—as she peeks from under it, walks on it, twists it in to various shapes, entwines herself in it, follows its length to the empty room where she meets her phantom lovers. Blanche Mains appeared in an immaculately white uniform which she could not bear to have soiled. Handling the sheets that Mr. Flagg has soiled in the night is unbearable to her and touching his soiled body is out of the question. On the other hand, Irene tries to mitigate the murderous actions practised by Blanche by spending all her working hours doing the laundry for her patients. Throughout her monologue, she carries up the soaking wet laundry from the underground boilers to be wrung out and hung up on the clotheslines spread all over her space. In the final segment, the patient in her white gown, who stands and jumps up and down on her bed and reaches her hands up to the light is as disembodied as one of Irene's ghosts.

What Schmidt does in *Tales* is to recreate an imaginary stage space which is recognizable as a hospital where human life is endangered rather than preserved. The only moral authority left, the compassionate Irene, is imprisoned in the basement because she knows too much. The robotic nurse Blanche Mains, who is running the place, represents the official state policies which allow the authorities to rob, maim and even kill their unfortunate charges in the name of providing care for them. When Blanche tells us: "I have nothing but the greatest respect/for human life/even the lives of these people" ("Cross"), she reveals herself as complicit with the discourses of state biopower circulating at the time. According to these discourses, still very much alive today in ever more virulent forms, nation states have the right to regulate "inferior elements of their society in the name of protecting the lives of "healthy" citizens.[5] In Schmidt's *Tales* the truly sadistic nature of the coercive biopower is no longer possible to deny because we are forced to witness it being practised on live bodies on stage. This "other" Alberta has become too real a place to deny.

Trevor Schmidt is an Edmonton-based actor/playwright/director/designer and the current Artistic Director of the Unconscious Collective. A graduate of the BFA in Drama from the University of Calgary, his output over the past ten years is enormous. Recent work includes *Tales from the Hospital*, which is the first in a series of "one voice" cycles, and was followed by *The Watermelon Girls* in 2000. The Unconscious Collective premiered his play *Treatment*, in the Spring of 2001. The fact that Schmidt had three of his plays nominated in the annual Sterling award category for best new play should

give some indication of both his merit and productivity. *The Watermelon Girls,* a play about unwed mothers, the companion piece to *Tales from the Hospital* received the award. Upcoming projects include *3 Very Lovely Girls... in Space,* a musical version of three sisters modelled on the three Brady Bunch sisters. In October 2001, a new piece, *Blood Oranges,* commissioned by Northern Light Theatre will be produced.

The Unconscious Collective was founded in 1995 with a simple mandate: To produce original works by Albertan Artists. This remains the case. In fact, through the last six years they have produced only original works by Albertans. Most of the projects have been creations of Artistic Director Trevor Schmidt who has embarked on an exploration of style that has given the Unconscious Collective an outstanding reputation garnering favour in the community, several Elizabeth Sterling Haynes nominations. Initially, Trevor placed focus on black comedy with oddball situations, witty dialogue and fascinating character roles particularly for women. He created the bovinesque Nurse Blister and the cold, dry psychic Helen for *The Calf Killers.* In *Precious Goods,* the morbid Lady Maule (who kept the head of her sister Mortadella in a bird cage) was balanced by the controlling madness of Lady Winter. The sardonic Rose unable to catch Mr. Right thanks to fits caused by the metal plate in her head was featured in *Tenderfeet. Land's Ending* introduced Ruby: the manipulative native with a diamond-eye.

The next style to come was the disco or rock-and-roll retelling of classic literature that the Collective likes to refer to as the "Extravaganza!". Trevor took John Ford to a teen ballroom dance competition turning *Tis Pit She's a Whore* into *Too Bad She's a Big Ole Slut;* where incestuous siblings Gianni and Bella were disqualified from the finals due to their relationship. He sent Otis to face monsters in production numbers in *Trippin',* an adaptation of Homer's *The Odyssey.* Shakespeare's *Measure for Measure* became *Swinging Without Annette* where he used a characterization of pop-icon Annette Funicello to represent the virginal purity of Isabella. Currently he is working on an adaptation of Anton Chekov's *Three Sisters* retitled *3 Very Lovely Girls... in Space* featuring the Brady girls longing to get to Mars. Trevor's imagination and wry wit have been deftly displayed in all of these productions which he also directed, designed and, with the exception of *Annette,* performed in.

Trevor began to find interest in writing monologues and, in line with his earlier work, writing especially for women. In 1996, he wrote the piece *Copper* with Angela Flatekval, Founding Member & Chairperson of Unconconsious Collective, in the lead role. When it played in Calgary and Provincial One-Act Festival, it was extremely successful, receiving several awards at both festivals. *Copper* was an inspiration for Trevor to continue exploration and expand it to create a compilation of several characters with common environment. *Copper* is now one third of the cycle, *The Ballroom.* The common denominator here is a legion hall made dance hall a few hours each week. Trevor has found a way to present two sides of a through two characters whose points of view alternate although they actually engage in dialogue. This cycle has not yet been produced.

According to Flatekval, who played the patient in the segment *Rising* in *Tales from the Hospital,* the actors faced a great challenge in

ways to bring the poetry off the page. They found the solution by "a musical approach to the work." The second installation of this type of work, *The Watermelon Girls* which features five women whose lives were changed by their experiences at a home for unwed mothers, added another layer of difficulty because it required the actors to transcend time to show the changing (and unchanging) effects of their situations.

NOTES

[1] While various forms of war, murder, population control and selective breeding were in place around the world in the late nineteenth and early twentieth centuries, the province of Alberta was the only jurisdiction in the British Empire to pass a Protection of Life, Sexual Sterilization Act in 1928 – almost a direct implementation of the ideology of justified killing in order to improve the life of others. Section 5, especially refers to the "multiplication of the evil by the transmission of the disability to the progeny." Operated by an appointed board of two medical and two lay people who made the final decision for every single operation, this board succeeded in sterilizing over 2800 people before the law was repealed in 1973.

[2] The most publicized case was Leilani Muirer, a young victim who made history when she won her suit against the government in 1997. As it turned out she was one of thousands of unwanted young girls supposedly of below average intelligence who were slated for sterilization as "unfit for parenthood."

[3] Marina Jimenez, "Alberta sterilizations victims also used as guinea pigs," *National Post* 28 Oct. 1998, A1. The same edition of the *Post* had several articles covering many details of the ongoing trials against the Albertan government.

[4] Trevor confirmed that he grew up with stories of what had happened to women like Leilani Muirer but that he had no direct models for the young girl in "White Hands" who has been sterilized without her knowledge. *Treatment*, a new play by Schmidt that premiered April 2001, is based on experiences his mother underwent in a psychiatric ward in 1959.

[5] Ann Stoler, *Race and the Education of Desire* (Durham and London: Duke University Press,1996) 84, quotes from a little known lecture by Foucault, *Les Temps Modernes*, 52. In the modern biopolitical state "the sovereign right to kill appears in a new form; as an "excess" of biopower that does away with life in the name of securing it." In *Tales from the Hospital*, Blanche justifies her treatment of the patients in such a way as to suggest that she believes that the more "degenerates" and "abnormals" she can eliminate, the more her life will be improved.

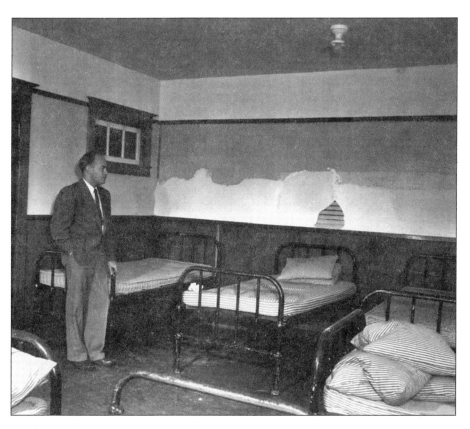

Dr. Leonard LeVann at the Red Deer Provincial Training School in the 1950s, where the now-illegal anabolic steroid norbolethone and the anti-psychotic haloperidol were administered. (Provincial Archives of Alberta)

The first production of *Tales from the Hospital* by the Unconscious Collective took place in The Arts Barns Open Space, Edmonton, in May 1998 with the following cast:

WHITE HANDS	Girl	Michelle Morros
CROSS	Nurse	Linda Grass*
DOWN	Nurse	Elizabeth Allison*
RISING	Patient	Angela Flatekval

Stage managed by the cast
Set, Lighting, Sound design by Trevor Schmidt*

*Equity Members

Production Notes on Staging

The Arts Barns Open Space – a cavernous, dark, warehouse space. Each of the four plays that comprise *Tales* were performed in isolated areas, with the audience required to move between said spaces in order to view each piece. The seating arrangement varied for each piece in terms of formation, distance, and proximity. Room was also allowed for spectators to stand.

Adding to the atmosphere, at specific points throughout the evening, smoke we released through grated portion of the floor, accompanied by a radiator hissing noise.

Stage directions were purposely not included in the text, but a physical exploration of each piece is greatly encouraged. Particularly useful to the company of the original production were a twenty-foot sheet (for WHITE HANDS), a wash bucket, gauze laundry, and multiple hanging clothes lines (for DOWN) and a metal hospital bed on rolling casters (for RISING).

Lighting was specific to each piece – uniformly harsh or "mood"y. Both of the "patient" monologues employed barred window gobos. All lighting reinforces a sense of confinement – if the actors were to move out of the defined light-space, they would be lost in the darkness of the cavern/warehouse.

Each piece was stage-managed by one of the other actors involved in the production.

TALES FROM THE HOSPITAL
by Trevor Schmidt

WHITE HANDS

GIRL stands, in a white hospital gown.

GIRL
At night
in the dark
in between the crisp sheets
i can hear the sound of her feet
padding down the hallway
across the checkered tiles of the Hospital
i can picture her white shoes with their
thick white soles
the sweater across her stiff white shoulders
the starch sound of her uniform
rustling.
Her face is a mask
her eyes like lasers
shooting her lasers into the darkened rooms
where weakened people huddle beneath blankets
pretending to sleep
trying not to draw her attention
hoping she won't come in

They've shaved between my legs
and keep taking things out from inside me.
i have a scar now from
side to side
and i know they're going to add another one
to bisect it from
mouth to mouth.
Or mouth to south.
The scar is still pink
and it hurts.

i lie in bed sometimes
and take internal inventory.
i can't figure out what they've left in me
and what all they've taken out.
A lung
Liver
Gall bladder
Spleen

Michelle Morros as the Girl and Linda Grass as the Nurse in "White Hands."
Unconscious Collective 1998.
(Photo by Mark Chalifoux, courtesy Trevor Schmidt and the Unconscious Collective.)

The women in white
gather in a small pool of light
beneath a desk
behind a desk
they speak in hushed whispers
soothing words that don't make sense to us
another language.
We, in the dark
sit and wait and watch and listen
while they fill their needles
and sharpen their knives.
and cool their stethoscopes.
Sometimes they laugh.

Someone shook me awake last night.
i was dreaming of somewhere else
and hands grabbed my shoulders
a voice hissed my name in my ear
i thought it might be her
but it was only Berta
her white hair like a halo
shaking my shoulders
feeling stitches stretching
"Jeesuz, Berta,
Whatchu want?"

Berta's crazy
thinks there's spiders in her bed

thinks they're crawling on her all the time
but she's just old and scared
so i drag myself out of bed
and we strip her sheets back
i sweep my hand across the bed
and say it's clean
and she cries and hangs on my neck
saying thank you
over and over.
We whisper, so they won't hear us
and we get back into bed.
Berta can't sleep right off
so she sings
quietly
she sings in a high, quavering
old church-lady voice.
i don't mind it so much
anymore.
i drift into sleep before she does
her songs in my ears.

Berta has worms
eating through her stomach lining
but every time she comes in here
to have them removed
they hide.
The doctors open her up
and can't find them
they hide
behind her intestines.
Berta's daughter used to visit her
but not anymore.

Berta isn't a very good singer
she hasn't got a very good voice
but it makes her happy.
i don't mind
as long as she's quiet.

The blinds snap up
crashing against the top of the window frame
and the sun comes into the room and slaps me
"It's almost nine, Sleepybones"
her voice sounds friendly
but her lasers flash
"Get up. You're wasting the day away."
She fusses around the room, her lips pursed
as Berta grumbles and we both try to shake the sleep
from our heads.
Normally, we'd talk
but not with her in the room
she's an intruder
and she listens
listens for secrets
to use against us
to take to the doctors
and have them cut us open
or put stuff inside us
or have us discharged.
She recommends needles.
She likes shooting people.

There's another woman in our room
we don't know her name
but the nurses treat her differently
and I've heard them whisper
"Terminal."

The woman is old
and terribly thin
with forty brown and white hairs
that slink across her head like a man
from one ear to the other
combed over carefully
by anyone with a comb
who cares
or feels bad.

Berta gets the bathroom first
and i am left alone with the nurse
while she looks after
the Terminal woman.
The nurse's name is Blanche Mains.
i have noticed it printed on her name tag.
She leaned across me once
and i pretended to be asleep with one eye.
Her hands are cold
long fingers of ice
poking
prodding
pressing
too hard.
She speaks in measured tones
pleasant, with manners
but the edge on it says that she doesn't like us
she doesn't care if we die or live.

Berta and i go to the common room
Berta is working on a jigsaw puzzle
of a giraffe and four balloons
the pieces are very large
it's an easy puzzle
but Berta can't seem to finish it
the pieces are large
it's an easy puzzle.

Everything is done under the watchful eye of a nurse.
Today it's Blanche Mains, R.N.

There's a man in the common room
everyday
he smiles and crosses to sit by me
he wears a purple housecoat
Berta warns me
she doesn't like him.
he sits near me and smiles

and grabs himself between the legs
He talks a lot
and breathes heavily
through his mouth
Berta calls him "Pervert"
but he just smiles
i don't mind
he never touches me
or says dirty things
he talks to me like a father
and nods understandingly
when i show him my scar.
i try to explain to Berta
i don't like him
but i don't dislike him either
and he doesn't scare me
like Blanche Mains does.

i don't look out the window anymore
it doesn't matter what's outside
i don't think i'll ever see it again
anyhow.
i've lost track of the seasons
the snow and rain
i haven't seen anything green for
a long time.

It's storming
through the window
i can see lightning
it flashes
sending huge shadows across the walls of the room
black and blue shadows like bruises.

Berta whimpers in her sleep
my stitches are bothering me
itching
and the Terminal woman
is rasping quietly.
i hear the familiar padding
of nurse's shoes on linoleum
slow measured sinister
i see a flashlight bouncing into rooms
reflected off the ceiling of the hallway
a light bouncing toward the door
a bed-check.

Closer
closer

i close my eyes and pretend to sleep
peering out from beneath the grill of my lashes

Her uniform glows in the moonlight
in the doorway
like a ghost
She stands
then moves in silently
softly padding
and stands in the window
flashing to view
when the lightning crashes against the panes
Berta mumbles
and she turns from the window
as i snap my eyes shut
into darkness.

When i open my eyes again
she is standing near the Terminal woman's bed
and in a flash of lightning
prying a large diamond ring off
the bony finger
i close my eyes
i press them tight
and when i open them again

it's morning
and the Terminal Woman is gone
the sheets are being peeled
back
like skin.

Berta mutters
"where'd she go where'd she go"
Berta mutters.
How should i know?

"Gone to God"
the nurse
with the white hands
and cold eyes
i dip my head to hear her
she's so quiet.
Berta whimpers
and her laser eyes

flash
"No sense crying
Won't bring her back
No way, no how"

When i ask what'll happen to
the body
she says
"No family"
When I ask what'll happen to
the ring
she says
"No ring"
When i ask again
she sends Berta to the toilet and locks the door.

"There was no ring. Not ever. If you saw one, you were imagining it. You
know how your mind plays tricks on you. We all know how you like to
make things up and tell tales. Perhaps i should tell the Doctor that you're
not doing so well."

and her hand
digs into my elbow
her white hand
with fingers
like a vise.

"You're putting on more weight"
she smiles

then Berta starts banging on the toilet door

She wants me to get fat.
She's fattening me up.
For The Kill.
Like Hansel
caught in the cage
in the kitchen
of the house made of
gingerbread
in the book
the blue book
back at the farm.

The farm was where i was
before.

i remember
but i don't really
remember
not good.

The man in the common room
the man in the purple housecoat
he smiled
when i told him about the ring
and Nurse Blanche Mains, R.N.

But i saw it
i almost saw the whole thing
and i may not be smart
but i'm smart enough to know
what i see
and what
i
do not.

Berta got mean today
getting locked in the toilet
she tore out pieces of her hair
like puffs of cloud
and let them drop to the floor
and she said
"I may be here because i got
smart worms
in me,
but you're here 'cause you're a
retard"
and for a minute
Old Berta
looks like the old man that i call
my father.
I'm not smart, i know
but i'm no retard.

"A retard could figure out your stupid
giraffe puzzle
you crazy old coot
you are so stupid that you're a bad singer
it's no wonder your daughter
don't come
no more!"

And Berta cries
and i just let her

i use my foot to sweep
the hair-puffs under
her bed
like dust-witches.
A retard wouldn't be smart enough
to think of that.
When Berta started singing to herself
all high and quavery
i sneak out into the hallway.

    Night.

i shouldn't be out of bed
if she catches me–
well, there's no telling what could happen
to me.

i sneak down the halls to get here
in the dark
in bare feet
here
in this room
this empty room
is where i save myself
i drag a sheet down here
and wait.
i wait
for my
Lover.
My magic Lover
comes to me here
and will save me.
He comes to me, under the sheet
close
his face so close it blurs
and i giggle
and the medicine
makes the room spin
and my Lover
stretches his wings wide
and his thing
makes me laugh again
and he doesn't say a word
just wraps himself into me.

He has hips like a woman
soft
and sometimes the face of that

man
who calls himself my father.
Sometimes he has great purple wings
and sometimes, when the lightning
flashes,
the face of the white nurse.
Those are the times I close my eyes
Tight i close them
and don't look again
until it's over
and he has flown away.

Then i lie on my back and pull my knees into the air
and wait
wait for it
to take.
That's what you do
so it'll get up there
inside
and make you have a baby.

Babies change everything.
i know
because i remember
far away
when the woman who used to be
my mother
grew fat
and laid down
and had a baby
it changed everything
that little, squalling, squirming
smart thing.
The man
my father
was soft
and cooing.
He turned
and looked at me with
blank eyes.

That nurse may be happy
i'm getting fat
but she doesn't know
that one time
maybe already
I got a baby in Me
a little boy

or girl
and there's no way the Doctor
would cut me open then
no way.
Because i still got the baby stuff
they didn't take that out
there's nothing wrong with that stuff.

Even if she's got the ring
even if she knows i know
even if the Doctor wants to cut me open
and move things around
even if that man and woman come back
and sign papers that say that they are
my parents
and give permission
even if it all happens–
a baby changes everything.

i can take care of a baby
i can take care of cows
and they're bigger.
it doesn't take a genius
to take care of a baby.
Love it
Feed it
Hold it
Help
it
See it
Keep it
Tell it that it's smart and pretty and you
Want it.

My mother is standing next to the sink. The light comes over her shoulder,
through the window. It is two o'clock in the afternoon. My mother has
brought the baby home. His name is Stuart. He came out of my mother's
tummy. She got fat and then she had him cut out of her. She showed me the
scar. That was when she told me about how the man's part does things to
the woman's thing, and then you do the knee trick even if he doesn't want
babies, even if he's afraid of having monsters. You can put your knees up
after he leaves and tell him later that it was a mistake, because babies are
gifts from God.

My mother holds the baby and the man who has been my father for my
whole life reaches his hand out to touch the baby Stuart's head. He coos and
smiles, like he never has with me. Not with the daylight streaming over his
shoulder.

And then my father turns to look at me, and his eyes get smaller, and they drop, slow, and my dress feels too thin in the places where it's gotten tighter lately, and he says, his teeth all uneven,
"Something gotta be done about that girl, mother. She's filling out. Sooner than later, they'll be sniffing around her. And she's slow. She'd end up the same as her mother. Slipping up and bringing another mouth to feed. Gotta find a place for her. Get something done."

And soon i get a new coat, and my hair done special, and my mother takes a picture of me holding Stuart, her miracle, her smart baby, and then i go up the long stairs to the Hospital and the man who calls himself my father carries the suitcase. i have red barrettes, with cherries on them. i look pretty.

They tell me that they have to check my tummy, to make sure things are alright. They put me in a shower and spray me hard. My hair gets wet and even though i tell them that my mother paid to have it done special, even though i try to hold the water away with my hands, it ends up ruined and i cry. They take my barrettes away, and i don't see my mother again.

They must have got in the truck—there'd be room now, without me—and drove away. They left me here.

Stuart was a good baby. Mine will be, too.
i am smart enough to know what to do.
I am smart enough to figure it out
Love it
Feed it
Hold it
Help it
See it
Keep it

Keep it

Keep it

Shh. She's coming. i can hear her feet.

Shh.

Shhh. She's coming.

Shh.

 Lights fade and she is gone.

CROSS

NURSE stands under a naked bulb.

NURSE
I was defending myself
He charged at me
Irene saw the whole thing
ask her
she saw the whole thing
he charged at me
It was normal
everything was according to
Procedure
I always do things
according to procedure
by the book
I run a tight ship here
on My Ward.

He came right at me
Irene saw the whole thing
she'll tell you
I was defending myself
out of fear
he was going to kill me

He would have killed me

I am not naturally afraid
I'm not
I'm a big woman
I can handle myself
all kinds of situations
through the year
I've lost
chunks of hair
I've got a scar
see
from a pencil-wielding–

countless scrapes
bruises
I'm not invincible
I've been damaged
but it's my job
my vocation
It's my calling,
really.

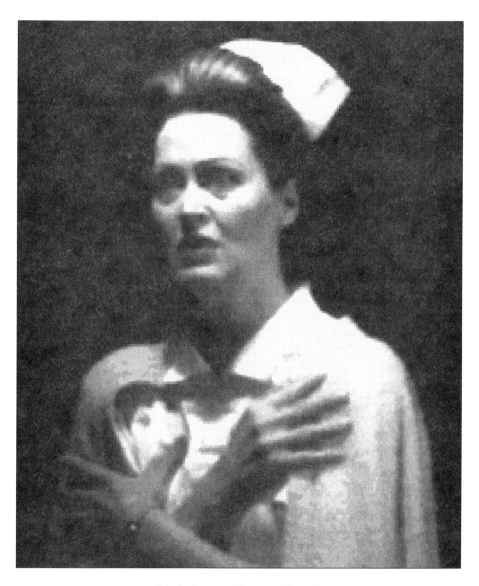

Linda Grass as Nurse in "Cross."
Unconscious Collective 1998.
(Photo courtesy Trevor Schmidt and the Unconscious Collective.)

There were tracks
in the snow
when I got out of the car
right next to the door
small tracks
I bent down
in the falling snow
bent down to peer close
tiny delicate
two two two
a rabbit, I figured
a small rabbit
a bunny
it would still be white
it could be anywhere
across the parking lot
out there somewhere
in the falling snow
looking at me
maybe.

I hurry across the lot
the wind is cold
and i keep
my face
pressed down into the collar
and I try not to look up
at the windows
that stare like empty eyes
dead
and sometimes the dead stand in them
their hands against the bars
their eyes calling out
something
to me
in the parking lot
walking away from the car
that takes me away
at the end of the day
or in the morning
when the endless night
has fallen into
a drugged stupor
and wandered off.

I follow the
rabbit tracks to
the single door

and lock myself inside with
the dead.

Irene will witness
she will
just ask
it's exactly like I said.
it had to be him or me
him or me
life or death
and it wasn't going to be me
no way, no how.

It was quiet
the lights out
most of
Them
were settled down for the night
all medicined up
tucked into beds
locked into room
finally quiet
only the soft padding noise of these
shoes
down the hall
the thin squeak across the squares of tile
that mark the path that separates us
the path that leads from the darkness
that leads out
that only we may travel.

The lightning cracks
flashes
the bodies of the dead under blankets
room after room
waiting.
but waiting
poised beneath blankets
like animals
ready to turn on us
we wait
beyond the fortress of a desk
in the only light
for the night-monsters to come.

A lightning bolt cracks
and a tiny light begins to blink
on the desk

"That's Mr. Flagg" Irene mumbles
"If he's wet his bed again–" and she lumbers down the hall
her wide whiteness
being swallowed up by the darkness.

I stand
and think about the bunny
hearing the murmur of voices
Flagg and Irene
low murmurs
soothing
and shortly the great white shape
bursts into light
and Irene hands me
a bundle of sheets
and says
"He'll need a bath.
I'll fix his bed and you
get him started in the
bath
room"

I have nothing but the greatest respect
for human life
even the lives of these people
great respect
But
I don't so much like
the thought of one of them
touching me unless it is
necessary in some
procedure.
But Irene is spreading the sheet
into the air
and as it floats down
to land on the plastic-covered
mattress
I take Mr. Flagg by the elbow
and we make our way down the hall
through the bowels of the Ward
to the room with the stainless steel tub
and the water pistols.
I grip him hard, making my fingers strong
to show him I am not afraid
"You ought to be ashamed of yourself.
A grown man, covered in his own filth.
It's disgusting.
I'm certainly glad you're not
my father"

That does the trick
and he gets smaller
his shoulders hunch over
and he cries a little.
He's not nearly so frightening
like that.

I loosen my grip the smallest fraction.

Things echo in that metal room
sounds bounce around
hard
turn the water on hot
hissing
then loosen the ties on his gown
cross and stand in the door
looking into the blackness for Irene
while he takes his gown off
the lightning flashes
making him look like an
obscene
black and white movie
the gown cracking and folding
to the ground around his feet
the steam rises
the dull thud of water on steel
where is Irene?
Never close the door
not when you're alone
that's Procedure

The black hallway
looks like a mouth
ready to swallow

I will not be afraid.
"Don't just stand there
Put it down the chute"
and he picks up the soiled gown and
crosses to the corner
and slides it into
the laundry chute.
Good
now the tub is between us
it means crossing away from the door
but
now there is metal
between us.

I touch the keys
that hang on a string
from my waist

they're not there now
they must have fallen off

We poise
on opposite ends of the room
my back to the door
to the dark hall
where the lightning flashes
illuminating the blunt form of Irene
lumbering toward us
between the rows of
doors
hurry hurry
he's naked now

Again
the lights flicker
the water spurts
hot
it's steaming

I can feel it on my sweater
he stands
ready to
I put the keys between my fingers
like a blade
a claw
don't let him see fear
don't let him grab me
oh hurry hurry Irene
he's shifting from
foot to foot
looking at me

"You're wasting time.
Get yourself in there
and clean yourself off
you ought to be ashamed of yourself"
quick look
what is taking her so long?
he hasn't moved
he hasn't moved
what is happening
have I lost control

my voice is steel
"Mr. Flagg"
a warning
he looks at me
his head shakes
"it's too hot, Ma'am"
and the way he says it
that one word
"ma'am"
I freeze
cold
with the steam on my sweater
he is poised
naked

Kill time
Kill time
hurry Irene
Anger bubbles up
fear and anger
my voice cracks out
"Get in.
My patience is wearing thin
MISTER Flagg
Get in or you know
what will happen"
and he lifts his leg to step into
the steam
I crane to look
down the flashing hall
Irene is half-in
a room
lightning flashes twice
a moan drifts down
and as I turn back

he leaps from the tub
toward me
his body red
water burns me
his scream
his hands toward my throat
at me at me
I choke
my hand swings up
the keys dig into his chin
he tips back
a squeak

a slide
a dull thud

He reached for my throat
charging at me
Irene would never have made it
in time
I had to do something.

He was getting up
steaming
red
red
fast
seconds
that's all I'll have
all it would take for him to finish me off

I had to do something
a swing caught my forehead
and I grabbed his ankles
hot wet
I had to keep him down
he had hit me
I couldn't let him get up, get out
not without Irene to help
so I grabbed his ankles
hard
and held them into the air
high
like a baby having it's diaper changed
a large, angry baby
a baby that wanted me dead
the water splashed onto my hands
face
scalding
screaming
his fists
red and steaming
banging out a dull tattoo
on the metal sides of the tub
he had hit me
he can't do that
that's not allowed
he knew that
that's not the way things run
on My Ward.
He knew that.

I don't allow hitting
especially not staff
and no bed-wetting
that is unacceptable
entirely unacceptable
completely.
He knew that.
I was fighting for my life
do you understand?
I had no choice
he turned on me
and by the time Irene got there
the lights flickering
she stood in the doorway
and I held his ankles high
in the air
She saw the whole thing, almost
she stood in the doorway
her eyes wide
like a bunny in the headlights
a round white bunny
staring at me

I did what I thought was best
what had to be done
to ensure my safety
and

I love my job
I do
it's not always easy
there's stress
but I can handle it
I can
it's all I have

I have stitches now
and some scalding
but that comes with the territory
the inmates are running the asylum, I guess

that was just a joke
I'm capable of being in charge
still.

Ask Irene.
She saw the whole thing.

She'll tell you what happened
just like I said.

> *The lights flicker for a moment and go out. The NURSE vanishes.*

Down

> *Cold blue. The figure of a NURSE rises from beneath the ground in a haze of hot steam.*

NURSE
Lots of time to think down here.
They like to turn the tables on you
Even after the best years of your life
blood sweat tears
pouring out you pour it out for them
willingly
but that ain't enough

no satisfaction from that
no
they gotta drag it out of you

Outcast
cast down here
sent down to the bottom
after years of faithful service

Hear that?
Hear them? They're back there, in the corners.
Scratching out a pattern on the floor, scurrying through the
walls, hearing everything, carrying it from one place to
another. Filthy buggers. Dirty little rats.

The Big Brass
sends you down here
banishes you to the basement
when you scare them
when you know too much
when you've seen too much
rather have you down here
with only the rats
to hear the truth

Sure

they still pay
but you have to think about it

Elizabeth Allison as Nurse in "Down."
Unconscious Collective 1998.
(Photo courtesy Trevor Schmidt and the Unconscious Collective.)

a lot more
when you're in the wash-room
near passing out from the heat
scrubbing sheets
and gowns
and underpants.
It's half a relief
to get to this part
cool down in this room
hanging things up
till i am surrounded by
thin ghosts
of the poor souls
that hover
up there
on other floors
far away

Of course, i see them, in a way… i know that these
sheets mean someone's slipped-up, that gown means some else
has grown bigger, these underpants mean … someone's gone.
Dead or home.

i miss them. Like they were my children.

Certain doors that used to open are locked to me now. But i stand outside,
on my way home and wave to the wall. They remember. They wave back,
standing on chairs, or beds, or at the end of hallways. Light, dark, snow or
rain. Always someone who remembers me. Misses me. One of my children.

i used to bathe them
every one my baby
some like to simply use
the pistols
blasting them clean
but not me
I'd rather have them
relax
soothe them
make them think of
Home
wherever that was
however far away
all the forgotten children

One girl
pulled from the bottom ward
transferred upstairs

the last one
we climbed the stairs
and i dropped her into the water
she raised her arms
her eyes closed
i lather her hair
beautiful blond hair
and she sings
her eyes closed
her hands reaching for…
something i will never see
something that
i hope she reaches.

the water runs
over their skin
white and soft
or red and weathered
and i scrub
though not too hard
i scrub them clean so they are
ready
i tuck them in
and some i kiss
and if they murmur in their sleep
if they call me
someone else
i let them

They don't know
some, like the girl with yellow hair
they don't even know that
they are not safe here
and i can't help them all
not with so much work to be done
suds and laundry
my hands are tied

i tried to start a garden down here once.
it's so dark
and damp
and there was no life
it seemed ideal for
mushrooms
i brought a window box from home
filled with earth
set it next to the steam
i would wring out the sheets into them

the blood sweat tears
of all the people from above
it will come to some
good
i thought

Faithful
without fail
like a mother
religiously
watching
waiting
no one knew
no one comes down here
but me
the white caps poked through the black earth
guarded by the empty forms of
gowns and sheets
a ghostly garden in the concrete
like the
so-many above
i will help something good
grow
in this concrete place

The Good Lord
never saw fit
for me to have any children of my own
none that...
well,
no sense dwelling on what
might have been
no sense
no sense
just gets you
dreaming
in slow motion
dreaming about my body
my body and the life trapped inside
that can't get out

i wanted
i so wanted
but when the time came
when it should have come out...
my body did it wrong.

It's alright
I'm alright
a baby won't change anything
i know that now.
It doesn't have to come from my body
no

i can love all my children here
even from the basement
even down there in the wash-room
they can hide me down here but they can't stop me
loving.

Each day
coming in
sneaking handfuls of dirt
fresh soil to add
packing it around the white caps
mushrooms
mushrooms
kept in the cool
nurtured, encouraged
loved.
That's the only way to make anything grow.

Did you hear that?
They're back.
Dirty buggers!
No-good dirty rats.
GET OUT OF HERE!
YOU'RE NOT WANTED!
GET IT?
YOU'RE NOT WANTED HERE!

DON'T YOU GET IT?!

Stinkin'... dirty...

They ruin everything.
I've found them
buried in bedding
baring their little teeth
their pink noses
their claws
sharp nails
tails pink like worms
stinking
dirty...

Why do they have to do that?
Huh?

Down here
i'm thinking all the time
and if i end up talking to myself
or sometimes singing,
well, it only figures
if it's not out loud
you won't be heard
and if you aren't heard
then you don't even exist.
The board isn't going to shut me up
lock me away, shut me up
and keep me quiet.

They don't know
none of them
that i would never tell
never
i wouldn't risk my job
not for anything
how could i give up my children?
how could i leave them?
who would watch out for them if i were to abandon
them?

Some nights
in the upper wards
it got to where i didn't even want to go home
at night
i would have just walked the hallways
back and forth
keeping the nightmares at bay
soothing the whimpers
smoothing hair back from fevered foreheads
i would have even crawled into beds with them
like a mother
until sleep had taken them again.

Of course, i never did that
well, hardly ever
it just wouldn't do, you see
Not Professional
Not Formal
Not Detached enough for some people's liking.
They told me
"You get too attached. They aren't worth worrying over. They're here

because no one else wants them. Surely you can see that. You certainly don't have to put so much investment in them. We're here to look after them, but clinically. This is a place of business."

How can some people go through their whole lives without... touching someone else? Just being ghosts... pale, see-through versions of themselves, wispy in the wind. No depth, no strength, no... no...

i don't know.

i don't know what I'm saying half the time. Go nuts locked away like this. Nuts. It's no wonder some of those kids end up in trouble, when they get locked up and forgotten. It's hard to hold onto what's... right... what's clean and white. Things get messy and crowded and unclear.

Like these sheets, these clothes. i sometimes gotta use so much bleach, just to get them back to white. So much bleach to get rid of the dark that i'm afraid it'll eat right through them. Sometimes things need that much cleaning. You gotta use the strongest solution possible and hope you don't destroy them in the process.

They're quite delicate.

Well, i snuck in handfuls of dirt, pocketfuls of peat, for near on three months. They never suspected. In the door, my hands in my pockets, down the back stairs to the cellar, and here, into the window box, where the soft white caps stretched higher and higher above the black soil.

Growing. In private. In secret. Without Them knowing. Something good, growing out of the concrete, cracking it's way through, breaking the hardness. i will help something grow in this hard place, this cold, hard place where nothing leaves until it dies.

i kept count. Careful count. Two... four... five... upwards of twelve white mushrooms straining to break free of the ground. Surrounded, not by ghosts anymore, no, but by... angels. Guardian angels that glow in the dark. Angels that circle the floors above, wrapping around the poor souls up there, absorbing the sadness, the evil, the sickness. Taking it all and returning here, where i scrub, with bleach, to make the angels pure again. They hang here, watching the window box, guardians even in rest, before i send them out again to some other lost child in need in one of the hundreds of rooms, forgotten.

Weeks of work. Months of waiting. Twelve white pillars of hope.

They ate them. The rats. The mushrooms, i mean. Chewed them to bits. Scattered chunks all over the hard cement floor. Destroyed. Tossed around like bits of stuffing out of a pillow. Not enough left to even piece together. i couldn't bear to try again. Not yet. But maybe. Maybe someday. Someday soon. Maybe tomorrow. Tomorrow after i get the wash done. Maybe then. Maybe.

Filthy little buggers. Taking up my time and energy i could be – should be giving to my children. Distractions.

i am still strong. i won't be broken, down here. They can work me, work me hard, like a horse, whip me like a horse, but they won't break me. Won't make me bend. They can pile it on me because i can take it. i can take it. The strongest bleach possible. i can put my hands into it, direct, and they

come out stronger, harder, tougher.
They need me to be strong. All the children.
My body will only do things right. Not like before. i am getting stronger,
smarter, and They don't even know. They hide me down here, but They
have no idea that one day… one day…
I'm gonna get those rats
I'm gonna get them
starting here
in the basement

I'll clean it out
and move my way up
floor by floor
until all the rats
are gone
I'm gonna clean this place out
and make it safe

once more
into the
mouth of Hell
into battle
thinking
thinking
always thinking
surrounded by
other angels.

> The NURSE sinks into the steaming ground and disappears.

RISING

> The PATIENT stands on a bed, the restraints hanging to the floor, her
> arms outstretched into a bright light.

PATIENT
There's only one window here
and it's so high
I can't even see out
but the sun shines in
golden orange
and if I stretch
far far far
my fingers can fit
into the path

Angela Flatekval as Patient in "Rising."
Unconscious Collective 1998.
(Photo courtesy Trevor Schmidt and the Unconscious Collective.)

I wash my hands in the light
i clean them
for my important work
my mission
I must be pure
I store up healing
and wait
I don't even go to the common room anymore
just stay here
in the room
and wait for the right moment

"And I shall come to you
on a mountain top
stretch my arms wide
and take you above

the heavens will open wide
to take us in
and we will leave these earthly bodies
and the cares that keep us down
and we will rejoice
forever amen"

That's from a kind of
Bible
except it's a
different one
that was written by
me.

It's just as valid
only some people don't think so.

I've been sent
that's my secret

I repeat it and repeat it
quietly to myself
so I don't forget
I've been sent

I used to be
in a different room
a room without a golden window
a room with walls
and a hard door
and in the night

a voice would slip
through the black hole in the wall
the hole-in-the-wall voice that said

"Go forth
Go forth
Rise up and take with you
all who need to be saved
take the one who will listen
the one from the depths
lift her up and
raise her soul to heaven"

I lay in the dark
and pulled my ears out
to make sure I was hearing right
and the silence bounced back at me
and I said

"Wwhaat?"

and there was nothing
no noise
I held my breath
until I was almost dead
and then it blew out like
a dandelion
and I heard it again

a voice from the hole
in the wall
whispered
"You heard me"

my head was so heavy
my neck near broke trying to
lift it
I dragged my lead body out of the bed
across the floor
I squatted
on my haunches
my lips pressed to the hole
in the wall

a tiny sliver of light
on my mouth

"I heard
I heard you
I heard
I'll do it
I'll do whatever you want"

a cool warm breeze came through
smelling of somewhere else
and I smiled
so it stroked my teeth
"You've been chosen"

I scrunch
lower
I press my eye to the hole
but there is nothing on
the other side
nothing new
just more walls
and halls
and darkness.

"Who are you?"
I ask
my mouth back to the hole
breathing in the sweet breath
like drowning
"Who are you?"

a long silence
silence
windy down the hall
before
finally
the answer floats through
and the name is whispered
as I press my ear to the hole
my hands on the door
and over the next many nights
the Gospels are revealed to me
and on the final night
I hear
"Go forth
and save her"

Who?
who?
how do I know who?

But the voice is gone
gone forever
it never comes back
gone
leaving only me

and the Gospels
which roll around in my head

I didn't like that room

I spent all my time
alone
I couldn't save anyone there
just me
and the hole in the wall that quit talking
only occasionally spitting out
bad food

I lay there
waiting
alone in the dark
waiting to start my work
waiting to save
someone
a woman from below
from the depths.

I called out
"Permit me to rise
Permit me to rise"

She came then
in white
beads of work on her forehead
rings of work under her arms
She cut me loose
lifted me up in her great arms
opened the hole in the wall
led me up
to this room
this room where I wait
in the gold.

She knew
that I needed to be here
out of that cell
down there

she let me help her
stretch the sheets out on this
my new bed
and when she began to leave
when I reached out to keep her with me
she said
she had work to do
a job
"Where?"
and she said
"Below.
Hell."

and I knew.
a gust of wind
shivered
down my back
and i knew
she was the one
the reason I was here
she was the one
to be saved
from the depths
from Hell
My mission was clear
Here in this golden room
she brought me here to
save her.

I stay
intensely focused
they try to distract me here
try to make me sleep
I lie awake in the blue of night
and listen
wait for the cool of wind
along my legs and face
or the voice that has never returned.
I watch
for the gold
to pour across the ceiling
slowly crawl across the room
then I call out

"Permit me to rise
Permit me to rise"

and they come
different ones
not her not the one I am sent for
different ones
they let me loose
and try to make me
do things
say things
they try to tell me to
give up
they try to tell me
I have no mission
there is no voice
they tell me
I will never reach the window
but they don't know.

I didn't always used to be so focused
when I was in the other room
down there

there was a battle going on
inside me
bad things
evil things
were fighting to overtake
the good
they had to tie me down
the evil was winning
black-thought headaches
I had horns
pressing their way
through my skull
pushing their path
through bones
horns
I couldn't stop them
and being locked down there
in darkness
didn't help
I tried
I tried to force them back in
but they wouldn't have it.

It's much better here
up higher
the air is better
there's an occasional breeze

it's much easier for the voice
to come to me–
if it wants to.

She brought me here to save me
and somewhere
somewhere in this place
she waits for me to save her.
I just need to be stronger.

I am getting better
everyone seems to agree
in tiny steps
always better
I wouldn't have been moved
up
to this floor
to this window
closer to the light
if there wasn't progress
being shown.
I feel lighter
a weight is lifted
Others shuffle the halls
door to door – looking for something
with empty eyes
sad
so much sadness.

I'm happy.
I know why I am here
where I was meant to be.
I couldn't fulfill my
purpose
without being here.
I am needed.
I am useful and must be put to work
So many to be saved
beginning with her.

"And the strength
will return
and one among you
that you do not know
will come forth
and you will see them
for what they are
and what they will become

and they will lead you
by the hand
out of the pit
up and
out
toward the light
from where you were
ignorant in darkness."

She is like the rest
everyone in white
they are in sleep
their minds
fogged over
they don't know
they don't listen to
their voices
they have grown accustomed
to life
without light
they've forgotten
that there is
somewhere else
that the light
we see
through a high window
comes from somewhere else.
They need to be saved.
one by one
they need to be told
so many in darkness

Turn
Turn

Turn toward the light
Turn and rise

Rise

Permit yourself to rise.

> *Her hands glow in the air and she smiles.*

> *The end.*

Dormitory at the Red Deer Provincial Training School in the 1950s.
(Provincial Archives of Alberta.)

SACRED TIME

by
Brian Webb

INTRODUCTION TO *SACRED TIME*

> Narratives are concerned not with isolated moments or particular acts, but with *sequences* of acts and events. They are orderings and interconnections of phenomenological perceptions, or the memories of these perceptions, in time and space.[1]

Through the media of solo and ensemble dance, live music, voiced narrative and large-screen video projection, Brian Webb's *Sacred Time* relates two parallel stories of predatory, brutalizing space. Profound and disturbing connections link the first story of an elk hunt west of Rocky Mountain House and the second, a stalking of a gay would-be lover in a large city, possibly Edmonton. This combination of verbal, visual, movement and acoustic texts attempts to define, as Webb observes, "a certain Alberta culture, one that recognizes the dichotomy between a spirituality rooted in the land and a brutality crystallized in the hunt for game." Both rural and urban settings explore an impulse toward mystery, an intuitive need to construct a sacred time.

The elements of this performance piece, captured here in recreated narrative, photos from the performance and a summary of the choreography, which Webb himself illuminated during an extensive interview, take several risks to present a physical reflection on spirituality. Seeing the hunt as a sacred activity, the sequence concerning the elk hunt is introduced first in an improvised monologue told in a deliberately casual fireside style. References to actual places and to familiar-sounding names of local hunters establish truth claims which compel the spectator to experience the excitement of the hunt right up to the particularly pungent details of the gutting and skinning. The unsentimentalized, sardonic delivery enhances the chilling moment when Brian, as the novice hunter, exchanges looks with the elk before he shoots him. The elk's return glance contains the knowledge of its impending death and a certain acceptance of its inevitability as part of the life cycle. It is this moment between life and death that is the sacred time of the title – sacred because it shows that energy is never simply created or destroyed but always in transformation between the two.

The unrelenting 25-minute ensemble dance which follows the monologue draws attention to the labour of the dance as a sacred activity in which energy is endlessly recycled. We watch the exhausted dancers drop out from time to time to rest for a moment, but the dance never ceases. A communal experience that must be witnessed, the dance invites our participation in the sacred creation.

In the second narration, the urban stalker, confused that a one-night stand in the "tunnel," a place of anonymous sex in the gay subculture, could be love, enacts the ecstatic moment of killing his dismissive "lover" in a deliberate reversal of the original roles of hunter and prey. The events, both taking place on Halloween, are meant to mirror each other. In the second sequence, the initiator, dressed in the devil's garb, transfixes his willing partner with his unmasked gaze after having sex with him, and seals the moment with an exclamation: "that was perfect/ that was even spiritual/ let's do it again." This is the transformational moment between sexual death and love which the initiator then fails to honour. The violation of that sacred moment leads to the further transformation of "love" into obsessive hate on the part of the man who had been pursued. Thus the prey becomes the stalker; the spirit of the elk who had recognized his impending death in the first narration, returns in the guise of the hunter. The transformation of Brian into the stalker narrator is enacted when he dons a head gear of elk antlers to tell the tale. At the climactic moment of the murder he wears his antlers and the blue-black cock feathers that were on his half-mask bird helmet on the fateful Halloween. In the eerie tradition of Edgar Allan Poe *cum* "American Psycho," he slips home, showers and falls asleep without dreaming. The energy has been transformed again in this consummate act of unspeakable and completely gratuitous savagery.

Brian Webb, Chair of the Dance Program at Grant MacEwan College, holds a BFA from the University of Alberta and an MFA from the California Institute of the Arts. A dancer, choreographer, teacher, visual artist, Brian's artistic output is enormous. Artistic Director of the Brian Webb Dance Company, he has choreographed over 40 dances for the company. In 1987, he began work on a series of self portraits that were created in collaboration with artists of other media. Since that date, his works have been presented across Canada. In 1997 he created *Project Desire: the mountains and the plains* which was presented in Edmonton, Calgary, Vancouver, Toronto and New York at P.S. 122. He receives numerous commissions from other arts and dance education institutes. In the past three years, he has created six new works including two commissioned by the Edmonton Symphony Orchestra and two by Catalyst Theatre. Some of his more recent works include *Sacred Time*, and, now, featuring a duo with Tania Alvarado, *A Summer Evening* which premiered on June 27 and 28, 2001, at the John L. Haar Theatre. Based on Marguerite Duras's short story *Blue Eyes/Black Hair*, the piece is intensely physical and highly erotic.

The Brian Webb Dance Company (BWDC) is an artistically driven organization with a mandate to "promote and encourage the development of original contemporary dance through the making of new dance in collaboration with artists of various media, the presentation of performances and workshops, the mentoring of younger emerging choreographers, and the encouraging of a context for contemporary dance making in Edmonton, in Alberta, and in Canada." Established in 1979, it continues to be the only professional dance company in Edmonton to present a full season of contemporary dance. Each year the BWDC brings in different companies from across Canada offering them different kinds of residencies in collaboration with Grant MacEwan College. As part of the 11-member CanDance Network, a national dance presenters organization, BWDC acts as an agent and represents these choreographers to dance presenters from across Canada. Brian is the newly appointed Artistic Director of the Canada Dance Festival. The recipient of many awards, Brian and the BWDC are an integral part of the Arts community in Edmonton.

NOTES

[1] Kim L. Worthington, *Self as Narrative: Subjectivity and Community in Contemporary Fiction* (Oxford: Clarendon Press, 1996), 14.

The first production of *Sacred Time* was performed at the John L. Haar Theatre, Edmonton, in November 2000 with the following cast:

DANCERS   Tanya Alvarado
             Dustin Anderson
             Walter Kubanick
             Doug Rachinski
             James Viveiros
             Brian Webb

MUSICIANS   Percussion: Trevor Brandenberg
             Keyboards and Trumpets: Allan Gilliland
             Bass: Graham Kidd
             Drums: Ron Samson
             Guitar: Dave Wall

Choreography by Brian Webb
Music by Allan Gilliland
Video by Tim Folkmann
Lighting Designed by David Fraser
Choreographic Monitor: Linda Rubin

SET

The stage was completely open and bare except for the row of standard issue turquoise plastic chairs lined up in a row upstage right, with water bottles beside them for the dancers. The band, crammed into the upstage left in the wing area, were visible to the audience. It was composed of a drum set, a keyboard, and some percussion instruments. A large white screen was set up in the upstage left area. The wings on both sides were not masked so that audiences could see what was going on off stage. The impression that was created was of scarcity and minimalism. The set was never transformed during the performance with the result that the stage always remained a space for dancing and movement.

VIDEO SCREEN

It was a constant presence, enriching the dancers' performance and creating its own separate text. A live video camera set up on the stage projected images onto the screen at various times. Thus the dancers became part of the video as well. The first image was of an enormous burning candle projected onto the screen from a video camera placed on the stage in such a way as to capture moments when the dancers were in the range of an actual candle which was kept lit during the entire uninterrupted twenty-minute dance sequence. Next came the footage of the forest whirling by as the elk herd approached, underlining Brian's story of the hunt and setting up resonances with it. The magnificent shot of an elk racing through the forest, followed by a still shot of his head and antlers caught in the camera's lens set up the moment for the life-death encounter that was the thematic centrepiece of the entire dance. The shapes and the movement of the elk herd running were echoed by the dancers in their violently energetic leaping and twirling and diving. Later the screen was used to project a gigantic silhouette of the elk man (Brian Webb wearing antler head gear). Later, the footage returned to different magical images of the forest with the light shining through the trees which served both as a backdrop for the dancers' solos and as a point of entry for them, since they often became part of the film when the camera picked them up. The last recurring spectacular image was of a burning tree. It became a mesmerizing focus for the dancers, drawing them to sit in front of it and watch it.

COSTUMES

The costumes were in keeping with the set. There was nothing extravagant or flashy about them. For the most part, it appeared as if the dancers were in their rehearsal clothes, each slightly different. They wore layers of tights and sweatpants, which they took off gradually when they got warm. There was no feeling that the clothing had some special meaning beyond being suitable to dance in. They did not transform the dancers in any way. At the place where Brian Webb narrated the urban tale of the psycho murderer, he stripped down to white underwear and a huge headdress made of elk horns which he wore for the duration of that sequence.

LIGHTING

It began by being unusually flat and dull, in keeping with the rehearsal feel of the piece. The sense that the piece was being improvised was maintained throughout by keeping the lighting very unobtrusive. The stage was often only semi-lit, so that it was hard to establish one point of focus. However, there were several special effects where dancers were caught in certain spotlights. For example, when James Viveiros sang "Only the Lonely," only his face and upper body were lit.

MUSIC

The live music written for the piece and performed by the composer and a small band was stunning. The score was perfectly tailored to meet the demands of the piece. The first long sequence that accompanied the twenty-five-minute dance captured the violent energies and barely contained rhythms driving the dancers. In general, the "liveness" of the music made the performance that much more vibrant.

PERFORMERS

The troupe was made up of one woman and five men. The stunningly beautiful Tanya Alvarado as the sole woman, often created a counterpoint to the predominantly male energy. Variations in age, height and body-type amongst the men added another dimension to the material. Brian Webb remained a central focus since he initiates the dance, narrates the two tales of the elk hunt and the urban stalker, and brings the piece to a close. However, each performer created a strong individual presence, especially in the solos that make up the third section of the performance.

Brian Webb narrates the hunter's tale.
Production at the John L. Haar Theatre, Edmonton, November 2000.
(Photo by Trout, courtesy the Brian Webb Dance Company.)

SACRED TIME
by Brian Webb

THE PERFORMANCE

> *The show began with Brian Webb coming on stage alone and beginning to dance in an unhurried impromptu manner. His movements had a certain dreamlike quality to them as if he were rehearsing them from memory. The sense of reverie was punctuated by several moments when the dance became sharper, with some jerky almost violent gestures, punctuated with slaps. After some time, Brian simply stops, and walks up stage to get a chair which he then brings down stage. Once in the chair and in a spot light, he begins to improvise the hunting story. The script that follows is in the notational score he used to improvise the monologue:*

1.

join in	moving to Lumbreck Falls
shooting lessons	
Chuck Lee –	best hunter in community
SMIRK	friend Ken
late October	end of hunting season
no snow	
elk hunt	during RUT

2.

go for four or five days
west of Rocky Mountain House

Camp ground	set up
afternoon	go scout area

Must Find:

1.	fresh tracks
2.	tree rub
3.	lots of droppings
4.	recognize wind direction

see them through binoculars
are they passing through or using meadows as feeding grounds

3.

Back at camp

proactive	GRUNT TUBE
	reed in mouth / plastic tubing

early to bed

must be up by 4:3–	before dawn

temperature drop / a hint of snow

It's cold	coffee

If I'm such a good shot – first shot
Chuck will second me
Ken will bugle the bull in

Dustin Anderson, Brian Webb and Doug Rachinski.
Production at the John L. Haar Theatre, Edmonton, November 2000.
(Photo by Trout, courtesy the Brian Webb Dance Company.)

4.
Drive up   –   two mile hike to meadow
just after dawn. ken's first bugle
several tries   a call returned
takes at least twenty minutes of play back and forth until we
finally   see the bull
gets closer   –   tree rub   –   turns north   –   broadside   –   turns
head to look at me
** EYE TO EYE he knows / I know **
one bullet
cheer   blah blah blah
          5.
Work to be done
hide is thick / strong hair / dulls 3 knives
Gut it   Stream / Heat   Covered in Blood
Find liver   vomit
take hind quarters first in plastic garbage bags, in oversize knapsacks
follow orange ribbons
tired   get to truck   and   back
load lighter but harder
I carry head — pull of antlers on brush — get to truck........

As Brian narrates the story, the dancers start to come in behind him and begin to whirl around. In particular Tanya moves with a certain frenzy. As the hunt story builds to the kill, the dancers who are moving in the dark, make certain movements that are reminiscent of Brian's original impromptu. As he talks more about the blood and the gutting and then the return back to camp with the elk's hoof 2' above his head, huge shadows are created by the dancers moving back and forth, until eventually they will call in to join them. At which point he removes the chair and joins them.

Now the candle is lit and imaged on the screen as the dancers watch. Then the wild, frenzied ensemble dance begins with everyone making the same movements which are reflected on the screen. The dance is an explosion of energy, almost threatening to go out of control with the dancers bending, thrusting, kicking, throwing their bodies to the ground. Dancers, especially Brian, but also the others, will go in and out of the dance if they get too tired or thirsty. The dance continues relentlessly, the beat unceasing, with Tanya and others often stepping out to observe and then reentering. The huge candle burns behind them on the video screen. There is a certain harshness to the music, and as the speeded up shots of the forest with the elk herd running through it start to appear on the screen, the dancers, the juxtaposition of the dancers with the screen images invite striking comparisons. The intricate patterning, the speed with which they move, their power and grace bear distinct resemblances to the elk. In time, the audience becomes aware that the energy that is being released has become unstoppable, and, perhaps, uncontrollable. Stops and starts on the part of the performers and the video images punctuate the speeding up. The

Tanya Alvarado.
Production at the John L. Haar Theatre, Edmonton, November 2000.
(Photo by Trout, courtesy the Brian Webb Dance Company.)

*dancers leave to get water or to remove some of their clothing. There are
some signs of tiring. Brian sits out and then returns, his movements more
jerky and violent. The dancing gets faster, the circle tighter as the elk races
through. The music stops and we are back to the image of the candle on the
screen.*

*In the darkness the dancers in their chairs fall over and off in sequence
against the candle reflections; some on the floor crawl towards the candle
with arms stretched overhead, like elks. The music is very delicate now and
the movements are slow and dreamy. The bodies are spread-eagled on the
chairs. The candle is approached and extinguished. The dancers reform
their chairs, except for Brian who is alone upstage, slowly composing
himself as he falls bends, reaches. Naked, except for his white underwear,
slowly puts on the elk antlers and moves stealthily about making circling
motions with his head as the others glide in and out of their chairs. Brian
dances with his antlers beside them as the screen reflects them with low
angle distortions. Then Brian, as elk man, begins to narrate his urban
stalker tale.*

You stupid fucking idiot
You stupid idiot
You fuck
I know you thought I'd never find you
you fuck
I phoned you three times
And, each time you had an excuse
Some spiritual moment
Halloween – three years ago – the tunnel
It was kinda cold but there were
still lots there looking for
the perfect stranger
the perfect match
the perfect
     one
you had on a goat mask, horns
flowing out behind – red
             lascivious
             tongue
and I
I had a half mask, a helmet
of blue / black cock feathers
We kinda circled each other
I smiled (a big smile)
and you laughed
And, after we were through
(we hadn't even taken the masks off)
you said

that was perfect
that was even spiritual
let's do it again
you took your mask off and kissed
me hard   you were beautiful
I took your phone number and
I took you at your word
And, when you were busy three times
I started to get irritated, but I thought
"Just one more time"
You sounded pissed off when you heard my voice
        Fuck you
I don't think this is such a good time
I'm not alone you know
I don't think you should call me again
I hung up

So, you can imagine my shock
when the elevator door opened
and there you were right in front of me
I had to step aside to let you pass
I started to get on, but
"No" I said
and turned
to follow you
You are So Stupid
I watched you try on three sweaters
buy a shirt
flirt with the sales girl
and then followed you out of the store
to the bus stop
stood right behind you
wanted to exhale slowly on the back
of your neck just to see you squirm
You idiot
we got on the "West 10"
I sat two seats behind you
"Why no car" I thought as I followed
you all the way out to the suburbs
When you got off, I didn't
This was Saturday
On the way back downtown I wondered
if you took the bus all of the time
Probably some bureaucrat
living in a pretentious house
Couldn't afford the car you wanted
Maybe you can't drive
alcoholic   illness

Anyway
I was there early Monday morning
waiting
Ten after eight you arrived
You smiled your smile
Fuck off   Pal
I followed you off at the eight street stop and right to the
Federal building
Then I waited a couple of days until
I accompanied you all the way home
saw you unlock the front door
and disappear inside
The rest was easy........
I got to know lots about you
You live alone
You shower right after you get home
each day and then parade from room to room
satisfied in yellow running shorts
You spend lots of time in the back
yard working on perennial flower beds
Delphiniums – pale blue
Orange poppies
Pale pink rose bushes
Cute
Each night
two hundred and fifty sit ups
Another shower and then to bed

I watched you by taking cover in
your well appointed shrubbery

    Laugh.

You're Such An Idiot
I laugh when I notice that one
of your basement windows is loose
And then when you're not there
I explore your whole haven
You're so tasteful
    so neat
    so tidy
even in your bureau drawer where
you toss knickknacks   jewelry   and pills
everything seems to be in place
I steal one of your pairs of yellow running shorts

I decide I want to be in the house with you
I'm there when you get home from work

I stay in the basement but hear you shower
hear you parade from room to room
hear you even sing a song
Orbison
And then I leave

The next time I come back, it's evening just past sunset, around ten ten
Once I make it into your back yard I see you ending your day
turning off the lights, pulling back the covers of your bed, closing the
thick drapes
I enter the house and when its very still
I go up the stairs one step at a time
I take all of the time I need

I'm calm,
I even feel peaceful
I get to your bedroom
Why didn't I know the door is closed?
I'm going to have to come back   Check this out

Next time I'm more prepared
I take the exact same path   follow my every step
Open the bedroom door   turning the knob with just the right amount
of
pressure
No sound
Takes me two more nights to put my head in the door
Four more to get all of the way in
You notice nothing
You sleep like a baby
I watch you for over a week as I devise my plan
I'm going to get you

On the chosen night
I follow my route exactly
All the way from my apartment
to the elm lined street
to the basement window
to the landing
to the bedroom door
step by step   silently
I turn the knob with same calm ease
I enter and I take the seven steps to the chair left of the foot of your bed
I sit and I listen to you sleep
(You're dreaming tonight   you do that sometimes)
You toss a bit   tonight you even cry
Such a Baby
When dawn comes   I'm still sitting there

wearing my helmet of blue / black cock feathers
nothing else

It's time
I stand up
I take the knife into my right hand that I've been hiding under the folds
of rust fabric at the base of the chair
I'm ready
I feel good   my muscles are alive
I feel just a hint of sweat on my upper lip
I smile
I crouch
I feel a tingle in the middle of my scrotum
And I leap
You Idiot
And just like that   I have you pinned down
sitting on your chest   your arms locked at your sides under the sheet
And You Are Mine
I smile and you begin to cry
I bring my face down close to yours and
I blow gently sweetly over your eyes
Stop It
I tell you how much I love you
I tell you how unfair you've been to me
I tell you how unkind it is to play
with other living beings
And then I cut your throat
your body convulses under my weight
And slowly come to rest
My heart is beating like a drum
I have to get out
I walk for a long time
I don't know what to do
but then I'm home
I shower
I have some orange juice
and I go to bed
I don't even dream about you

*As he speaks, he is reflected on the screen, a huge man-beast standing
perfectly still, presiding in some way over the dancers who perform
sculpted movements from their chairs, gracefully falling over each other's
bodies in fluid undulating movements. As the story develops they move
their chairs into a straight line and continue to hold each other as they
slide up and down over each other's bodies in slow motion. Tanya comes
downstage and lies down moving seductively. When Brian is telling the
story of being in the man's bedroom, she is involved in an intricate
moment of seduction with one of the male dancers. As the dancers move*

in very slow, very uniformly choreographed stealthy movements, the piece builds to its climactic kill. At the moment of the kill, the chairs are reassembled, facing in different ways. The stage fades to black.

Then the beautiful face of James Viveiros appears out of the darkness; he sings Roy Orbison's "Only the Lonely" in a moment of perfect whimsy which offsets the stalker's grotesque brutality.

Now the dancers return to their chairs which have been realigned in a straight row and each one in turn performs a solo expressive of their individual state to a background projection of what appear to be multi-coloured swirling lights but are eventually recognizable as light reflecting though raindrops glistening on leaves in the forest. These images are in turn cut by the appearance of the gigantic image of the burning tree with its branches outlined by the flames swirling around it. As each new solo happens, the other dancers reposition themselves to watch or not as they wish. At one point, everyone gets up and dances slowly in unison and then some of them move in to watch the burning tree as it gets reduced to ashes. Some of the dancers are reflected inside the fire itself. Increasingly the focus of everyone is on the burning tree image.

The closing sequence focuses on an abject Brian who has separated from the group and is slumped up against the upstage right wall. While all of the other dancers are watching the burning tree, Brian begins a slow tortured diagonal crawl across the darkened stage. Caught in a dim light, he makes his way downstage.

The end.

l to r: Walter Kubanick, Dustin Anderson, James Viveiros,
Brian Webb, Tanya Alvarado, Doug Rachinski.
Production at the John L. Haar Theatre, Edmonton, November 2000.
(Photo by Trout, courtesy the Brian Webb Dance Company.)

LOVE'S KITCHEN

by
Anna Marie Sewell
and Cathy Sewell

INTRODUCTION TO *LOVE'S KITCHEN*

> Music may serve as a model of self. One can find one's self in music's
> ways of happening. One can also recall one's self on rehearing music.
> Music is a key resource for the production of autobiography and the
> narrative thread of self.[1]

Set entirely in the kitchen of Sarah Roy, *Love's Kitchen* is, as its name suggests, a love-in for the departed Auntie Isobel (A.K.A. Auntie Love), a
beloved matriarchal force in the lives of Roy and her sister Imogene. The fact
that Auntie Love's body has been laid out in one of the most fundamental
rooms of the house in a homemade coffin on wheels makes her stage presence
enormously powerful and, at times, humorously grotesque. Forced by
Imogene to recognize that they owe it to their Aunt to fulfill her last request
to bury her from home, Sarah has first to come to terms with her own discomfort at this more traditional practice. Ostensibly the more serious character, an educated community development worker, she represents a woman
active in the larger community, while the impish Imogene, a mother of four,
serves as her down-to-earth complement. Together they are enjoined with the
task of honouring their Auntie's unfailing love and interpreting its meaning
for them and the larger community, which is sketched as a kind of Aboriginal
Anytown, a generic community that could be either a Reservation or Metis
community anywhere in contemporary Canada.

As they explore their own relationships through witness and song, the
sisters gradually acknowledge the pain and aspirations of their personal lives
and intimate relationships. Their first duet, "Where do you go? Where do you
go? / Children lost to the wind," is a lament for all the children who have
been lost in their community. The condoms that Sarah has been handing out
to them to replace the baggies—which some youth have been using as do-it-
yourself prophylactics—become a sign of hope for the future. When the topic
turns to questions of Sarah's husband, Richard, her confession that he falls
short of being an ideal partner also turns into an ironic song which salves
some of the hurt by highlighting how unrealistic her expectations were. The
next song revolves around a much sadder truth, since we know about
Richard's lost sister and her dead child. Balancing the story of Richard's
obsessive mourning for his losses is the equally legendary story of Imogene's
husband Olin and his cooking, celebrated in the Bannock Song.

Love's Kitchen is a play of songs and signs. The healing that the sisters are
undergoing accelerates as the presence of Auntie Love begins to manifest
itself through various signs, beginning with the vision in the sky of the
round-bellied woman and her mysterious message, "I'll be there soon." As
they rock the coffin in time to their song, Imogene reaches in and pulls out a
letter from their dead relative. Auntie Love's magical return has already happened, they learn, in the recognition that the barren Sarah is, like her sister,
also newly pregnant. The powerful message of rebirth and regeneration in
Love's Kitchen grows out of its deceptively domestic preoccupations with the
small details of the everyday lives of the sisters. As the joyfulness of the wake

crescendos into a final song, "The Heart of a Nation," Anna Marie and Cathy Sewell craft a play that speaks through the personal empowerment of Sarah and Imogene to prophesy the rebirth of Aboriginal communities. The Sewells are of Mi'gmaq, Anishnabe and Polish heritage, and came of age in a climate of fairly intense change and renewal. They use Sarah and Imogene to give voice to some of the changes and challenges they have lived.

The music-punctuated talk which takes place around and about the coffin is anything but morbid: birth, marriage and new beginnings are their form of singing Auntie on her way. The sisters' conversation is not exclusively "l'écriture feminine"; that is, it is not wholly in a register which rebuffs patriarchal values, redresses women's exclusion and mimes the rhythms of women's bodies. While it is true that they see their husbands as far from ideal, the sisters do not disallow the possibility of understanding by men and of communication with them. The music of the play, a property of bodily being, is the agent of their accumulated and gendered awareness. As De Nora's study *Music in Everyday Life* speculated, music in *Love's Kitchen* is a means of realizing identity and of moving toward a greater structure that one wishes to complete. The sisters' celebration of "Love," as a person and an emotion, permits them to revisit their past, acknowledge different values and retain a belief in the mythical possibilities of signs.

Writer/performer Anna Marie Sewell studied poetry as part of her BA in Drama from the University of Alberta. She also studied Creative Writing at the En'owkin Centre, an Aboriginal Arts College in Penticton, B.C. In Edmonton in 1998 she founded Big Sky Theatre, an Aboriginal theatre company dedicated to producing new works. Her work has been anthologized and produced in various formats, and in 1999, she was a recipient of the Prince and Princess Edward Prize in Aboriginal Literature, due in large part to her work *Heart of the Flower*, which tells of her experiences as a Halfbreed Canadian teaching English in Japan. Cathy Sewell co-founded the internationally-known Aboriginal women's vocal ensemble Asani. She was also a journalist who worked in print, radio and television. Cathy held a degree in Native Studies from the University of Alberta, and worked for the Office of Native Student Services until her death in August of 2001. In recognition of her academic and community work, including teaching the first post-secondary course in Contemporary Indigenous Music, she was posthumously awarded her Masters in Education in International Intercultural Education.

Love's Kitchen, began as two sisters sharing music, and the Sewells employed a process Anna Marie calls "bonescripting," melding indigenous storytelling modes with collaborative techniques of modern western theatre. A central image was drawn from the experience of holding Big Sky Theatre Society's first Annual General Meeting in a church basement; there was a wake upstairs that night. The presence and proximity of death, and its acknowledgement as part of the circle of life, became central to *Love's Kitchen*.

NOTES

[1] Tia De Nora, *Music in Everyday Life* (Cambridge: Cambridge University Press, 2000), 158.

Poster from Edmonton Fringe production, August 1999.
(Courtesy T. Sewell and M. Henderson.)

Love's Kitchen, written for inclusion in the Sk'wak'lum Buckskin Theatre Festival, a national Aboriginal theatre showcase hosted by the En'owkin Centre, debuted on March 19, 1999 with the following cast:

IMOGENE   Anna Marie Sewell
SARAH   Cathy Sewell

Directed by Anna Marie Sewell and Cathy Sewell

Love's Kitchen was also performed at the Edmonton Fringe in 1999, directed by Mark Henderson, and, as part of Big Sky's touring repertoire, it has been produced in schools, at conferences, in a prison, and as part of the 1999 World Indigenous Peoples' Conference on Education in Hilo, Hawai'i.

SETTING
Sarah & Richard Roy's kitchen, with a table and two chairs centre. There is a guitar stage left. On the table there is a small ratcheting wrench set.

LOVE'S KITCHEN
by Anna Marie Sewell and Cathy Sewell

In the dark, we hear a pot of tea and cups set out on the table. As SARAH begins to chant "WEYAHO" off stage, lights come up on IMOGENE Nolan, SARAH's sister, as she enters from the other side, pushing a long box on wheels, humming. She sets box down centre, picks up guitar, and picks up the refrain for about 8 bars, then subsides. Enter SARAH.

SARAH
Why do we have to do this?

IMOGENE
Hi. Good day at work?

SARAH
I don't want to talk about work right now. I want to know why that cow Donna isn't taking care of this. I mean, she's got the nerve to tell me to tell you that you'd better not laugh like at Uncle Harley's – and you'd better not, Imogene–

IMOGENE
Sarah, don't you know–

SARAH
Know what? Why you were laughing? I don't care why you were laughing. She did have a point you know–

IMOGENE
No, I'm not talking about Uncle Harley's wake. I'm talking about this one. This is what she wanted.

SARAH
Donna?

IMOGENE
As if! Auntie Isobel herself.

SARAH
What? I thought she wanted it here because the hall burnt down last week.

IMOGENE
No, that's what you call a happy coincidence. Though I wouldn't put it past her to arrange it so she could get her way.

SARAH

What are you saying? You're talking like she planned to die.

IMOGENE

Well, planned is a strong word, but she sure was ready to go; counting down ready to blast off – ten... nine... eight...

SARAH

Imogene!

IMOGENE

What? It's not the end of the world, dying. Seven...

SARAH

Have some respect!

IMOGENE

I'm trying to. That's what I'm trying to tell you. This is what Auntie Isobel wanted. She told me so herself. You weren't there. That's why Donna's giving you such a hard time, you know. You should have seen it. Bunch of us sitting there around her bed and that Donna comes barging in; and she starts right in on us – "It's my mother's funeral, it's my mother's wake, I know what my mother wants," and then her mother rears up in bed and looks her in the eye and says, "Donna, I want you to shut up."

SARAH

She actually said that?

IMOGENE

You should've seen it. Donna's face falls bang on the floor and Auntie says it again. "Donna, you just shut up. Sarah and Imogene have been daughters to me all my life, and I want them to take care of me now. I'm through listening to you. This is my last days and my last wish, and this is how it's gonna be – I'm getting buried out of my own old kitchen, and those girls are gonna get me ready, and sing me on my way. That is if it's okay with them..."

SARAH

But–

IMOGENE

Don't worry. I answered for both of us. I told her we'd be honoured. I told her you'd be here, and help me out. Her last days, her last wish. Honestly, I don't know how you could go to work–

SARAH

How could I not? Those kids need to know at least one adult in this community cares for them. They're important.

IMOGENE

But this is more important. This is family. You should have come as soon as you got the message.

SARAH

What message?

IMOGENE

The one I left you, as soon as they brought her?

SARAH

I didn't get a message.

IMOGENE

Well I left one at the office.

SARAH

With whom?

IMOGENE

Who else?

SARAH

That idiot receptionist the Chief hired because she's got great big… "community connections?"

IMOGENE

Well, anyhow, she's been here all day and we've been waiting for you.

SARAH

Well, I would have come if I'd known, and I didn't know and that's why I didn't come. Well, where is she? (*IMOGENE indicates box.*) In my kitchen?!

IMOGENE

Well, yeah. I knew you'd be home soon, so I'm making tea–

SARAH

There's a dead body in my kitchen.

IMOGENE

I couldn't leave her all lonely by herself.

SARAH

There's a dead body in my kitchen.

IMOGENE

Oh stop it! It's not like I laid her out right here, all dead bits hanging all over your kitchen table.

SARAH
Well where–

IMOGENE
I washed and dressed her in your bedroom.

SARAH
In my bed?!

IMOGENE
No, on the floor. Of course on the bed. What's the matter with you? (*as SARAH exits*) Too good to give a bed to your poor auntie, just cause she's dead?

SARAH
(*off*) But my Bed!

> *SARAH returns and carries a laundry basket of sheets across the kitchen, avoiding the coffin as best she can.*

IMOGENE
You're prejudiced, that's what it is. When I think of all the times she had us over to stay when this was her place and we were kids. What did she always say, Sarah? What did she say? "Oh Sarah, love," she'd say, "my little Imogene; you girls have my bed. I'll sleep on the couch. No, no, I insist. Nothing's too good for my special girls."

SARAH
But a body–

IMOGENE
And now look at you. First time she turns up dead, and you won't have anything to do with her. Oh, sit down, Sarah. Here. I made you wild mint tea, just like she used to. (*pours herself a mug*) Only I didn't find your sugar.

SARAH
Sugar causes diabetes.

IMOGENE
Not even any honey in this house.

SARAH
Aboriginal people have several times greater risk of developing adult onset diabetes than the rest of–

IMOGENE
(*rummaging in SARAH's handbag.*) You got any of them mints they give out at the dentist?

SARAH
It runs in our family, you know.

IMOGENE
(*pulls out some condoms*) Ooh. Candy. (*She starts reading the packages, joking about flavours, etc.*)

SARAH
(*seizing a condom from IMOGENE*) You want to know about work?

IMOGENE
Sure.

SARAH
Today I found out what some of the junior high kids were using for condoms.

IMOGENE
Oh really? Do tell.

SARAH
Baggies. Tied on with rubber bands. Imogene, it's not funny. Those kids are putting themselves at risk. They're crazy.

IMOGENE
No, no… twist ties, now that would be crazy.

SARAH
It's not funny, Imogene. You'd think by now there's enough information around that they'd know. And it's my job to teach them, before they all catch AIDS–

IMOGENE
They could cut off the circulation. It could fall off!

SARAH
Stop it.

IMOGENE
Or get rubber band hickies. All bruises on it. Ow-eeyah! Now with a twist tie… hey, baby, gotta bag before we snag. Got me a baggie – supersize. But don't you worry little lady, I got me a twist tie, gonna snug it up real good. Ooh. That feels…

SARAH
Stop it, Imogene. That's just like you. Always joking about everything. Get serious for once in your life. Life hurts. Death hurts. Death happens.

IMOGENE
So does life.

SARAH
Those poor kids.

"WHERE DO YOU GO?"

> *This song is very slow, accompanied by guitar, with a descant that is entwined within the lyric. Lead lyric sung by SARAH.*

Where do you go? where do you go?
children lost to the wind
is there a way for you to stay
forever innocent, untouched by flame?

where do you go? where do you go?
carried away by the stream
where do you go? covered by stone
is it dark? is it cold? are you calling to me?
where do you go? where do you go
tell me where do you go?

> *Descant sung by IMOGENE.*

where do you go, wildflower children, buffalo children, where do you where do you where do you go?

IMOGENE
Hey, isn't Dick supposed to be home by now?

SARAH
Richard. His name is Richard.

IMOGENE
Oh, pardon me – Richard. So, where's Richard working today? He is working, isn't he? He was just leaving when I got here this morning, and he said–

SARAH
Be serious, Imogene.

IMOGENE
You mean, gasp!, he lied?

SARAH
Well, lied is a strong word, but – thank God I've got a good job that pays all the bills. I know I said "for richer or for for poorer," but, I don't know, Imogene. He's just not the man I married.

IMOGENE
Aw, they never are.

"I THOUGHT MY LOVE"

Rhythm is provided through using the tool set.

SARAH
I thought my love was an eagle
soaring high above the plain
but he turned out to be a turkey

IMOGENE
too stupid to come in from the rain.

SARAH
I thought my love was a river
flowing swiftly to the sea
but he turned out to be a puddle

IMOGENE
splashing mud all over me.

SARAH
I thought my love was a cedar
swaying proudly in the breeze
but he turned out to be a little tiny shrub

IMOGENE
couldn't even come up to my knees.

SARAH climbs up on the table for the final verse.

SARAH
I thought my love was a mountain
and that he'd be as strong as stone
but if he's supposed to be my tower of strength, tell me

She leaps, and IMOGENE stops playing.

(*spoken*) why am I standing here alone?

Richard Roy, I stood behind you when no one else in this community would. When your sister came back from East Hastings, you said, "Sarah, we've got to take her in, she's got no one else. We're family." And so we did. And we asked nothing of her, no money for rent, for groceries, nothing. It wasn't until later that we found out that she was pregnant, and that she was HIV positive. And when little Nicky was born, do you think she even cared about him? No! She was out there drinking and drugging and doing God knows what.... I'm the one who looked after him. I'm the one who held him and cuddled him and loved him. And one evening I woke up because he was crying and I noticed she was gone. No note, nothing. She had taken everything we had given her. She even stole the $500 we had saved for her treatment. But you know what, Richard, I was glad she was gone. And I said, "We've got to take care of him. We're his family." And those five months were the happiest of my life. We were finally a family. It was wonderful to be a Mom. To see him smile. To hear him laugh. And so wonderful to see you be a Daddy. To see you playing with him. To see you show him how to be a man. Until he left us too. I woke up that morning to feed him, and he was lying there in his crib. Cold. And now you're out there, every day, looking for her. "Oh Sarah, we've got to find her. She's got to know." Well guess what Richard? She doesn't want to know. She doesn't care. She never cared. She's gone. She's gone and she's not coming back. I'm here. And it kills me to see you dying a little every day. Bleeding – like you're some kind of sacrifice to bring her back. Sometimes... sometimes I think you want to die.

"HE ONLY WANTS"

Standard folkie kind of song.

CHORUS
He only wants to be Jesus Christ
he only wants to die for everyone
i only want to be some kind of friend
walk with him in the morning sun

How can you love such a thorny man?
how can you reach him through his crown?
how can you meet him and not fall down on your knees?
how can you bear him to the ground, when

CHORUS
...feel the sun coming round
coming round come around come around come around come around (x2)
sun coming round

How can you reconcile loving with breaking
the only thing he thinks makes him strong?
how can you set him back on his feet when his feet are bleeding?
how can you tell him that he's wrong? is he wrong when

CHORUS
...how sweet the sun
coming round come around come around come around come around (x2)
sun coming round

He only wants to be
He only wants to be
He only wants to be Jesus Christ
and i live on the ground
right here on the ground.

IMOGENE
So you do still care.

SARAH
Of course I do. Just cause we're not single-handedly doubling the population here, like you and Olin–

IMOGENE
Don't you start on Olin.

SARAH
Well really, if you want to poke fun, what kind of name is that? Olin Nolan?

Next lines over each other, ending on "he does? Dick" and "Rawhide."

IMOGENE
It's a perfectly good name. Not like Dick. Dick. Ha! Is that what he is, or what he does? Dick.

SARAH
Olin, Olin Nolan, Rollin, Rollin, Rollin, Rawhide! Is that what you use for condoms, Imogene? Rawhide? That why you got a whole herd of little Nolans? Here. (*throws her a condom*) A present for you and Olin. Think you can learn him how to use it?

IMOGENE
Stop it, Sarah. That's just like you. Think you're so much better than me, because you got an education and all I do is pump out more kids.

SARAH
Imogene, you know I don't think–

IMOGENE

Yes you do. You're always talking down to me. And Olin, too.

SARAH

Aw, come on, Imogene.

IMOGENE

No, you don't understand.

SARAH

I don't understand?! You don't understand. Don't you know I'd give anything to have what you've got? I lost my child, and you've got four.

IMOGENE

Five.

SARAH

What?

IMOGENE

That's what I'm trying to tell you. It's too late. I'm pregnant again.

SARAH

Oh Imogene!

IMOGENE

Go ahead and say it. I'm stupid. Stupid. Stupid. Stupid (*throws condoms at SARAH*)

SARAH

You are not stupid. (*throws condoms back at her*)

IMOGENE

Yes I am. It's not like I don't know where they come from. And it's not funny, Sarah.

SARAH

Yes it is. Like you say, "Life happens."

IMOGENE

It's not like Olin wants it to happen.

SARAH

Olin isn't happy about this?

IMOGENE

No. He's freaked out. He said…. He said…. He said… he doesn't want it.

SARAH
But he loves his kids.

IMOGENE
But don't you know? Every time I get pregnant he gets scared. And
I thought he'd get used to it. The first time, it's natural to be scared – even
the second. But every time. Sure he gets over it. But what if this time he
doesn't get over it? Men do leave, you know.

SARAH
Not Olin.

IMOGENE
You haven't seen him. Every time.

SARAH
Every time?

IMOGENE
Every time.

SARAH
You should have told me.

IMOGENE
How was I supposed to tell you? Your baby had just died, the first time.
And I thought it would get easier, and the babies kept coming and it
didn't get easier and meanwhile, there you were, super-woman, getting
an education, changing the community, becoming somebody. Why would
you want to hear that Olin doesn't want what you and Richard gave
everything for, and lost?

SARAH
Hey, you could have told me. I'm your sister. Look, he'll come around. This
is Olin we're talking about. Olin the King of the Daddies.

IMOGENE
I don't know.

SARAH
I do. I was there. Remember, how everyone used to say how Olin Nolan
was getting his Granny to teach him how to cook? And you said "Big Olin,
the carpenter? This I gotta see." And you dragged me along for cover, so we
could pretend we were just walking by his house. And then he called us in.
Not even embarrassed or macho or anything. Hey, girls, he said, come and
try this bannock. I think I finally perfected the Nolan Roll. All flour up his
arms, on his clothes, in his hair. And I looked at him looking at you, and
you looking at him and I knew right then why he was learning to cook…

"The Bannock Song"

> *They sing an ode to Bannock, complete with chanting, drumming and a pow-wow dance break. [For cultural reasons, this song remains unpublished.]*

SARAH
So you see, you've got a good man, too. Come on, let's have some tea. (*pours tea for IMOGENE*)

IMOGENE
Yeah. I guess.

SARAH
And listen. There's something else. I knew you were pregnant.

IMOGENE
You knew? That Olin told you!? Why, that–

SARAH
No, no,no, it wasn't like that at all. Listen. The thing is… don't laugh, eh?

IMOGENE
Who me, laugh?

SARAH
I saw a sign.

IMOGENE
A sign. Like what – "baby on board?"

SARAH
No, I mean I saw a sign. Listen. Today, I was walking to work. This dust devil came right in front of me and so I stopped and I looked up and right there in front of me, the sun was behind this cloud. Bluest sky you ever saw all around it, and this one cloud; it was a woman; and I knew I knew her. And she was cradling her big round belly. And then she was holding a child, and then she drifted away from the sun. And I heard a voice say "I'll be here soon."

IMOGENE
Really?

SARAH
Really. Imogene, I guess the thing is, after the baby died, I pretty much lost my faith. But don't you get it?

IMOGENE
No. What?

SARAH
Don't you see? That was her, I know it. Auntie Love.

IMOGENE
You believe that?

SARAH
Just because I lost my faith doesn't mean I don't still believe. That was her.
And she was telling me to tell you that she wants to come back.

IMOGENE
So maybe, this is her?

SARAH
Could be. And I bet you Olin would feel a whole lot different if he knew
that.

IMOGENE
That this is Auntie Love wanting to come back and live with us again?

SARAH
Yeah. Look how much he loved her.

IMOGENE
He made her this coffin.

SARAH
You see?

IMOGENE
(*They drink tea; suddenly she starts to laugh.*) That's pretty funny though.

SARAH
What?

IMOGENE
It's got wheels.

> *SARAH inspects coffin, starts moving it. They burst into song in rhythm
> to her rocking it. Rollin Olin Nolan…*

Oh, no, stop! Oh, Auntie, I'm so sorry.

SARAH
It's okay, she'll understand.

IMOGENE

No. (*IMOGENE pulls letter out of coffin.*) …she told me to make sure I gave this to you.

SARAH

(*reads letter*)
"Sarah Love;
I know how you are about good-byes, and i do understand – but i want very much for you to understand too. You have to say good-bye so you can say hello again. Think about it; you can see it all around you. The winter has to come, so the earth can rest and renew herself. And so on… and I've had my time, my summer and my fall – support girdles notwithstanding. The thing is, i want you to know how proud i am of you; maybe you don't know it, but your dad he was always proud of you too; took a lot of love for him to share you with me, but that's the kind of heart he had—just like you—a lot of heart. The way you try so hard to take care of everything and everyone. You think Richie's the bad one, letting his life go all to pieces trying to put his sister back together. Well, you're right. But you won't do him any good if you do the same. I've been praying for you, you know. And i figure, closer i get to the spirit world, more pull i've got. I'm just a little old lady, but i figure if i'm lucky, Creator might see his way clear to letting me see you again soon. Let's just say i got a hunch. Anyways, i know this. You and Richie will make good parents.
Well, not to be too flippant, but i gotta go.
But never too far.
Love always from your Auntie Love.
P.S. Tell Imogene she owes me five bucks. I knew she'd forget to give this to you."

…I don't understand.

IMOGENE

Yes. You do. Think about it. I'm three months along. You're a public health educator. Use some math. You think Aunty Love planned for me to get pregnant before she even died?

SARAH

But I've tried, before. We've tried.

IMOGENE

Maybe that's what she was saying. You've tried so hard.

SARAH

I'm late, but I thought it was just because Auntie died.

IMOGENE

And the vision didn't tip you off. No, no it wouldn't.

SARAH
I just thought it must be for you.

IMOGENE
That's just like you. You think Richard's bad for giving too much, but look at you. Trying to give me your sign. Come on. That's a real spiritual cheap shot, sending a vision just to help me calm down Rollin Olin Nolan.

SARAH
Don't call him that.

IMOGENE
I will too, if I want to. And I'll tell him that hey, he knows where they come from, too. As for me, I don't care whose auntie they were in another life, they're coming to be born to me in this one – born to us. And he can just accept that; life comes when and where it will, and our job is to love it the best we can.

SARAH
Like she did. She always had room for whoever came to her door. My door, now, and my kitchen. I'll do my best to keep it as well as you did.

"HEART OF A NATION"

CHANT
Hi, hiya hi, heya heya hey hiya hey ho.
Hi, hiya hi, heya heya hey hiya hey ho.
Heya heya hey hi.
Heya heya hey hiya hey ho.

VERSE
The Cheyanne people say that whatever enemy we face
No Nation is defeated if the women's hearts beat strong.
When keepers of the fire, wisdom, courage and desire
Survive to face tomorrow, then the people carry on.

BRIDGE
Centuries of subjugation (living in chains)
Ancient wisdom could not claim (hidden away)
Cultural continuation (spirit remains)
Sacred mysteries remain.

CHORUS
The Heart of a Nation beats within me
The strength of the spirit is carrying me
The pride of the people, true brave and free
The heart of a nation beats within me.

CHANT
(Add harmonies and counterpoint line.)
Hi, hiya hi, heya heya hey hiya hey ho.
Hi, hiya hi, heya heya hey hiya hey ho.
Heya heya hey hi.
Heya heya hey hiya hey ho.

VERSE
The Hopi people told in one of their prophesies of old
How light would lift the darkness when the Eagle touched the Moon.
And now that time has come; now the healing has begun
Of five hundred years of sorrow and colonization's ruin.

BRIDGE
Praying for elucidation (show me the way)
Strength to guide me through the pain (show me the way)
Grandmothers my inspiration (show me the way)
Comes from your long walk of faith.

CHORUS

CHANT

VERSE
Now it's been told to me that the answer's there for those who seek.
In our hearts we are connected to the ones who have gone on.
We're keepers of their fire, wisdom, courage and desire.
Their vision brings tomorrow. In our children we live on.

BRIDGE
Strength of seven generations (fire in the veins)
Is running through my blood today (you are the flame)
Grandmothers my veneration (spirit unchained)
Your strength and courage mine to claim.

CHORUS

CHANT

CHANT

SARAH
Here's to Love.

IMOGENE
To Love. (*They drink tea.*) Well, it must be getting to be time.

SARAH
Right; I guess people will be coming to see her soon.

IMOGENE
So, are you okay with her being in your living room for that?

SARAH
Guess so.
IMOGENE
Cause we could still whoosh her over to my house–

SARAH
And let Donna ever say we didn't do it like Auntie wanted? As if. Well, Auntie, you've carried us all your life. Now it's time for us to carry you.

IMOGENE
Sarah, it's got wheels.

Song: "Weyaho," sung while keeping drumbeat on coffin, and with footsteps. IMOGENE and SARAH roll coffin off while continuing to sing. Exeunt omnes *stage left.*

The end.

[1] for Big Sky Theatre's productions of *Love's Kitchen*, condoms were donated by Feather of Hope Aboriginal Aids Education Society. These condoms are individually packaged in cardboard wraps which sport such sayings as "have a safe Indian Affair."

[2] to the tune of the old western "Rawhide."

MY PERFECT HEAVEN

by
Jonathan Christenson
and Joey Tremblay

INTRODUCTION TO *MY PERFECT HEAVEN*

> And you want to believe it. You want to believe in the magic of where you are, up, up, and way up, so high above the city, in a penthouse bedroom that seems to scrape a hole in the sky and reach right up to heaven; lying there naked with this Rhinestone Cowboy whispering some sweetness in your ear. You need to believe that as you look through the window of this cowboy's penthouse bedroom you really do see that little bluebird soaring freely in the sky.
> (Christenson and Tremblay, *My Perfect Heaven*)

Jonathan Christenson and Joey Tremblay's *My Perfect Heaven* takes us on a journey of such endlessly expanding imaginary spaces that it eludes easy categorization. Written originally for a Loud n' Queer festival, *My Perfect Heaven* carves out a fantasy space where a queer little farmboy might exist in a new version of prairie gothic. Performed by Joey alone on stage, "painted pale blue from head to toe" and sitting up high over the stage "in a large barbed wire nest," the piece depends heavily on the images and emotions created through the intense lyricism of the spoken lines which recount the adventures of the outcast "barefoot boy" as he leaves the farm for the big city. Punctuated by the introduction of romantic hits from '50s musicals, Joey's renditions of the well known lyrics added another dimension to the depth of the yearning for love informing his narrative. Jonathan's live accompaniment backstage reinforced this extension of the text.

Wildly imagistic, Joey's monologues paint a kaleidoscope of colours and shapes and sensations of exquisite beauty drawn together by the image of the "tiny fragile bluebird" soaring in the sky and looking down on the world below. As the bluebird, Joey creates a vantage point from which to narrate the tale of the "barefoot boy." By zooming in and out on the barefoot boy at various key moments, Joey brings him to life so vividly that he becomes a distinct character directly experiencing his own bewilderment and pain. Identifying him with Crazy Walter and his magical sparkling glass junkyard prepares us to feel the same sympathy for him as we do for Walter when his sapphire trailer explodes to the cheers of the townsfolk. As such, Joey's narration intervenes to open up a space for the spectator to see the farm boy without being able to judge him simply as a misfit. Through the immensely skilful narration, the boy's naive wonderment and pleasure in his sexual adventures are kept alive as he moves from the country to the city turning tricks with the "cowshit boys."

The power of Joey's narration is such that he succeeds in creating a "Third Space of enunciation, which makes the structure of meaning and reference an ambivalent process" and in so doing, allows for resistant interpretations to emerge.[1] The barefoot boy's depth of feeling and love of beauty serves him well in the city since it helps him to sniff out the deceptions that the Rhinestone Cowboy has in store for him. Humiliated one last time when the Cowboy rejects him and throws him back on the street after a night of lovemaking, he refuses to cry any more. The glorious coda that ends the play

is an explosion of beautiful colours and images describing Joey's full transformation into the bluebird and the barefoot boy all in one. It ends the play
on a note of exuberant joy and laughter.

My Perfect Heaven is a stunning piece of theatre with a wonderful twist.
In opening up a third space which moves queerness from its outlawed status
to a place of fantastic beauty, it offers the spectator a chance to experience its
alterity. It is not the "barefoot boy's" homosexuality which is at issue here, but
the internalized homophobia that results in his being punished for it.

Jonathan Christenson, a second generation Canadian, the son of a
Lutheran clergyman and a social worker, received his MFA in Directing from
the University of Alberta in 1996. Jonathan has directed productions of
Shakespeare's *Macbeth* and *Richard III*, Charles Mee's *Orestes*, Georg
Buchner's *Woyzeck* and his own production *At the Still Point of the Turning
World*. His work has been honoured with awards for direction, writing and
sound design in both the U.K. and Canada.

Joey Tremblay was born in Birtle, Manitoba and grew up in the tiny hamlet of Ste. Marthe in Southeastern Saskatchewan. He received a BFA in Drama
at the University of Regina (1987) and a Diploma from the Vancouver
Playhouse Acting School (1989). In 1992 Joey co-founded Noises in the Attic,
a theatre company mandated to produce new Canadian plays. For Noises in
the Attic, Joey directed such plays as *Tofu and Donuts*, *Justice*, *Fat Girl Sings the
Blues*, and *Dysfunctional Documentary* – which he co-wrote with Sarah
O'Leary.

In 1995 Joey and Jonathan wrote *Elephant Wake*, which went on to tour
Canada and the U.K., garnering critical acclaim and winning numerous
awards, including a Sterling Award for Best Actor at the Edmonton Fringe
Festival and a nomination for *Stage Magazine*'s Best Actor at the Edinburgh
Fringe Award. In 1996, Joey and Jonathan began as Artistic Co-Directors of
Catalyst. Shortly thereafter Heather Redfern was hired as General Manager.
Together they moved the company into an abandoned warehouse in the
funky district of Old Strathcona and transformed it into what is now
Edmonton's only professional black box theatre. There, under a new man-
date, they launched their first full season of original work by the artistic
co-directors. Since then, they have written/directed an adaptation of *Electra*,
The Abundance Trilogy, *Elephant Wake*, *My Perfect Heaven*, *Songs for Sinners* and
The House of Pootsie Plunket, which, combined, have garnered over thirty
awards and nominations for outstanding work. On each of these projects they
have returned to working with actors Julianna Barclay, Dov Mickelson, and
Siân Williams, and designer Bretta Gerecke, all Artistic Associates at Catalyst.

In 1997 Catalyst took *Elephant Wake* and in 1999 *The House of Pootsie
Plunket* to the Edinburgh Fringe where both productions received awards for
outstanding new work. In May, 2000 they were the only English-language
company invited to the prestigious festival, Carrefour International du
Théâtre in Québec City, where they performed *The House of Pootsie Plunket* to
enthusiastic audiences. *Pootsie* had a very successful run at the Vancouver
East Cultural Centre, played in Regina, and then toured for six weeks in the
United Kingdom in the Spring of 2001. Their next piece, already in workshop,
will be a large scale musical entitled *The Blue Orphan*.

Under the Artistic Co-Directorship of Jonathan Christenson and Joey Tremblay, Catalyst Theatre, which was founded in 1978, is establishing a unique position for itself on the arts scene in Edmonton and Canada. It is Edmonton's only professional creation-based theatre company, a company dedicated to producing the original work of its artistic co-directors, artists with a unique creative voice that defines the Catalyst aesthetic. Committed to touring its original work nationally and internationally each year, the company no longer presents a season of performances as other established companies of its size do, but instead works on a project-to-project basis, inviting the audience to see the work as it progresses.

NOTES

[1] Homi K. Bhabha, *The Location of Culture* (London & New York: Routledge, 1994) 37.

My Perfect Heaven was first produced at Loud n' Queer festival, Edmonton, in November, 1995, with the following cast:

Barefoot Boy   Joey Tremblay

Directed by Jonathan Christenson

MY PERFECT HEAVEN
by Jonathan Christenson and Joey Tremblay

BAREFOOT BOY
It hurts inside
My perfect dream
Waits.
The longing…
The pining…
The waiting…

At night, to put myself to sleep, I don't count sheep. No, no. Instead,
I place thirty-eight pretty flowers side by side in a rainbow of thirty-eight
vibrant colours brightening the darkness of my mind. And as I bend down
gracefully to lift each individual flower and place it gently in a precious
vase of finest Chinese porcelain, I linger for a moment, letting each flower
whisper its own special secret of a particular moment from a particular year
of my blessed "slash" cursed life. Sometimes the flower is a delicate pink
cherry blossom which hints at a soft and warm memory and I sigh.
Sometimes the flower is a fiery fuchsia which breathes a memory that burns
hot and mean and I cry. But please don't worry. I don't linger long. I place
each pretty flower carefully in its place in the vase and move to the next
and to the next and to the next until each individual flower, each beautiful
blossom, has joined with the others to form a dazzling bouquet of unearthly
beauty. Then, with the greatest of care, I take in the palms of my gently
cupped hands a tiny, delicately crafted, ornamental bluebird and place it
gently atop my bouquet. And as I drift effortlessly to sleep, that tiny fragile
bluebird, inspired by the beauty surrounding it, flutters its delicate wings,
tips back its head, and takes flight, soaring up, up, and up, so high above
the world, singing its refrain as it disappears from sight.

"Knee deep, knee deep, knee deep."

I don't know…
This dream, so light, so heavy,
Twists in my stomach like a knife,
Beyond my grasp,
Rots in my head like a cancer.
I reach.
I stumble.
I lose.

You look.
You say I'm crazy.
I'm insane.
I say I don't care because you don't understand.

Joey Tremblay as Barefoot Boy, August, 1996.
(Photo by Howard Silverman.)

You don't understand
My perfect dream
Waits.
The longing…
The pining…
The waiting.

"Knee deep, knee deep, knee deep."

A bluebird perches ever so delicate on a weather-beaten water tower, listens carefully to the wind whispering wild across the prairie, then sings its reply.

"Knee deep, knee deep, knee deep."

At just the right moment, that same bluebird, with graceful, open wings, dives, beautiful and weightless, into the whistling air.

Down and down, spiralling down, the bluebird descends toward a grey and dusty town; dives toward its twisted metal rapping endlessly in the dusty wind; plunges toward its dust-covered pick-up trucks with grey, somber faces staring vacantly through mud-smeared windows; plummets toward its cowshit boys drinking coke and smoking cigarettes, James Dean-like, on their post office stoop.

This town is tired and worn.
This town is giving up.
This town is ugly.

But where's the barefoot boy?
Where's the barefoot boy?

Invisible against the clear blue sky, the bluebird weaves his way through the dangling telephone wires and across the railway tracks to a yard with two black dogs, chained to a clothes line, barking and snapping, their mouths dripping with sparrows, their mouths trickling with bird blood soup and spittle.

Invisible against the clear blue sky, he circles the house which stands in the yard with the barking black dogs, who lift up their noses and snap at empty air.

This house is broken down.
This house is hopeless.
This house is ugly.

But where's the barefoot boy?
Where's the barefoot boy?

Invisible against the clear blue sky, the bluebird swoops down toward the house, slips in through a broken window, and perches on the sunken bedpost of a bare-mattress bed in the bedroom of Big Fat Momma. She snores loud, bologna arm across her forehead. Jack Sprat Daddy lies grey and twisted beside her, farting and swallowing. His adam's apple bobs up and then down, up and then down.

This room smells of sour booze.
This room smells of broken dreams.
This room is ugly.

But where's the Barefoot Boy?
Where's the Barefoot Boy?

Down the stairs the bluebird floats toward the dirty kitchen. Pots and pans fester: scum brown, scum green, scum grey. Only Little Sister here, hair like dried thistle, tears washing little rivers across her dirty cheeks into an ocean of drool, of snot, of piss; a circus freak girl who pulls her rubber legs across the greasy grey linoleum.

This girl is hungry.
This girl is forgotten.
This girl is ugly.

But where's the Barefoot Boy?
Where's the Barefoot Boy?

In the basement, no doubt. No doubt he sleeps on his nest of dirty clothes, dreaming pretty colours, dreaming pretty music, dreaming pretty ballerinas falling pretty from the sky.

But the Barefoot Boy is gone,
Fled from the dirty nest,
Fled from the house,
Fled from the yard with the barking black dogs.

"Knee deep, knee deep, knee deep."

Invisible against the clear blue sky, the bluebird flies, following the footprints of the Barefoot Boy, following the footprints of the Barefoot Boy, following the footprints of the Barefoot Boy.

I have been in certain penthouses,
In certain highrises,
On certain streets,
In this particular city;
Up, up, and way up,
So high above this particular city;

So high above this pulsing, oozing, festering scab of a city;
So high above this gob-splashed, piss-stained, shit-smeared craphouse of a city.

"Knee deep, knee deep, knee deep."

But where's the barefoot boy?
Where's the barefoot boy?
Spying on Crazy Walter, no doubt. No doubt he hides in a beat-up old buick spying on Crazy Walter.

Crazy Walter's tin trailer was set in the middle of a junk yard just on this side of town. It was painted sky blue, a blue sapphire that fell from the sky and sparkled in a sea of gorgeous twisted rust.

Crazy Walter wore his white hair long, long and gorgeous; long, white hair he could scoop up into a gorgeous bun and secure with a pin. Well, at least this was the case on days Crazy Walter walked into town to do some shopping.

You can imagine the looks. You can imagine the noses turning up. You can imagine the jaws dropping smack on the sidewalk.

But Crazy Walter didn't seem to notice. He just walked through that grey town, proud and pretty, like a bolt of coloured lace saying: "How do you do, Mr. Johnson? Good day, Clive Becker. Mabel Parker, how is your mother?"

There was a beat-up old buick on the edge of Crazy Walter's junkyard. It was easy for the Barefoot Boy to crawl in the back seat of that beat-up old buick and stare and spy through the broken back window; stare and spy, unnoticed, as Crazy Walter busied about making his junkyard rich, making his junkyard perfect, making his junkyard gorgeous.

Crazy Walter collected blue glass bottles: Milk of Magnesia, Noxema, Cote D'azure perfume.

Crazy Walter would smash the bottles, ever so carefully, and glue the shards of broken glass to the twisted, rusted metal that surrounded his gorgeous blue trailer. When you squinted your eyes everything sparkled; a huge rhinestone broach that fell from the sky.

The Barefoot Boy thought:
"This place is rich.
This place is perfect.
This place is gorgeous."

Crazy Walter made flowers, gorgeous arrangements transformed from paper and plastic, transformed into magic cherry blossoms, showy peonies, blue bells and lady slippers; frenzies of gorgeous colour which Crazy Walter created in a flurry of graceful movement; colours which seemed to dance as Crazy Walter sang:

Listen to the bluebirds gayly sing
Happily and joyful do they bring.

Crazy Walter would set his flowers in tin can vases and place them carefully about the twisted metal of his junkyard; a Garden of Eden sprouting from the dirt of a dusty dry town.

The Barefoot Boy thought:
"This place is rich.
This place is perfect.
This place is gorgeous."

They say that when Crazy Walter's sapphire trailer caught on fire the propane tank threw a blue flame straight up towards heaven, kissing a hole in the sky.

They say that the fire was so hot it melted Crazy Walter's trailer into a pool of blue lava.

They say that a week later, as Crazy Walter's junkyard smouldered black and empty near the dull grey town, a shower of blue ashes fell gently from the sky.

"Good riddance," Mabel Parker's mother said. "Good riddance to bad rubbish."

When a Barefoot Boy first comes to the city he's amazed at how far away he can really be from that grey and dusty town. He can measure the distance with a series of yellow lines cracking and peeling on a six-lane highway. He can scrub clean those dirty black feet, buy himself a pair of shiny new shoes, and pack up that grey and dusty old town in the box those shiny new shoes came in: in goes Big Fat Momma and Jack Sprat Daddy; in goes Circus Sister and two barking black dogs; and in goes a hockey team of hip-checking, cross-checking cowshit boys.

"Fuckin' woos! Fuckin' fairy! Fuckin' figure-skating momma's boy!"

"Knee deep, knee deep, knee deep."

If you squint your eyes, till the teardrops blur your vision like a broken glass, you can follow in the footsteps of the Barefoot Boy.

"Knee deep, knee deep, knee deep."

Listen to the heartbeat of the Barefoot Boy.

"Knee deep, knee deep…"

Here they come.

Run you little bastard with your dirty black feet.
Run for your life through the ripening wheat.
Fly you little fucker!
Fly!
Up!

But the Barefoot Boy he falls–
"knee deep"–
from grace–
"knee deep, knee deep."

Listen to the heartbeat of the Barefoot Boy.

The cowshit boys! The cowshit boys!
Cower from the boot heels of the cowshit boys!
The cowshit boys! The cowshit boys!
Bleeding from the boot heels of the cowshit boys.
The cowshit boys! The cowshit boys!
Stinging from the arrows of the cowshit boys!

STOP!
I AIN'T NO–
STOP!

Listen to the heartbeat of the Barefoot Boy.

Blood bath, blood bash, blood bath, blood bash.

Stupid fucking cowshit boy with dirt under your fucking fingernails,
smelling like shit, smelling like barnyard pig pen, smelling like fucking
fried bologna.

Stupid fucking cowshit cornholer standing, pants down, all hard and horny.
Standing, pants down, with your dirty pecker in a calf, sucking you off,
with calf slobber running down your fucking leg.

Stupid fucking cowshit cocksucker, shooting fucking slingshots, shooting
bluebirds dead off fucking telephone poles.

Through the swelling
through the prism
through the heartbeat
through the pain...

four and twenty bluebirds fall from the sky.

When a Barefoot Boy first walks the beat his heart pulses with the traffic on
a Saturday night;

pulses scared and excited at the same time;

pulses neon pink: on, off, on, off.

And when a horn blows he turns his head...

A Barefoot Boy in a big big city has to eat.
Well, he has to eat.
He has to eat.

In my prime for an unforgettable time. Call Dallas.
Handsome, healthy and hung. Call Tex.
Spank me skinhead. Call Norm.
Shy and from the farm. Call uh... uh... Blue Boy?

Blue Boy...

Barefoot Boy... floating on a dugout pond; floating lazy in a rubber
doughnut; bobbing up and down dreaming... perfect... heaven.

Suddenly, up through the murky, muddy water, up through its scum green
surface, a cowshit boy.

Now we all know that a cowshit boy is mean because he has a little wire
element, electric-like, inside his brain that glows hot and makes him see
everything in the colour of red.

Not blue, like looking through coloured glass making everything pretty. But
red... mean fucking red that makes him want to swing his fist and knock
out some lights. Boom, boom.

Red that makes him want to push the pedal to the metal and floor it baby
floor it. Vroom, vroom.

Red that makes him so hot and horny he's gotta... he's gotta... he's gotta
get some. Va-voom.

"Hey, don't hurt me. I didn't do nothing," says the Barefoot Boy.

"I'm not gonna hurt you. I'm not here to hurt you," says he.

And with that he takes a barefoot toe in his cowshit mouth and tows the Barefoot Boy to shore. He drives the Barefoot Boy six miles out of town, six miles out of town on a back road near a field of golden wheat, six miles out of town in the back seat of a new blue buick.

A cowshit boy can be kind of cute when he's not seeing red. I mean when a cowshit boy is acting… uh… shy… acting tender… acting sweet in the back seat of his new blue buick… you can't help but notice… you can't help but notice there's a sadness and a hope… in those rough and tumble hands. You can't help but notice how easy it is for him to reach down inside you and grab hold of your beating heart.

You want to believe this. Don't you? You want to believe in the magic of lying there naked with this… new and tender boy heavy on top, heavy on top with his hardness pressing hard against your belly.

And you need to believe this. You need to believe you hear him whisper some sweetness in your ear. You need to believe that if you squint your eyes and look through the back window of the new blue buick you can see that little bluebird soaring freely in the sky.

It takes a cowshit boy six minutes and sixty-six humps before he shudders on your naked belly. It takes him six big deep breaths of air before he pulls away from the sticky mess and pulls on his jeans and buckles his belt. It takes a cowshit boy about six seconds to start seeing red when he sees you lying there staring out the window.

"Don't you tell a living soul or I'll wring your pretty neck," says he.

And he picks you up, smacks you hard across the face, and throws you out on your bare ass. Vroom, vroom.

And that's how it is.
That's how it is.
That's how it is when a Barefoot Boy walks six miles barefoot all the way home.

I have been in certain penthouses,
in certain highrises,
on certain streets,
in this particular city;
up, up, and way up,
so high above this city;
so high above this scum-infected city
that it sparkles like a…
sparkles like a…
Rhinestone Cowboy.

The Barefoot Boy will walk nervous down a certain city street, stand nervous outside a certain city highrise, speak nervous into a certain highrise intercom:

"This is me," he will say.
"This is Blue Boy."

The Rhinestone Cowboy, up, up, and way up, so high above the Barefoot Boy, so high above his head, will answer. And the door of that certain highrise lobby will open with a "buzz."

Ten... Fifteen... Twenty...
The barefoot Boy will stand nervous in the ascending elevator...
Twenty-five... Twenty-seven... Twenty-nine...
Will notice his reflection in its stainless steel doors...
Thirty... Thirty-one... Thirty-two...
Will feel compelled to wipe his black and dirty feet...
"Ding!"

The Barefoot Boy will rap gently on a certain penthouse door, will open that penthouse door, and, with one deep breath, will step in.

This place is rich.
This place is perfect.
This place is gorgeous.
Polished chrome and sparkling glass...
A Crazy Walter junkyard lifted to the sky.

And the Rhinestone Cowboy, smoking imported cigarettes, smoking Winstons, will walk him through each gorgeous room, talk him through each gorgeous view of a cowboy's three hundred and sixty degree dream.

The Barefoot Boy will notice as they walk from room to room, will be unable to help but notice as they talk from view to view, the sweet-smelling scent of thirty-six perfect white lilies perfectly arranged in a large blue glass vase, a Crazy Walter centerpiece which will sit in the middle of the Rhinestone Cowboy's perfect penthouse paradise.

"Smell 'em," he'll say, "they almost smell real."

And you want to believe it. You want to believe in the magic of where you are, up, up, and way up, so high above the city, in a penthouse bedroom that seems to scrape a hole in the sky and reach right up to heaven; lying there naked with this Rhinestone Cowboy whispering some sweetness in your ear. You need to believe that as you look through the window of this cowboy's penthouse bedroom you really do see that little bluebird soaring freely in the sky.

In the morning the bright sun burns red and hot,
burns away the evening mist,
burns away the night's magic.

You wake up lonely.
You wake up confused.
You wake up startled by a stranger staring angry at your feet…

"You should leave now," he says. "Get dressed, boy, and get out."

Fuckin' homo asshole!

May I speak honestly? May I chirp my honest song? Will you hear me, my friends? Will you sit perched and patient as you are showered with the sweet-smelling flowers of my perfect perfect dream? Huh? Will ya?

In my dream I stand naked, surrounded by a forest of giant porcelain vases; ten foot tall glazed porcelain vases of translucent bone china, like nothing you've ever seen before. And each magnificent vase is bursting with colour, is a volcanic eruption of every hue, every tint, every tone, every shade, every… nuance of colour; an exploding firecracker of damson blue, coral pink, lilac, magenta, saffron, vermilion, indigo, dusty rose, violet and turquoise.

Resounding through this forest of floral delights are the dulcimer tones of a chorus of knee deep… knee deep… knee deep… divas, which send a chill up my spine, leaving in their wake a ripple of goosebumps.

As I stand there, naked, my skin eggshell blue, my goosebumps swelling outrageously, my transformation begins.

And as I feel the pulsing, swelling, throbbing, burning pressure of my new self pressing itself outwards through every tiny follicle of my skin, it begins to rain, a refreshing shower of ruby red rose petals gently soothing me into my new life.

When I know my transformation is complete I spread out my arms, tip back my head, and launch into flight.

And as I do, that forest full of blue-sky bluebirds open their wings and, in a single, harmonious wave of movement, we soar up, up, and way up, beyond the luxurious penthouses of this rhinestone-sparkling city.

And as I fly higher and higher, I feel the delicate heartbeat of the Barefoot Boy begin to pulse in my chest. And I begin to laugh. And I laugh and laugh, my silly little laugh.

"Knee deep, knee deep, knee deep."

You have to admit…
You've gotta love that.

The end.

LA MAISON ROUGE

by
Manon Beaudoin

INTRODUCTION TO *LA MAISON ROUGE*

> You shouldn't have taken my place maman.
> I sometimes imagine that it could not have been worse.
> You thought you could fix everything, but you couldn't maman.
> It was too heavy maman, trop lourd pour moi.
>
> (Beaudoin, *La Maison Rouge*)

Manon Beaudoin's *La Maison Rouge* echoes the traditional prairie gothic genre in its revisiting of an ancestral home abandoned twenty-five years earlier, but here the realistic elements have become dreamlike fragments delineating subconsciously charged encounters between characters who randomly move between past and present searching for meanings that forever elude them. Physically based, the actions and gestures of the characters are telling a deeper truth than words can convey. The House itself, red from the stain of their shame and silence, lives and breathes with them through its haunting music and thoughtful speeches. It opens and closes the play with observations which deepen our sense of the psychic spaces where it stores the terrible secrets its inhabitants have suffered. The long delayed homecoming occasioned by the mother's impending death suggests an event of tragic proportions comparable to the Oresteia, where Electra and Orestes must kill their mother in repayment for her slaying of their father. However, in this case, there are variations which resist the patriarchal script, for while there is an Ipheghenia figure in the form of the drowned Blanche, the Mother, unlike Clytemnestra, has already paid for her infidelities.

The variations on the classic themes increase the resonances of what is now acknowledged as the search for the lost mother, for the matriarchal space, not in order to punish but to embrace. Thus Mother and House are identified as one when the play begins and the mother wakens from her bed to watch for Rose's return. Her empty bed, as the only real furniture in the house, represents all aspects of her as a living, loving, sexual, and, now dying being, as well as an absent figure for her children. It becomes the focal point for much of the action of the play as it is the place from which she will try to access all of her children in order to say good bye. The skeletal outline of the House, which besides the mother's bedroom, had an entrance platform, a door, a few window frames and a two-storey outside staircase, provided the multiple locations necessary to reenact the story as well as to powerfully represent the mother's entrapment within.

The action of the play, heavily gestural and dreamlike, moves slowly, often ritualistically, towards a replay of the past events that brought about the dissolution of the home. Trauma theorists have identified the "foundational moment of consciousness as a responsibility towards others in their death (or potential death)" and have further argued that "this encounter with the real cannot simply be located either inside or outside the dream, but has to be located in the moment of the transition between the two, in the movement from the one to the other... [or] in what Lacan precisely calls "the gap that constitutes awakening."[1] Beaudoin has created a *mise en scène* in which these terrible moments come to be acknowledged through the transitions where the jagged relationships between the characters get connected.

Thus, although in the case of Rostand there is no present-day reconciliation with the mother who waits in vain to see him, there is a replaying of his relationship with the beloved Blanche over whose death he had experienced terrible guilt. A laughing water spirit, Blanche, takes him on the journey towards an acceptance of her death. Her tragic loss, symbolic of his loss of innocence when he found his mother with her lovers, is dramatically conflated in the sound of the gunshot he hears in the same instant that the ice cracked on the day of Blanche's drowning. His own loss of innocence, a result of witnessing his mother receiving her lovers, compounded by seeing her after the murder, are replayed in fragments over several scenes and in juxtaposition with his three attempts to enter the house in the present. By the same token, his mother realizes that he is never going to come inside to say goodbye just as she and Rose are drawing together.

The painful "gap" between Rose's ability to accept her mother, without ever being able to tell her why she murdered her mother's lover, is captured by the reversed arrangement of the scenes. Rose's violation is only replayed after she and her mother have shared their most intimate moments. Although Rose will never have to carry around the trunk with the memories of the lovers again, the gap opened up by her not being able to share the truth with her mother will never be closed.

However, the skillful retelling of the events in a climactic order ending in the violent crime implicates the audience because we have been let in on the secret and granted another level of understanding denied to everyone but Rose. We share in her isolation when her plea for her mother's forgiveness goes unheard, and recognize her suffering when her mother dies believing that she had sacrificed herself because her daughter was angry at her. The deeply painful ambiguities remain, never to be resolved.

Nevertheless, something has been changed in Rostand and in Rose when they meet outside the house at the end. Their confessions, that neither of them could speak to her, brings them the release of sharing their failures with each other. In representing the unspeakable moments, *La Maison Rouge* gives us glimpses into those life-altering moments in our ancestral spaces where the truth can only be faced by looking at the gaps.

Manon, originally from Quebec where she earned a B.Ed. from the University of Montreal, has been working in the Albertan theatre community since 1987. She is a freelance artist – playwright, director and actor who is widely accomplished in all three areas. She has written *Quatre heures et demie* (text commissioned by the ATFC for La Journée mondiale du théâtre); *Terre bleue* (created at L'UniThéâtre, Edmonton); *Laura* (created at Le Théâtre de La Licorne, Montreal); *Glorious Liars* (created at Catalyst Theatre, Edmonton); *La Valise* (created for *Les Contes d'appartenance*, Sudbury and published in *Les Contes d'appartenance* at Les éditions Prise de Parole); *The Suitcase* (created at Northern Light Theatre, Edmonton); *Longing*, co-written with Binaifer Kapadia (created at Catalyst Theatre, Edmonton); *La Maison Rouge* (created at Le Théâtre du Coyote, Edmonton), with the English version of *La Maison*

Rouge created at the University of Alberta, Fine Arts Dept. She is working on a new play, *Dans les bras d'un géant*.

Manon's acting credits include roles in: *The Oedipus Project* for Northern Light Theatre; *La Valise, La Déposition, La Locandiera* for L'UniThéâtre; *Electra, The Abundance Trilogy* for Catalyst Theatre; *Shimmering Garden* for New Heart Theatre; *Macbeth, Richard III* for the University of Alberta. She directed: *The Tourist,* Periphery Theatre; *La Maison Rouge* and *États d'âme,* Théâtre du Coyote; *Art, Indemne, Seins innocents,* L'UniThéâtre; *Glorious Liars, Longing,* Catalyst Theatre. She has worked closely with L'UniThéâtre, a francophone company in Edmonton since 1993.

Manon was the Artistic Director of Le Théâtre du Coyote from 1987 to 1994, a company dedicated to creating francophone plays. She also participated in the creation of clownesque plays that toured festivals and schools in Western Canada: *Le Circus Bop et Zézelle, Il était une fois un fou, oups, une folle du roi!, Le Fossé/Vacancy, Pas si différent*!

NOTES

[1] Cathy Caruth, *Unclaimed Experience: Trauma, Narrative, and History* (Baltimore & London: Johns Hopkins University Press), 142-3, especially notes #9, 11.

La Maison Rouge was first presented by le Théâtre du Coyote at the theatre of La Cité francophone in Edmonton, Alberta, Friday, June 13, 1997 with the following cast:

BLANCHE	Vanessa Porteous
LA MÈRE	Anne Mansfield
ROSE	Denise Kenney
ROSTAND	John Ullyatt
CELLIST	Christine Hanson

Directed by Manon Beaudoin
Choreographed by Bobbi Westman
Set designed by Bretta Gerecke
Costumes designed by Peter Field
Lighting designed by Melinda Sutton
Stage managed by Gisèle Lemire and Martine Tremblay
Composer: Christine Hanson
Visual consultant: Doug Jamha
Publicist: Gisèle Lemire

La Maison Rouge was first presented in its English translation at the University of Alberta, Master of Fine Arts, Directing program Saturday, February 18, 1999, with the following cast:

BLANCHE	Beth Graham
THE MOTHER	Blair Wensley
ROSE	Kate Banigan
ROSTAND	Tony Sharkey

Music director/keyboardist: Gail Olmstead
Violinist: Sarah Card
Percussionist: Darren Cook

Directed by Deborah Hurford
Movement coach: Wendy McNeil
Design consultant: Tanya Lampey
Assistant directed by Ryan Farrell
Movement advisor: Linda Rubin
Directing advisor: Kim McCaw
Stage managed by Kris Heuven
Assistant stage managed by Melissa Cuerrier
Light operator: Seth Collins
Light/sound advisor: Nico Van der Kley
Technical director: Don MacKenzie

CHARACTERS

ROSE   A Woman. 38 years.
ROSTAND   A Man, brother of Rose. 33 years.
BLANCHE   A soul/spirit, sister of Rose and Rostand
THE MOTHER   Their mother
THE HOUSE   A voice
THE VISITORS   Five pairs of shoes

Family ties... the ones we want, the ones we don't want.

SETTING
The story unfolds in the family home, which embodies their past lives. Rose
and Rostand return to the family home after a 25-year absence. Their mother
is dying. Blanche's spirit has come too; she drowned 25 years earlier. Rose,
who stays at her mother's bedside, is desperately trying to share her secret.
Rostand who never enters the house is waiting for Rose. He is struggling with
the memory of Blanche's death.

AUTHOR'S NOTES
The text in the present is aligned on the left side of the page; memories,
impressions, the ghostly presence of Blanche are aligned further on the right.

Rose, Rostand, Blanche and their mother are bound by what was, or was not
– memories, desires, impressions, emotions. The family should have a sense
that they are physically connected, so when one moves the others are affect-
ed. Lighting and music also contributes to create this interdependence.

The music should convey those reminiscences, desires, impressions, emotions. It is the memories of the house, it is the voice of the objects, it is the
pulse of the story. It announces, warns, accompanies sensations, emotions.

Movement is integral to the world of the play. As well as the text, the bodies
are telling the story: the corporeal language of each character, the abstract
movement with the poetic text, the dynamics with the symbolic objects.

The Mother's visitors are pairs of shoes, they are not a bodily presence. They
are represented on stage by the physical handlings of the shoes and the family reactions. Rose is carrying a trunk for a suitcase, like a burden. The men,
the five pairs of shoes are hidden in her trunk.

The empty bed is the "dying mother;" the absence of the mother in Rose's life,
Rose's desire and inability to connect with her mother. Rose sees the Mother
only towards the end when she is facing her inner truth.

The first production of La Maison Rouge helped me to clarify the visual world
of the play. Those visual elements essential to the play became part of the
written text. But I also want to share the images that did not end up in the

text. They made organic sense in the first creation of the play; they are not meant as direction but more as inspirational material.

• *La Maison Rouge*. Red is for shame, for silence. Blue atmosphere was prominent in the first production, the house surrounded with water, red came in patches – the Mother's red dress, the revolver wrapped in red cloth, Rose's red dress, the blood. The arrival of Rostand was marked by sharp red lighting. Red for real, flesh and bone. Rostand is staying outside of the house, he is carrying the line of the story.

• The window in the mother's bedroom was a suspended frame like an opening, a threshold. Rose and her mother had an active, physical relationship with it.

• An immense staircase in the middle of the house was the stage for Blanche's drowning. Her drowning was slow, we saw her losing life while Rose struggled with her own violent memories. The stairs were also a dynamic element to connect the different levels of the house and also to connect the outside and the inside of the house.

• Rose and Rostand cross a bridge to get back to their family home, like there is a gap between the real world and the world of their childhood. We did not have a concrete bridge, this image was symbolic. Rose and Rostand entered from the audience.

LA MAISON ROUGE
by Manon Beaudoin

PROLOGUE – THE FAMILY HOME

The house awakens, its voice is melancholic.

THE MOTHER is asleep in her bed, pale.

BLANCHE is there. Opalescent, reminiscent of water. BLANCHE is not a child, she has a child spirit, her presence is light. She is playing alone, collecting pebbles and meticulously placing them on the river bank.

ROSE is travelling from the "real" world to come back home. She is carrying a trunk on her shoulders. ROSE is strong, guarded. Her clothing is armour, hiding her shape. Underneath, she wears something delicate.

THE HOUSE

THE HOUSE
I opened my eyes

THE MOTHER slowly awakens as if the house's words give her life. She wears a delicate, white slip. She finds the strength to get up and put on her best dress. A beautiful, deep red dress. The arrival of her children will help THE MOTHER revisit her life before her death.

She was there
by the edge of the river
Her shoulders crying

She appeared to me
more frail, more alone
smaller
After so long an absence

I wasn't waiting for her anymore.
I thought she would never come back.

The murmurs have been silent for a long time
All those walled up memories
Reminiscence hidden in cracks
The forgotten nooks

> ROSE crosses the bridge. In sight of the house, she puts down the trunk, out of breath. She rests a moment. THE MOTHER is watching her daughter's return from the window.

But she came back
We will again be together.

ROSE'S VISIT

> ROSE's trip has been a long one, she takes a moment along the river. She is back home, everything is different, everything is the same. BLANCHE watches her.

>   BLANCHE
>   (surprised, really happy to see her big sister) Rose? (She approaches, ROSE does not see or hear BLANCHE.) Rose.

>   ROSE
An exile, hoping to forget,
my memories watching over me
wherever I go.

I am a beacon,
I am a window,
     translucent glass,
a distorted mirror,
I light up the road this being travels
she always ends up in the same place.
A home, red with tears.

> ROSE tries to pull her trunk, it won't move. She leaves it there and heads for the house. BLANCHE is curious about her sister's trunk. As her hands touch it, the trunk sounds a warning. ROSE looks back and moves slowly towards it. She feels BLANCHE's presence. Finally, ROSE walks back to the house. She hesitates, then enters the family home. There's a swoosh — smells, dust, a doorway, the stairs, it's the home of her childhood — joy and pain. Her mother has come to the door but ROSE does not see her. THE MOTHER is taken by surprise, she touches her own face lightly, wondering.

> ROSE enters her mother's bedroom.

>   ROSE
(to her dying mother in the empty bed) Maman?

> No response. ROSE is drawn nearer to her dying mother. BLANCHE has followed her mother into the bedroom. They watch ROSE. BLANCHE

approaches ROSE, she lightly touches her sister's face and lips with her fingers. ROSE sighs, she cannot stay in this house. She leaves.

BLANCHE and her mother stay together in the bedroom. THE MOTHER sits on the bed, BLANCHE's head on her knees.

ROSE goes back to her trunk, calms down. She then takes out red paper and writes to ROSTAND, her brother that she has not seen in years. She writes to announce that their mother is dying – he should come. As she seals the red envelope and hides it in her pocket, ROSTAND, in his house, receives the letter. He opens it, reads it silently then…

Mother is dying. Come. Rose.

Rose is Staying

ROSE knows she has to go back, she is dying inside. She also knows that she will stay till the end. ROSE pulls her heavy trunk to the door, then walks into the house. As ROSE makes her way towards the house, THE MOTHER quietly leaves BLANCHE in the bedroom and exits.

ROSTAND is in his house, he is struggling with his decision. He wants and doesn't want to go back to his childhood home, both at the same time.

ROSE
(to her dying mother in an empty bed) Maman, it's me Rose.

ROSE's memory, sometime after the disappearance of her father.

THE MOTHER *appears in the cellar, she is burying her husband's clothes as well as a revolver, she wraps it in a red cloth. ROSE goes down the stairs, she is thirteen years old. THE MOTHER is startled.*

THE MOTHER
Rose *ma chouette*, it is late, go to bed. *(THE MOTHER tries to compose herself. All ROSE wants is her mother's arms around her.)* Rose, don't cry. You're my big girl. *Allez, va te coucher.*

ROSE
Maman. Why?

THE MOTHER
I don't know Rose. I don't know that
Your father. *(She searches for the right words.)* Sometimes he

was so far away, lost in his own darkness. His silence.
He had only small moments. Tiny sparks.
Not enough to want to stay.

Allez Rose, it is late.
(pause, to herself)
He told me I was his muse. A long time ago.
And it was enough then.
I loved him.
A vulnerable soul.

THE MOTHER cuts a lock of her hair and buries it with the relics.

ROSE
(savouring the last words of her mother)
A vulnerable soul. *(THE MOTHER disappears from the cellar.)*

ROSE
(to herself)
Oh maman, don't go, not yet.
I have so many things to tell you.

Directly to her mother in the hope of reaching her;

Maman, I wrote to Rostand.

At ROSE's announcement, ROSTAND leaves his house and moves toward his childhood home. BLANCHE, overjoyed, runs to the front door. THE MOTHER finds the best spot in the house to watch for her son's arrival. ROSE stands at the bedroom window.

They are all waiting for ROSTAND.

ROSTAND

ROSTAND arrives. He is happy-go-lucky, a bit of a "goof." He says what he says without past and future weight on it. He is wearing his best clothes for this visit, they are tattered. He has in his pocket ROSE's letter, worn, torn apart and stuck back together again.

BLANCHE recognizes ROSTAND, her favourite friend/brother. But he doesn't see her.

ROSTAND
Wow, just the way I pictured it, *(He closes his eyes.)* almost.

ROSTAND crosses the bridge.

BLANCHE
Rostand? *(She tries to reconnect physically with her brother.)*

ROSTAND
(doesn't see or hear her)
It's been almost twenty-five years to the day.
I have a picture at home. With the date written on it. In red.
A picture of the whole family. Except Blanche.

A cold breeze – BLANCHE is disappointed.

ROSTAND stops himself at the door, he can't go in – it's BLANCHE, a pale memory of her passes in his head and pulls him back toward the river. She accompanies him.

I don't want to be alone with mother.

In the bedroom.

ROSE
(towards her dying mother in the empty bed) Maman?

ROSTAND
I'll wait for Rose.

Pause.

Ostie qu'ça sent bon, ici. It smells good. *(He goes to an old tree.)*
Oh my God, the apple tree. Every spring. I could not stop sneezing.
It was the flowers of the apple tree. Always sneezing. The flowers did it.

But the apples didn't.
(remembers) Rose.
When Rose picked an apple, she would make it disappear in her dress,
and she would rub it for a long, long time until it shone, bright red.
One for me, one for her.
We ate so many apples. In the winter we'd steal them from the cellar.
Mother didn't like that.
(He picks at the tree, he is surprised by his own feelings.)
God, it feels good to be here. I am eight again, my nose wiggles.
It smells like my childhood. The smells, and the colours of my childhood…

Pause.

BLANCHE is still there, physically close to ROSTAND. She remembers his presence, their games.

Me and Rose, every day we would roll like crazy in the grass.
And then we'd compare our calves, how fat and floppy they were.
Sitting really close, one against the other. Hers were floppier.
I was very small, five maybe, when Rose showed me how.

>*Pause.*

In the fall, I'd lay down on the ground, covering myself with leaves,
right there under the weeping willow, right close to the river.
I'd fill my head, all my body with the smell of the wet dirt.
I'd close my eyes. And I'd listen.

>*Pause.*

Then I'd become water. I knew that winter was coming.

>*A chill – BLANCHE loses her balance.*

I don't like winter.

>*BLANCHE loses interest, walking away from her brother. She gets absorbed in her own game.*

Sometimes, a shiver would crawl down my whole body. I wouldn't move.
The smell of brown leaves,

>*ROSTAND sees his mother in his mind. THE MOTHER in the house appears, she's so happy to see her son.*

autumn, always makes me think of my mother,

>*Pause.*

telling me I was gonna catch my death.
Always telling me to stop wasting my time.

THE MOTHER
Rostand?

>*Pause, ROSTAND doesn't really hear her.*

Rostand. *(She confides to him, disappointed.)* You never came to see me.

ROSTAND
(doesn't want to hear her) Autumn always makes me think about mother.
Must be because I was born in the fall.

THE MOTHER disappears. Pause.

(light, sincere) Sometimes, I think about this. The morning my mother's
water broke.
And it was because of me.
She was holding her huge belly, frowning and grimacing.
And it was because of me.
I was her second, Rose was the first. But I was the first boy, the only boy.
And me. I pushed and shoved, desperate to get out, to get out of there.
And my mother. She was in pain.

Pause.

It was because of me.
When I think about this, I know that I am alive.

Pause.

That day. I was someone. Everything was possible.

A chill – BLANCHE falls. ROSTAND stiffens.

I don't like winter.

*BLANCHE is not hurt. She stands up slowly, shakes off her feathers like
a bird and runs in the house.*

THE PRINCESS

In the bedroom.

ROSE
(to her dying mother in the empty bed) It's Rose, maman.

Pause. THE MOTHER is there, listening to her daughter.

Maman. *Des fois, je vois papa.* I see him.
His back. Leaving.
My eyes follow him.
Until he's no more than a little black dot in the horizon.
He never looks back.

Pause.

The past has engulfed me completely.
(She shivers, then vehemently;)
My bones have exploded to all four corners of this house and I can't salvage all of the pieces.

ROSE, disheartened, stands at the window.

BLANCHE is far away at the top of the world.

BLANCHE
(big) Me, I am a princess
And one day, my wings are going to grow and grow and grow.
I will fly.
And I will travel the whole world like a wild goose.

A tableau with THE MOTHER, BLANCHE and ROSE. Each in their dream.

LONELY

At the riverbank.

ROSTAND
Wasting my time! I've thought of that often.
Time isn't lost. It just seeps in. But you do forget.

Pause.

Here.

The tableau breaks; ROSE returns to her mother's bedside, THE MOTHER looks at herself in a mirror and BLANCHE comes back into the house.

Time stopped twenty-five years ago. And before that. *(He tries to remember.)* I don't know.

Pause.

If I waited in silence, right there underneath the weeping willow,
like when I was young, I wonder.
I wonder if the river would take me in her arms.
Maybe time would carry me along and I would visit every hidden nook and cranny of my life.

A faint image in ROSTAND's head.

BLANCHE
(calls looking for her brother) Rostand. Rostand.

BLANCHE comes running in, looks under the bed. She sees ROSE and takes her hands.

Oh Rose, did Rostand come in the house to hide?

ROSE surprised, smiles, and shakes her head no. BLANCHE runs out of the room. ROSE looks at her lovingly.

ROSTAND
I don't know if I want to remember this.

(laughs) Blanche and me, sometimes we sat close, one against the other.
We compared our calves, how fat and floppy they were.
Mine were floppier. It's *me* who showed *her* how.
Sometimes, we said nothing. We'd just travel.

> *BLANCHE finds her mother and runs into her arms. ROSE looks on, she remembers this.*

BLANCHE
Maman, it's me *ta princesse. (BLANCHE is her mother's joy. They are close together. She whispers in her mother's ear.)* Maman, call Rostand. Just to play a trick on him. *(The two laugh. ROSE is still watching them.)*

ROSTAND
My mother. Can't imagine her now.
Time has made a hole, and my mother has slipped inside.

I suppose that's why you were scared to come here, it's like visiting a spook.

She's in there, waiting for me. And I am here underneath my tree.
She'd say, "Rostand, you are wasting your time again, I don't know where you'll end up, your head's always in the clouds, *(smile) tête de linotte*, she'd say."

THE MOTHER
(calls out to ROSTAND from a window) Rostand.

ROSTAND
(almost hears his mother) Maman?

THE MOTHER
(louder) Rostand.

ROSTAND feels their presence. He turns, believing that he will see them. BLANCHE and her mother snicker. A chill – ROSTAND turns away.

THE MOTHER
(laughing) Rostand, you should see the look on your face! You look like you've just seen a ghost.

ROSE at the window, gives a faint smile.

ROSTAND
Maybe I should go in.

ROSTAND walks to the door, he wants to enter. BLANCHE and her mother look hopefully at ROSTAND.

ROSE
(in the bedroom) Sometimes maman, a soft light sneaks into my head. Not for a long time.
But I know it is there.

ROSTAND
(makes up his mind, he returns to the riverbank)
I'm fine right here. I'd rather wait for Rose.

THE MOTHER is disappointed, BLANCHE takes her in her arms.

ROSE
(to her dying mother in the empty bed) Maman... maman... *(sigh)*

L̲A̲ D̲A̲M̲E̲ ̲D̲U̲ ̲L̲A̲C̲

ROSTAND
In summer and in winter both, Blanche and I played along the riverbank.

Pause.

The river was a magnet for us. Blanche said that there were diamonds in the water. And that one day, she'd become a fish and that she would be rich. But she'd still talk to us anyway.

ROSTAND's memory.

His mother is brushing BLANCHE's hair, BLANCHE is bursting with laughter.

La dame du lac, featuring Denise Kenney as Rose, John Ullyatt as Rostand, Vanessa Porteous as Blanche and Anne Mansfield as La Mère.
La Cité francophone production of La Maison Rouge, *Edmonton, 1997.*
(Photo courtesy Ed Ellis.)

THE MOTHER
Blanche stop moving

BLANCHE
Maman, tell us the story of *La dame du lac.*

THE MOTHER
Not again? *(THE MOTHER cannot refuse BLANCHE.)*

ROSTAND
And she loved to hear that story, over, and over, and over.
The lady of the lake.

THE MOTHER
(spoken) Viens mon grand, allez viens.

ROSTAND joins them and sits down on the ground.

The storytelling of La dame du Lac *is a warm family moment that the children enjoy.*

Rose, you're not coming?

ROSE shakes her head no. THE MOTHER smiles at her. She listens to the story from a distance.

When I was very small, ma grand-maman, she tucked me in every night. I often cried before falling asleep in her arms. When I cried, she would tell me the story of *la dame du lac* so I would slip gracefully into the arms of Morpheus.

And this is exactly how she told the story to me:

The lady of the lake appeared from out of the mists.
She was all white, translucent.
We heard her song, from far away, smooth like honey.

(to herself) Sometimes, it seemed that I was truly hearing her.

BLANCHE
Was she a ghost?

ROSTAND
A fairy?

THE MOTHER
(smiling) She was a fairy, a soft fairy.

Her melody caressed all those who had a sad heart,
embracing their souls . Then, their bodies lightened and
they glided softly on the water right to the middle of the
lake. And there, they danced all night with her, the water
twinkling around them.
In the morning, they woke up, a smile on their rosy lips.

BLANCHE
Maman, is she dead, *la dame du lac*?

THE MOTHER smiles weakly.

For a moment, time is suspended.

A VISITOR

The doorbell rings.

THE MOTHER
Rose, go answer the door. *(The tableau breaks.)*

*ROSE exits the room. THE MOTHER adjusts her hair, her dress
and heads towards the front door. BLANCHE and ROSTAND
follow her playing and teasing each other.*

*ROSE walks outside the door, opens the trunk, gets a pair of shoes
and closes the trunk. She returns with the visitor, THE
MOTHER is there. BLANCHE and ROSTAND stop their game.*

THE MOTHER
(welcoming the visitor, the children are polite) Bonjour.

Here Rose, finish brushing your sister's hair.

*THE MOTHER heads towards her bedroom with the visitor, the
children follow, sneaking, cheerful. Their mother looks back, they
are caught.*

*ROSE brings her sister to a comfortable place to brush her hair.
ROSTAND still looks toward the bedroom but then, bored, he
tries to divert his sisters' attention to play with them.*

---

*Simultaneously, THE MOTHER is in her bedroom with the
visitor, he is flirting with her. She is flattered by his attention.*

The children are aware of the laughs from their mother's bedroom, ROSTAND is becoming more and more disruptive. ROSE is impatient.

ROSE
Rostand

ROSTAND leaves the house and runs to the riverbank. He lays by the river.

The visit ends. THE MOTHER lovingly disposes of the visitor/shoes, as relics. She displays them in a chosen spot in her home.

ROSTAND'S DREAM

ROSE is still brushing BLANCHE's hair.

ROSTAND
(at the riverbank) The smell of Rose when she was brushing Blanche's hair, the smell of the ice on the river, right there along the shore, in winter.

BLANCHE, teasing, breaks away and runs to hide in the house.

BLANCHE
You can't find me. *(A game – ROSE disappears looking for BLANCHE.)*

ROSTAND
I am missing some pieces. Large pieces.
My brain is cracked.
My memories, my imagination. Everything is mixed up.

BLANCHE reappears, alone. She plays by the riverbank, her game becomes more and more daring during ROSTAND's dream. Until she loses her balance.

I dreamt yesterday. *(He sees his dream in telling it.)*
I am on a bridge. A long bridge, really narrow. I am running and running.
There are many people screaming and watching the river below.
There is a blue car.
My mother is there. She says. "Rostand come see." I don't want to go there.
At the other end, I see a big metallic door. Rusted.
In my dream, all that I want is to open that door, to close it, to be on the other side of it. To look back. And for everything to be over.

I was running again, I couldn't stop myself. *(pause)* But the whole time
I had the feeling of being in the same spot. Running on the same spot and
I couldn't stop myself running. *(ROSTAND shivers.)*

> *Pause.*

My girlfriend tells me all the time that if something exists in your
imagination, it's because it's real.
My brain flips when she says that. I don't understand when she says that.

> *Pause.*

I wanted to bring her here but finally I didn't. I don't know why.
I decided to come by myself.
I think I made the right decision, she doesn't like to waste her time either.

My girlfriend, in cahoots with my mother, that's a scary thought.
(smile) I am better alone anyway.

> *THE MOTHER appears in the house.*

ROSTAND
Rostand admit it, you were not able to tell her that you don't remember
your mother, or your sister Rose. I can't even form an image of Rose in my
stupid head.

> **THE MOTHER**
> Rostand. *(pause)* Why didn't you ever come to see me?

> *The peak of BLANCHE's game; she looses her balance and falls on
> the ground. She stays there, motionless.*

> *ROSTAND sees BLANCHE on the ground. A faint memory. He
> goes towards her, hesitates before touching her. BLANCHE opens
> her eyes, shakes her feathers off softly, makes sure that nothing is
> broken and runs away. ROSTAND, surprised, sits back down
> watching her go.*

> *ROSTAND wonders if he really saw BLANCHE.*

ROSTAND
Rose, for Christ's sake. Tell me where you are.

> *ROSTAND sits at the riverbank and takes off his shoes.*

THE GIFT

ROSTAND's memory.

> *THE MOTHER arrives home carrying a gift. She sees ROSTAND alone on the riverbank. She walks quietly behind him and covers his eyes with her hands.*

ROSTAND
Blanche? Rose?

THE MOTHER laughs, ROSTAND recognises her.

ROSTAND
Maman. *(He sees the gift.)* Is that for me, maman?

THE MOTHER
No Rostand, it's for Rose. *(She opens the box and shows him the dress, holding it up and frivolous, she twirls in front of him.)*

ROSTAND
Maman. *Je m'ennuie de papa.*

THE MOTHER
Moi aussi mon grand. I miss him too.

Pause.

ROSTAND
Maman, who was he? Who was that man yesterday?

> *THE MOTHER doesn't know what to say, uncomfortable. She attempts to distract ROSTAND, teasing him and trying to put the dress on him.*

ROSTAND
(insistent) Maman

> *The doorbell rings. ROSTAND freezes, anxious. They look at each other. The doorbell rings again. THE MOTHER puts the dress back in the box quickly. She leaves ROSTAND without adding a word and enters the house.*

> *ROSE answers the door, BLANCHE joins her sister. ROSE walks to the trunk, gets a pair of shoes. When ROSE comes in with the visitor, THE MOTHER is there, happy to welcome him. She invites him into her bedroom. ROSE stays with BLANCHE. She brushes her sister's hair.*

————————————

This visit is cheerful, more sexual. The visitor and THE MOTHER engage in foreplay games around the bed.

———————

ROSTAND sees or hears what's going on in his mother's bedroom. ROSE is very aware of the noises coming from the bedroom. Her gestures become more absent, she pulls BLANCHE's hair, by mistake. BLANCHE wriggles away to free herself.

ROSE
Blanche stay still

BLANCHE
(sulking, then playfully) Rose, *moi, je suis une princesse.* And one day, my wings are going to grow . And I will fly and travel all around the whole world like a wild goose.

ROSE smiles listening to BLANCHE. BLANCHE twirls and twirls with ROSE, then disappears. ROSE, dizzy, stays by herself.

———————

Simultaneously, the visit ends in the bedroom and THE MOTHER lovingly puts away the new pair of shoes in display with the other pair.

———————

ROSE regains her composure.

ROSE
(to her dying mother) Maman, sometimes, a soft light slides into my mind. *(Rose shivers.)* God, it's cold in here.

Pause.

(Rose, now close to her dying mother.) Maman, I always have a feeling of crying inside. In my shoulders mostly. Not in my eyes anymore. *(without looking at her mother)* Punishment in the face of my silence, I suppose.

Pause.

Maman, I have a poison inside of me, it gives me a bad taste in my mouth.

THE MOTHER appears with the gift in her hands.

(to her dying mother) Maman?

THE RED DRESS

ROSE's memory.

THE MOTHER stands, offering ROSE the gift. ROSE sees her.

ROSE
Maman.

Her mother gives her the gift. Delighted, she slips on the dress and dances in front of her mother. She is very proud.

———————————

Simultaneously, BLANCHE and ROSTAND join each other in a secret spot along the riverbank. They are close to one another, they are comparing how floppy their calves are.

———————————

At home, ROSE dances during her sibling's discussion. Her mother watches her tenderly.

———————————

ROSTAND
Blanche. Rose said that father is not coming back.

BLANCHE
It's not true. Rose is a liar.

(seeing the lady of the lake far away) She's there. Rostand, she's there.
Do you see her? *(BLANCHE stands up obviously excited.)*

ROSTAND
(looks in the same direction, then disappointed)
I don't see anything, Blanche.

ROSTAND
Sometimes. Blanche scared me.

BLANCHE
Moi, je suis une princesse. Then. One day. My wings are going to grow and grow and I will fly all around the whole world like a wild goose. I will return only in winter. Then I will tell you all about my magic adventures.

ROSTAND
She was never scared. She reminded me of an amazon. Or an angel from one of my books.

ROSE
(*stops turning and takes her mother's hands*) Merci maman.

The doorbell rings. THE MOTHER lets go of ROSE's hands and, excited, prepares herself. ROSE, deflated, goes to get the visitor.

ROSTAND
God damn bell. I wanted to pull it out so that everyone would just leave us alone. I just wanted us to stay by ourselves. Blanche, Rose, *moi et maman.*

ROSE opens the trunk, gets another pair of shoes and brings them back into the house, THE MOTHER is there.

THE MOTHER
(*welcomes the visitor, then*) Rostand, why have you never come to see me?

ROSTAND
Sometimes I still hear that damn bell. I freeze. And I wait. Wait till it's over.

THE MOTHER returns to the bedroom with the visitor. They make love on the bed. This visit is more aggressive.

———————

BLANCHE
(*firmly tells her story*) Moi, je suis une princesse. Then. One day. My wings are going to grow and I will fly and I will travel around the whole world like a wild goose. Then I will float on the soft water, twinkling.

———————

The doorbell rings again. ROSE goes to get another visitor.

———————

I will meet the lady in white in the middle of the lake.
She is so beautiful, translucent.
She told me she would wait for me. Until the end of time.

She exits.

———————

ROSE
(*with the shoes in her hands*) Maman. (*ROSE is embarrassed in the visitor's company.*)

———————

THE MOTHER
(on the bed, to ROSTAND) Rostand. Why have you never
come to see me?

ROSE
(more loudly) Maman!

ROSE leaves the visitor alone, she puts down the pair of shoes.

*She cannot bear to hear the noises coming from the bedroom. She
puts her hands over her ears and closes her eyes.*

BLINDMAN'S BLUFF

Memory, impression of ROSE's inner world.

*BLANCHE enters running, she takes ROSTAND and brings him
into the house to play Blindman's Bluff, one of their childhood
games. They enter and see ROSE, alone.*

BLANCHE
Don't look, Rose.

ROSE keeps hers eyes closed, the game starts cheerfully.

---

*Simultaneously, THE MOTHER puts away the two pairs of
shoes lovingly, displaying them with the others. Sadness seeps in.*

---

*ROSE does not succeed in touching BLANCHE or ROSTAND,
or maybe she gives them a second chance if she does. The children
are having fun but they become more and more reckless. They pull
and push ROSE.*

*ROSE has had enough, she defends herself and explodes.
BLANCHE and ROSTAND, stunned, run out of the house.*

*ROSTAND reappears laughing, he sits down at the riverbank,
BLANCHE watches her brother from a hidden spot.*

ROSE calms herself, she is back with her dying mother.

ROSE
I feel a fire inside of me, maman.
In my head, my chest, sometimes in my whole body.
There is a blade inside. Sometimes I see it.

Pause.

You shouldn't have gone in my place mother. *(pause)* I'm holding on by a thread maman.

ROSTAND
Sometimes, it's as if there is something broken inside of me. I am crushed from within, empty of us all.

BLANCHE disappears.

THE MOTHER CONFIDES

THE MOTHER is looking at ROSTAND.

THE MOTHER
Rose?

ROSE
Maman?

THE MOTHER
(approaching ROSE) Rostand is not coming to see me.

ROSE is troubled.

ROSTAND
Maybe I should go in.

For the third time, ROSTAND walks to the door. He can' go in. He sits down.

Mother, *(shakes his head)* she's in there, inside of me. In my heart. All over. Warm.
And at the same time, I hate her.
I became so small. I became an oyster.
I am not capable of moving.

A chill – BLANCHE's death creeping in.

Fuck, I can't breath.

ROSTAND walks away from the door. He exits.

The Mother confides, featuring Denise Kenney as Rose and Anne Mansfield as La Mère.
La Cité francophone production of La Maison Rouge, *Edmonton, 1997.*
(Photo courtesy Ed Ellis.)

THE MOTHER
Rose, why is he not coming up?

ROSE
I don't know.

THE MOTHER
Things don't always happen the way we want them to happen.

Pause.

I would like him to come inside and see me.

I wanted to be the oasis.
I am very sorry. *(Rose is having a hard time hearing this.)*
I have been drying up.
In the depths of my being.
I have become a bottomless well,

In my womb, ghosts are complaining endlessly.
I can't sleep anymore Rose.
I can't sleep anymore.

Pause.

Blanche comes sometimes and soothes me.
I melt. Her husky voice awakens lost memories from too long ago.
Then I run after them. I never catch them.
And right there, Blanche laughs.
And it hurts Rose. It hurts.

THE MOTHER approaches ROSE, they are close to one another.

BLANCHE'S DEATH

ROSTAND's memory.

THE MOTHER and ROSE are together in the bedroom.

BLANCHE
(enters all excited, ROSTAND is following her) Rostand.
Rostand, come.

ROSTAND
(afraid) I don't want to go there. *(pause)* Blanche, I'm cold

BLANCHE and ROSTAND reach the riverbank. A dangerous spot.

The death of Blanche, featuring Denise Kenney as Rose and Anne Mansfield as La Mère,
Vanessa Porteous as Blanche and John Ullyatt as Rostand.
La Cité francophone production of La Maison Rouge, *Edmonton, 1997.*
(Photo courtesy Ed Ellis.)

BLANCHE
(*looking far away*) One day. I will grow wings. Orange ones.
Then I will float on the soft water. Twinkling. I will meet the
lady in white from the middle of the lake.
Do you see her Rostand? (*She holds his hand to reassure him.*)
She is so beautiful, translucent.
Do you hear her song?
She said she would wait for me. Until the end of time.

ROSTAND
I'm scared Blanche.

BLANCHE
(*ventures a little further, lets go of ROSTAND's hand*) Rostand.
The rest of you will not see me, and you won't hear me. I
will become invisible because I will be a white angel.
(*She ventures out further onto the ice.*)
Do you see the lady in white?

*ROSTAND hears a gun shot. He is disconcerted, his attention
turns toward the house. The ice cracks, BLANCHE falls. She
disappears in the water.*

ROSTAND
(*realising that BLANCHE has disappeared*) B l a n c h e

ROSE SEES HER MOTHER

ROSE and THE MOTHER are still in the bedroom.

THE MOTHER
Rose. The day that Blanche died, I lost everything.

ROSE
(*to herself*) I lost everything too maman.

THE MOTHER
Things don't happen the way we want them to sometimes.
A living death. I am a living death, Rose.

Pause.

All my life, I fought to escape them.

ROSE
Who are you talking about, maman?

THE MOTHER
Rose, they caught me. Then they caught my children, all my children.
Except Blanche. Maybe.

ROSE
Maman?

Searching for consoling words, she sees her mother.

The ghosts of the past are insidious, maman
Our feet get stuck in the muck of the family dirt. I know that.
Do you remember maman.
You said that: I'm struggling like the devil in holy water.
You remember? I was laughing.

———————————

ROSTAND
(on the riverbank where BLANCHE disappeared)
I could not see the lady in white, Blanche.
If I had known, I would have walked onto the water with you.
I didn't see the lady in white.
I wanted to leave too, but I was scared.
You disappeared, Blanche.

———————————

ROSE
Nevertheless,
you gave me this maman.
An inhuman hope.

My innocence,
my pride broken.
It's been so long.

———————————

ROSTAND
(immersed in BLANCHE's death) I was mad at you for a long time, Blanche.
I should have taken you by the hand and told you to stay.

The doorbell rings. ROSE freezes.

And after all this, everything is fuzzy in my head, *(The doorbell again.)*
There's nothing but red in my head.

The doorbell rings again.

———————————

ROSE
I am not dead, maman.

ROSTAND
Rose damn it, if I had known that you weren't coming, I wouldn't have come.

THE VIOLATION OF ROSE

ROSE goes to answer. Her mother waits a moment then gets up painfully.

ROSE opens the trunk and gets the last pair of shoes. She welcomes the visitor. Her mother is not around, so she waits with him. She is holding the shoes in her hands. He makes her laugh, compliments her. He touches her shoulder, she laughs. Brushes against her breast, she is embarrassed. Touches her breast again. She wants to call her mother, she can't.

The visitor violates her sexually. ROSE can't scream. During the aggression, her face, her body become more and more neutral, something dies inside of her.

When ROSE comes to her senses, she sees her aggressor. She runs away. She runs, totally lost, totally alone.

ROSTAND
(while ROSE runs away and hides)
There's nothing but red in my head and it's bigger than me.
The river was like a magnet for you, Blanche.
You said all of the time that there were diamonds in the water
and that one day you would be rich.

It seems to me that I was scared all my life
I wanted so much for Blanche to come back.

Inside, THE MOTHER welcomes the visitor and invites him into her bedroom. They attempt making love but THE MOTHER is worn out. She is disillusioned, her movement has no life.

ROSE enters the house, she wants to call her mother but she is not alone. She goes down to hide in the cellar, takes off her dress and cleans her body in a rage. She digs the ground up to hide her dress. She discovers her father's clothing.

The violation of Rose, featuring Denise Kenney.
La Cité francophone production of La Maison Rouge, *Edmonton, 1997.*
(Photo courtesy Ed Ellis.)

And the revolver.

She hears her mother's laugh.

A chill – something has died inside.

ROSE leaves the cellar. She approaches her mother's bedroom with the revolver wrapped in the red cloth. Her mother and the visitor are on the bed. ROSE walks in without being seen, she stops beside the bed, aims at the man and pulls the trigger.

A gun shot, the same that ROSTAND heard when BLANCHE disappeared in the water. The visitor falls.

Blood.

ROSE drops the gun on the bed.

ROSTAND
(at the riverbank where BLANCHE disappeared, remembering)
B l a n c h e

ROSTAND runs in the direction of the house.

<u>In the Bedroom</u>

THE MOTHER
Rose?

ROSE realizes what she did, what her hands did. Astounded she looks at her guilty hands, she panics.

The mother understands that ROSE found her father's revolver hidden in the cellar.

The visitor is dead.

It's me, Rose, that you should have killed.

ROSE
Maman, I'm scared.

THE MOTHER
I want to disappear.

ROSE
Mother, I'm cold.

ROSE doesn't manage to tell her that it is not her who is guilty, but him. Her throat is mute.

THE MOTHER
Mon Dieu Rose.
Why?

ROSE runs to hide in the cellar. THE MOTHER, empty, sits on the bed.

Memory of THE MOTHER.

ROSTAND arrives in the bedroom. Red in his head. He can't say anything.

Silence.

The doorbell rings. THE MOTHER is startled. ROSTAND runs to the door. ROSE, in the cellar, is petrified. She caresses her father's clothes for comfort.

The doorbell rings again. THE MOTHER takes the revolver in her hands and desperately cleans her daughter's fingerprints off it. The doorbell again. ROSTAND opens the door and runs outside.

Authorities are in the house.

THE MOTHER responds to their presence. She has the revolver in her hands. She takes the blame, becomes the accused. She bears the physical posture of the accused.

She exits the bedroom.

Blackout.

THINGS DON'T HAPPEN THE WAY WE WANT THEM TO SOMETIMES

BLANCHE is there. Opalescent, reminiscent of water. She is playing alone, collecting pebbles and meticulously placing them on the river bank.

ROSTAND sits at the riverbank.

ROSE finds her way to her dying mother's bedside

ROSE
I wanted to forget the smells of my youth.
I wanted to crush the memories, hide them in a cell.

> *Simultaneously, THE MOTHER enters. Fragile, she is dressed in her white garment. She sits down on the bed, listening to ROSE.*

I covered my shame, soothed it with a balm.

> *Pause.*

But hidden memories pile up. And, in the end, there is no more space.
They overflow. All my denied memories circling me and choking me.
And my throat can't even scream.

> *THE MOTHER lies down.*

You shouldn't have taken my place maman.
I sometimes imagine that it could not have been worse.
You thought you could fix everything, but you couldn't maman.
It was too heavy maman, *trop lourd pour moi.*

(sensing the death of her mother) Maudit maman. Don't die,
I still need you, a little bit longer maman.

ROSTAND
(to BLANCHE) The river was like a magnet for you Blanche.

ROSE
Why are you dying in my arms maman?
It is Rostand that you want to see, and he stays down there by the river.

ROSTAND
You were always saying that there were diamonds in the water
and that one day you would be rich.

ROSE
It's me, maman. It's me, Rose, that's here with you.
I wanted you to forgive me, *(pause)* to hear it from you.
To tell you how I regret, I don't know exactly what.
I am sorry, so very sorry.
I just wanted you to hear me.

> *ROSE is kneeling very close to her mother, now.*

THE MOTHER dies.

At the moment THE MOTHER dies, BLANCHE looks at the house. She gets up slowly, delicately shakes her feathers like a bird, she makes sure she is not broken. She has a last look for ROSTAND. And she leaves. Forever.

ROSE covers her mother's body.

ROSE
Pardon maman.

ROSE, shaken, leaves the bedroom.

THE HOUSE
(while ROSE is leaving the house)
Her frightened ears,
the softness of her soul
where truth lives,
her core. Bruised.
Only the violence stayed
The fear of the violence
possible violence,
human.

REUNION

ROSE arrives at the riverbank. She looks at ROSTAND. He finally sees her.

ROSTAND
(getting up) Rose?

Pause.

ROSE
Rostand, she is dead. *(pause)*
She would have liked to have seen you.

A long silence.

ROSTAND
I couldn't.
I wouldn't have been able to speak to her.

ROSE
Me neither Rostand. *(pause)* I couldn't.

ROSTAND and ROSE sit together. Alone.

EPILOGUE

THE HOUSE
They all came back
Losing and finding themselves
Their story is carved here

Pause.

The blood that flows in our veins has no age.

The end.

LA MAISON ROUGE

Dans la version originale de cette pièce, de laquelle Manon Beaudoin a traduit et écrit la version anglaise, le retour d'une soeur (Rose) et d'un frère (Rostand) à la maison familiale évoque des mémoires d'événements passés, sanglants, et fantomatiques. L'action de *La Maison Rouge* est symbolique. Le texte poétique, plein de douleurs, désirs, solitudes et secrets, convoie un sens d'assèchement et d'étouffement. La mère mourante voudrait être l'oasis, mais désolée, elle s'est asséchée. Elle admit à sa fille: "Je suis devenue une morte vivante." Le fils ne peut pas approcher ni parler à sa mère. La fille ne sait pas communiquer avec sa mère non plus. Les fantômes du passé sont insidieux. Les personnages de cette pièce se rendent compte du fait que, comme Rose l'observe, "on s'enlise en pataugeant dans une boue familière." Pour cette famille la maison contient et symbolise leur histoire gravée, l'histoire d'un viol, d'un meurtre, et du silence.

La pièce *la Maison rouge* a été créée par le théâtre du Coyote à la salle de la Cité francophone, le vendredi 13 juin 1997 dans une mise en scène de l'auteure.

BLANCHE	*Vanessa Porteous*
LA MÈRE	*Anne Mansfield*
ROSE	*Denise Kenney*
ROSTAND	*John Ullyatt*

VIOLONCELLISTE: *Christine Hanson*

Chorégraphie: *Bobbi Westman*
Scénographie: *Bretta Gerecke*
Costumes: *Peter Field*
Éclairage: *Melinda Sutton*
Musique originale: *Christine Hanson*
Consultation visuelle: *Doug Jamha*
Régie: *Gisèle Lemire et Martine Tremblay*
Publicité: *Gisèle Lemire*

PERSONNAGES

ROSE	Une femme. Trente-huit ans
ROSTAND	Un homme, frère de Rose. Trente-trois ans
BLANCHE	Soeur de Rose et Rostand, morte à l'âge de six ans
LA MÈRE	Leur mère

LES VISITEURS	Cinq paires de souliers
LA MAISON	Une ou des voix

Cette pièce se déroule dans un seul lieu, le domaine familial. L'espace théâtral et la temporalité ne sont pas réalistes; ils permettent le voyage de chacun des quatre personnages.

Rose et Rostand reviennent à la maison après vingt-cinq ans d'absence; leur mère est mourante. Le spectre de Blanche est là; Blanche est morte noyée, vingt-cinq ans plus tôt. Rose, au chevet de sa mère, tente de révéler son secret. Rostand, lui, n'entre jamais dans la maison, il attend Rose. Il reste aux prises avec le souvenir de la mort de Blanche.

LA MAISON ROUGE
de Manon Beaudoin

LA MAISON S'ÉVEILLE

La maison s'éveille, mélancolique.

LA MÈRE dort dans son lit, pâle.

BLANCHE est là, opalescente. Elle joue seule, elle collectionne des pierres qu'elle place méticuleusement au bord de la rivière.

ROSE pendant ce temps voyage vers la maison, elle porte une lourde malle sur ses épaules. ROSE est forte. Ses vêtements cachent ses formes féminines, une armure. Dessous, elle porte quelque chose de délicat.

LA MAISON

LA MAISON
J'ai ouvert les yeux

LA MÈRE s'éveille lentement, la Maison lui redonne vie. Elle porte un jupon long, blanc. Elle trouve la force de se lever et d'enfiler sa robe, la plus belle; une robe d'un rouge profond.

Elle était là
au bord de la rivière
Ses épaules pleuraient

Elle m'est apparue
plus frêle, plus seule,
plus petite
Après tant d'absence

Je ne l'attendais plus.

Les murmures se sont tus depuis longtemps
Tous les souvenirs emmurés
Les réminiscences logées dans les fissures
les recoins oubliés

ROSE traverse le pont. En vue de la maison, elle dépose sa malle, essouflée. Elle se repose un moment. Par la fenêtre, LA MÈRE observe l'arrivée de ROSE.

The Princess, featuring Denise Kenney as Rose and Vanessa Porteous as Blanche.
La Cité francophone production of La Maison Rouge, *Edmonton, 1997.*
(Photo courtesy Ed Ellis.)

Mais elle est revenue
Des retrouvailles inespérées.

Une Visite de Rose

> *La route a été longue, ROSE reste un moment près de la rivière. Elle observe la maison familiale, tout est différent, tout est pareil. BLANCHE est là.*

BLANCHE
(surprise, heureuse de revoir sa soeur) Rose?
(ROSE ne la voit pas.) Rose.

ROSE
Un interminable voyage,
j'ai porté mes racines à travers le monde,
pour oublier.
Mais,
je suis un phare,
je suis une fenêtre,
un miroir distordu.
Et j'éclaire la route de cet être
qui aboutit toujours à la même place.
Une maison rouge de larmes.

> *ROSE tente de tirer sa malle à quelques reprises, la malle ne bouge pas. Elle la laisse là et se dirige vers la maison. BLANCHE, curieuse, touche la malle; un son alarmant. ROSE se retourne et revient lentement, elle sent la présence de BLANCHE. Finalement, ROSE repart vers la maison. Elle hésite, puis entre. Émoi – les odeurs, la poussière, un seuil, les escaliers, la maison de son enfance, des souvenirs heureux, d'autres plus douloureux. LA MÈRE est venue l'accueillir à la porte, ROSE ne la voit pas.*

> *ROSE entre dans la chambre de sa mère mourante.*

ROSE
(à sa mère mourante, dans le lit vide) Maman?

> *Pas de réponse. ROSE se poste à la fenêtre un moment. BLANCHE s'approche d'elle, elle effleure de ses doigts le visage, les lèvres de ROSE. ROSE soupire, sent la présence de BLANCHE. Émoi – elle ne peut rester dans cette maison plus longtemps. Elle sort.*

> *BLANCHE et LA MÈRE restent ensemble dans la chambre. LA MÈRE s'assoit sur le lit, BLANCHE à ses pieds, pose la tête sur ses genoux.*

ROSE ne quitte pas le domaine, elle s'arrête à la hauteur de la malle. Elle écrit à son frère ROSTAND, elle ne l'a pas vu depuis des années. Elle lui écrit pour lui annoncer la mort imminente de leur mère. ROSTAND reçoit la lettre.

notre mère est mourante. Viens. Rose.

ROSE RESTE

ROSE tire sa lourde malle jusqu'à la porte. Elle sait qu'elle restera jusqu' à la fin. Elle entre et va au chevet de sa mère mourante. BLANCHE est toujours dans la chambre.

ROSTAND, chez lui, est troublé par cette nouvelle. Il veut et ne veut pas retourner à la maison de son enfance, les deux à la fois.

ROSE
(*à sa mère mourante, dans le lit vide*) Maman, c'est moi Rose.

Souvenir de Rose, quelques temps après la disparition de son père.

> *Une lumière perce au travers de la porte du cellier, elle avance. LA MÈRE est là, elle enterre des vêtements du père et un revolver qu'elle enveloppe d'un tissu rouge. ROSE descend et comme lorsqu'elle avait treize ans, elle prend une pièce de vêtement et la porte à son visage. LA MÈRE sursaute, leurs regards se rencontrent.*

> **LA MÈRE**
> Rose ma chouette, i est tard, va te coucher.
> (*ROSE se réfugie lentement dans les bras de sa mère.*)
> Rose, pleure pas. T'es ma grande.

> **ROSE**
> Pourquoi, maman?

> **LA MÈRE**
> Je le sais pas Rose.
> Ton père. (*Elle cherche ses mots.*)
> J'avais l'impression qu'i vivait dans la noirceur.
> I avait juste des, petits moments. Des petites étincelles.
> Pas assez pour vouloir rester.

> Allez Rose, i est tard.

ROSE part lentement mais elle entend sa mère.

I me disait que j'étais sa muse.
À un moment donné ça pu suffit.
Je l'aimais.
Une âme vulnérable.

LA MÈRE coupe une mèche de ses cheveux, l'ajoute aux reliques qu'elle enterre, puis les recouvre. Elle disparaît.

ROSE
(savoure les derniers mots de sa mère) Une âme vulnérable

ROSE
(à elle-même) Maman va-t'en pas, pas tout de suite.
J'ai trop de choses à te dire.

Un silence.

(vers la mère mourante, dans le lit vide) Maman, j'ai écrit à Rostand.

À l'annonce de cette nouvelle, ROSTAND quitte sa maison en courant; BLANCHE se précipite vers l'entrée de la maison; LA MÈRE se poste à l'endroit idéal pour surveiller l'arrivée de son fils; ROSE, elle, reste à la fenêtre de la chambre.

Elles attendent toutes l'arrivée de ROSTAND.

ROSTAND

ROSTAND arrive, désinvolte. Il porte son habit du dimanche, une cravate, ses habits sont dépenaillés. Il a dans la poche la lettre de ROSE, chiffonnée, déchirée et recollée. Il avance lentement.

BLANCHE reconnaît ROSTAND, son frère, son ami. Lui, ne la voit pas.

ROSTAND
Me semble que ça pas changé, *(se ferme les yeux)* pas tant que ça.

BLANCHE
(heureuse) Rostand? *(Elle veut renouer contact physiquement avec son frère.)*

ROSTAND
Vingt-cinq ans presque jour pour jour que j'ai pas mis les pieds ici.
J'ai une photo chez nous avec une date d'écrit dessus, en rouge.
Une photo de toute la famille. Sauf Blanche.

ROSTAND hésite avant d'entrer dans la maison. Il ressent le poids de ses souvenirs, le poids de la mort de BLANCHE qui le tire vers la rivière. Il décide finalement d'y rester. Il rit.

J'ai pas envie de me trouver tout seul en face de la mère.

Dans la chambre.

ROSE
(vers sa mère mourante, dans le lit vide) Maman?

ROSTAND
Je vas attendre Rose.

Pause.

Ostie que ça sent bon ici. *(Il voit un arbre décrépit.)*
Quand j'étais petit, les fleurs de pommier ça me faisait tout le temps éternuer.
Pas les pommes par exemple. On en as-tu mangé des pommes!
Rose.
Rose quand a cueillait une pomme, a la faisait disparaître dans sa robe, pis a la frottait longtemps jusqu'à temps qu'a brille, rouge.
Une pour moi, une pour elle.
L'hiver, on allait les chercher en cachette dans cave.
(Il arrache une petite branche de l'arbre.)
Ça fait du bien d'être ici.
Ça sent mon enfance? Les odeurs, pis les couleurs de mon enfance...

Moi pis Rose, des fois, on se roulait dans l'herbe.
Pis après on comparait notre gras de mollet. Collés un sur l'autre.
J'étais tout petit quand Rose m'avait montré comment.

Pause.

BLANCHE est toujours là, physiquement tout près de ROSTAND. Elle se rappelle sa présence, leurs jeux.

L'automne, je me couchais par terre au pied du saule pleureur,
dret-là au bord de la rivière.
Pis je me remplissais les narines à craquer, le nez dans terre mouillée.
Je me fermais les yeux. Pis je devenais l'eau.
Je le savais que l'hiver s'en venait.

Un frisson – BLANCHE perd son équilibre.

J'aime pas ça l'hiver.

> *BLANCHE se désintéresse de ROSTAND, elle reste autour mais absorbée par son propre jeu.*

Des fois, un grand frisson me traversait le corps. Je bougeais pas.
L'odeur des feuilles brunes,

> *ROSTAND se rappelle de sa mère, elle apparaît dans la maison. LA MÈRE est heureuse de voir son fils.*

l'automne, ça me fait toujours penser à la mère,

> *Pause.*

a me disait que j'allais prendre mon coup de mort.
A me disait toujours d'arrêter de perdre mon temps.

LA MÈRE
Rostand?

> *Pause, ROSTAND ne l'entend pas vraiment.*

Rostand. *(Elle lui confie, déçue.)* T'es jamais venu me voir.

ROSTAND
(ne voulant pas entendre) L'automne, ça me fait toujours penser à la mère.
Ça doit être parce que chu né en automne. *(LA MÈRE disparaît.)*

> *Pause.*

(léger, sincère) Des fois, je pense à ça.
Un matin. Les eaux de la mère ont crevé, pis c'était à cause de moi.
A tenait sa grosse bedaine en grimaçant, pis c'était à cause de moi.
J'étais le deuxième, Rose était la première.

Mais j'étais le premier garçon, le seul.
Là. Moi. J'avais poussé, acharné pour sortir, sortir de là.
Pis la mère. A l'avait eu mal.

> *Pause.*

Pis c'était à cause de moi.
Ben quand je pense à ça, je sé que chu en vie.

> *Pause.*

Ce jour-là. J'étais quelqu'un. Pis tout était possible.

> *Un coup de froid – BLANCHE tombe. ROSTAND se raidit.*

> *Pause.*

J'aime pas ça l'hiver.

> *BLANCHE se relève lentement, s'ébroue. Elle entre dans la maison en courant.*

La Princesse

> *Dans la chambre.*

ROSE
(à sa mère mourante, dans le lit vide) C'est Rose, maman

> *LA MÈRE entre dans la chambre et s'assoit sur le bord du lit, elle écoute ROSE.*

Maman. Des fois, je vois papa. De dos.
Partir. Moi, je le suis du regard.
Jusqu'à temps qu'il soit plus qu'un petit point noir à l'horizon.
Il se retourne jamais.

Pause.

Le passé m'a ensevelie complètement.
(avec véhémence) On dirait que mes os ont explosé dans les quatres coins de cette maison puis j'arrive pas à récupérer tous les morceaux.

> *ROSE reste à la fenêtre, pensive.*

> *BLANCHE est loin, au sommet du monde.*

> **BLANCHE**
> Moi, je suis une princesse.
> Puis, un jour, i va me pousser des ailes.
> Et, je pourrai faire le tour du monde comme les oies sauvages.

> *Un tableau de LA MÈRE, de ROSE et de BLANCHE. Chacune dans ses rêves.*

<u>SEUL</u>

ROSTAND
(sur le bord de la rivière) Perdre mon temps! J'ai pensé à ça souvent.
Le temps, ça se perd pas. I s'imprègne. Mais on oublie.

Pause.

Ici.

> *Le tableau se brise. ROSE retourne au chevet de sa mère. LA MÈRE se lève, elle se rend à son miroir et se regarde. BLANCHE revient dans la maison.*

Le temps s'est arrêté y a vingt-cinq ans. Pis avant ça. *(Il essaie de se rappeler.)* Je sé pas.

> *Pause.*

Si j'attendais en silence, comme quand j'étais petit pis que je me laissais emporter par la rivière dret-là en-dessous du saule pleureur.
Peut-être que le temps m'amènerait visiter toutes les racoins cachés de ma vie.

BLANCHE
(crie de loin) Rostand. *(plus fort)* Rostand.

> *BLANCHE arrive à la course dans la chambre. Elle cherche ROSTAND sous le lit, elle regarde par la fenêtre. Elle voit ROSE dans la chambre.*

Rose, Rostand es-tu venu se cacher dans la maison?

> *ROSE surprise, sourit, lui fait signe que non. BLANCHE sort de la chambre. ROSE la suit du regard.*

ROSTAND
Chu pas sûr que je veux ça.

(rires) Blanche pis moi, des fois on s'assoyait, collés un sur l'autre.
On comparait notre gras de mollet. C'est moi qui y avais montré comment.
Pis des fois, on disait rien. On voyageait.

> *BLANCHE court se blottir dans les bras de LA MÈRE. ROSE les regarde.*

BLANCHE
Maman, c'est moi ta princesse. *(BLANCHE est le soleil de sa*

mère. Elles tournoient toutes les deux. Puis BLANCHE lui chuchote à l'oreille.)
Maman, appelle Rostand pour lui jouer un tour. *(Elles sont complices.)*

ROSTAND
La mère. Chu pas capable de l'imaginer asteur.
Le temps a fait un trou, pis ma mère a glissé dedans.
J'imagine que c'est pour ça que t'avais peur de venir ici,
c'est comme visiter une revenante.
Est là, a m'attend. Pis moi chu ici en dessous de mon arbre.
A dirait, "Rostand tu perds ton temps encore une fois, ché pas où ce que tu
vas te retrouver avec cette tête de linotte." *(sourire)*

LA MÈRE
(rit, appelle ROSTAND) Rostand.

ROSTAND
(croyant entendre sa mère) Maman?

LA MÈRE
(plus fort) Rostand.

ROSTAND sent leur présence. Il se tourne, croit les apercevoir.
BLANCHE et sa mère pouffent de rire. Un froid – ROSTAND se
détourne.

LA MÈRE
(moqueuse) Veux-tu ben me dire d'où tu sors?
Change de face, on va croire qu'on est le diable en
personne.

ROSE, à la fenêtre, a un faible sourire.

ROSTAND
Peut-être que je devrais entrer.

ROSTAND se dirige vers la porte, il veut entrer. BLANCHE et LA MÈRE
s'immobilisent, espoirs.

————————————

ROSE
(dans la chambre) Des fois maman, une lumière douce se glisse dans ma tête.
Pas longtemps. Mais, je sais qu'elle est là.

————————————

ROSTAND
(prend une décision, retourne au bord de la rivière.)
Chu ben ici. J'aime mieux attendre Rose.

LA MÈRE est déçue, BLANCHE la prend dans ses bras.

ROSE
(à sa mère mourante) Maman… maman… *(soupir)*

LA DAME DU LAC

ROSTAND
Été comme hiver Blanche pis moi on allait sur le bord de la rivière.

Pause.

La rivière c'était comme un aimant pour nous autres.
Blanche disait qu'y avait des diamants dans l'eau.
Pis qu'un jour, a deviendrait un poisson, pis qu'a serait riche.
Pis qu'a nous parlerait quand même.

Souvenir de ROSTAND.

> *LA MÈRE brosse les cheveux de BLANCHE, BLANCHE rit
> aux éclats.*

LA MÈRE
Blanche, arrête de bouger.

BLANCHE
Maman, raconte-nous l'histoire de la dame du lac.

LA MÈRE
Une autre fois?

LA MÈRE ne peut rien refuser à BLANCHE.

ROSTAND
A l'adorait que la mère y raconte c'te histoire de…
la Dame du lac.

LA MÈRE
Ben viens, mon grand.

ROSTAND va les rejoindre et s'assoit par terre.

Rose, tu viens pas?

ROSE fait signe que non. LA MÈRE lui sourit. ROSE écoute de loin.

Cette histoire racontée aux enfants est un moment familial heureux, chaleureux.

Quand j'étais toute petite, ma grand-maman me bordait tous les soirs. Quand je pleurais, elle me racontait l'histoire de la dame du lac et je glissais doucement dans les bras de Morphée.

Et c'est exactement comme ça qu'elle me la contait:

La dame du lac apparaissait à la brunante parmi les vapeurs du lac.
Elle était toute blanche, transparente.

On entendait son chant, lointain, onctueux comme du miel.

(à elle-même) Des fois, i me semble que je l'entendais vraiment.

BLANCHE
Est-ce qu'elle était un fantôme? *(Sa mère lui fait gentiment signe de se taire.)*

ROSTAND
Une fée?

LA MÈRE
Elle était une fée, une douce fée.
Sa mélodie berçait tous ceux qui avaient le coeur gros et leur âme se gonflait. Alors ils s'envolaient et glissaient doucement sur l'eau jusqu'au milieu du lac, et là, toute la nuit ils dansaient avec elle, sur l'eau. Au matin, ils se réveillaient un sourire aux lèvres.

BLANCHE
Maman, est-ce qu'elle est morte la dame du lac?

LA MÈRE sourit faiblement.

Un tableau de la famille. Ensemble.

PREMIER VISITEUR

La sonnette de la porte résonne.

LA MÈRE
Rose va répondre à la porte.

ROSE se dirige vers le vestibule. LA MÈRE ajuste sa robe, soigne ses cheveux. BLANCHE et ROSTAND, insouciants, jouent autour d'elle.

ROSE ouvre la malle, en ressort une paire de souliers, puis ferme la malle.

Lorsque ROSE revient vers le vestibule, LA MÈRE est là. BLANCHE et ROSTAND arrêtent leur jeu.

LA MÈRE
(accueille le visiteur, les enfants sont polis) Bonjour

Rose, continue à brosser les cheveux de ta soeur.

LA MÈRE se dirige vers la chambre avec le visiteur, les enfants, enjoués et curieux, les suivent. LA MÈRE se retourne et les surprend, en flagrant délit.

ROSE va s'assoir avec BLANCHE, elle lui brosse les cheveux. ROSTAND essaie d'attirer l'attention de ses soeurs, d'interrompre leur activité.

Simultanément, LA MÈRE a amené le visiteur dans la chambre. Cette première visite a un ton de coquetterie, de séduction.

Les enfants sont intrigués par les rires venant de la chambre. ROSTAND devient de plus en plus dérangeant. ROSE s'impatiente.

ROSE
Rostand?

ROSTAND sort de la maison et court s'étendre au bord de la rivière.

La visite se termine. LA MÈRE emporte affectueusement les souliers et les expose dans sa chambre, comme des reliques.

LE RÊVE

>*ROSE brosse toujours les cheveux de BLANCHE.*

ROSTAND
(sur le bord de la rivière)
L'odeur de Rose quand a brossait les cheveux de Blanche,
pis l'odeur de la glace dans rivière, l'hiver en bas de chez-nous.

>*BLANCHE, taquine, se dégage et court se cacher dans la maison.*

BLANCHE
Tu pourras pas me trouver.

>*ROSE disparaît à la recherche de BLANCHE.*

ROSTAND
I me manque des bouts. Des gros bouts.
J'ai la cervelle fêlée.
Mes souvenirs, mon imagination. Tout est mélangé.

>*BLANCHE réapparaît, seule. Elle joue au bord de la rivière, son*
>*jeu devient de plus en plus audacieux durant le rêve de*
>*ROSTAND. Jusqu'à ce qu'elle perde son équilibre.*

J'ai rêvé hier. *(Il voit son rêve en le racontant.)*

J'étais sur un pont. Un pont long pis étroit. Je courais, je courais.
Y avait plein de monde qui criait, pis qu'y regardait en bas, la rivière.
Y avait une auto bleue.
Ma mère était là. A disait: "Rostand viens voir." Je voulais pas y aller.
À l'autre bout, je voyais une porte en fer. Rouillée.
Dans mon rêve, tout ce que je voulais, c'était d'ouvrir la porte, de la fermer,
d'être de l'autre côté. De regarder en arrière. Pis que tout soit fini.

Je courais encore, je pouvais pas m'arrêter.
Mais j'avais tout le temps l'impression d'être à même place.
Je pouvais pas m'arrêter. *(ROSTAND frissonne.)*

>*Pause.*

Ma blonde a me dit tout le temps que si ça existe dans ton imagination, c'est
parce que c'est vrai. Ça me fait flipper quand a dit ça.

>*Pause.*

Je voulais l'amener ici pis finalement j'ai laissé faire. Je sé pas pourquoi.
J'ai décidé de venir tout seul.

Je pense que j'ai ben faite, elle non plus a l'aime pas ça perdre son temps. A l'aurait pu faire connivence avec la mère. *(sourire)*

> *LA MÈRE apparaît dans la chambre.*

En quelque part Rostand, tu voulais pas y dire que tu te souviens ni de ta mère, ni de ta soeur Rose. Chu même pas capable de me faire une image de Rose.

LA MÈRE
Rostand. *(pause)* Pourquoi t'es jamais venu me voir?

> *L'apogée du jeu de BLANCHE, elle tombe et reste là, inerte.*

> *ROSTAND voit BLANCHE par terre. Il va vers elle. Il hésite avant de la toucher. BLANCHE ouvre ses yeux, s'ébroue doucement, s'assure qu'elle a tous ses morceaux et se sauve. ROSTAND, surpris, revient s'assoir en la regardant partir.*

> *ROSTAND se demande s'il a vraiment vu BLANCHE.*

ROSTAND
Rose, crisse. Veux-tu ben me dire où ce que t'es.

> *ROSTAND s'assoit au bord de l'eau, il enlève ses souliers.*

Le Cadeau

> *Souvenir de ROSTAND.*

> *LA MÈRE arrive à la maison, elle apporte un cadeau. Elle voit ROSTAND seul, sur le bord de la rivière. Elle se place en catimini derrière lui et lui couvre les yeux avec ses mains.*

ROSTAND
Blanche? Rose?

> *LA MÈRE rit, ROSTAND la reconnaît.*

ROSTAND
Maman. *(Il voit le cadeau.)* Est-ce que c'est pour moi, maman?

LA MÈRE
Non Rostand, c'est pour Rose.

Elle ouvre la boîte, lui montre la robe. Elle l'essaie devant elle et tournoie, frivole, séduisante.

ROSTAND
Maman. Je m'ennuie de papa.

LA MÈRE
Moi aussi, mon grand, je m'ennuie de papa.

Pause.

ROSTAND
Maman, c'est qui, qui est venu hier?

LA MÈRE est mal à l'aise. Elle tente maladroitement de distraire ROSTAND en lui essayant la robe.

ROSTAND
(*insistant*) Maman

La sonnette de la porte sonne. ROSTAND fige inquiet. Ils se regardent. La sonnette de la porte sonne de nouveau. LA MÈRE remet la robe dans la boîte en vitesse, mal assurée. Elle quitte ROSTAND et entre dans la maison.

DEUXIÈME VISITEUR

ROSE répond à la porte, BLANCHE surveille. ROSE ouvre la malle, prend une paire de souliers, referme la malle. Lorsque ROSE revient dans le vestibule, LA MÈRE est là pour accueillir le visiteur. Elle l'invite à sa chambre. ROSE reste avec BLANCHE, elle brosse les cheveux de sa soeur.

―――――――

Cette visite est enjouée, plus sexuelle. LA MÈRE et le visiteur initient des jeux préliminaires autour du lit.

―――――――

ROSTAND voit ou entend ce qui se passe dans la chambre. ROSE est attentive aux bruits venant de la chambre. Ses gestes deviennent plus absents, elle tire les cheveux de BLANCHE, par mégarde. BLANCHE se dégage.

ROSE
Blanche, reste tranquille!

BLANCHE

Moi, Rose, je suis une princesse.

Puis un jour, il va me pousser des ailes.

Et je pourrai faire le tour du monde comme les oies sauvages.

ROSE sourit en écoutant BLANCHE. BLANCHE entraîne ROSE dans une ronde puis disparaît, ROSE reste seule.

────────────

Simultanément, la visite se termine. LA MÈRE emporte la nouvelle paire de soulier et l'expose tendrement avec la première paire.

────────────

ROSE se ressaisit.

ROSE

(à sa mère mourante, dans le lit vide) Maman, des fois, une douce lumière se glisse dans mon cerveau.

(Rose frissonne.) Y fait froid ici,

Pause.

Maman, j'ai toujours l'impression de pleurer à l'intérieur.

Mes épaules surtout. Je ne pleure plus par mes yeux.

(sans regarder sa mère) Une revanche en face de mon silence, je suppose.

Pause.

J'ai un poison en-dedans maman, ça me donne un mauvais goût dans la bouche.

Pause.

Maman?

La Robe

LA MÈRE, le cadeau à bout de bras, l'offre à ROSE.

ROSE

Maman

ROSE court vers sa mère et prend le cadeau. Ravie, elle enfile la robe et danse devant sa mère. Elle est très fière.

────────────

Simultanément. BLANCHE et ROSTAND se rejoignent au bord de la rivière. Ils s'assoient collés un sur l'autre, ils comparent leur gras de mollet.

À la maison, ROSE tournoie sur elle-même, sa mère l'observe tendrement.

ROSTAND
Blanche. Rose a dit que papa reviendrait pas.

BLANCHE
C'est pas vrai... Rose c'est une menteuse.

(apercevant la dame du lac au loin) Elle est là. Rostand, elle est là. La vois-tu? *(Elle se lève, excitée.)*

ROSTAND
(regarde dans la même direction que Blanche, puis déçu)
Je vois rien, Blanche.

ROSTAND
Blanche, des fois, a me faisait peur.

BLANCHE
Moi. Je suis une princesse. Puis. Un jour. I va me pousser des ailes et je pourrai faire le tour du monde comme les oies sauvages. Je vais revenir seulement en hiver. Pis je vais vous raconter mes voyages magiques.

ROSTAND
Elle, a l'avait jamais peur. A me faisait penser à une amazone. Ou à un ange que j'avais vu dans un de mes livres.

ROSE
(arrête de tourner et prend les mains de sa mère) Merci maman.

La sonnette de la porte résonne. LA MÈRE lâche les mains de ROSE et sort en hâte pour se préparer. ROSE, déçue, va chercher le visiteur.

ROSTAND
Maudite sonnette.
Je voulais juste l'arracher, pour que tout le monde nous laisse en paix.
Je voulais juste qu'on reste nous autres. Blanche, Rose, moi pis la mère.

ROSE ouvre la malle, prend une autre paire de souliers et la ramène dans la maison. LA MÈRE est là.

LA MÈRE
(accueille le visiteur au vestibule, puis)
Rostand, pourquoi t'es jamais venu me voir?

ROSTAND
Des fois je l'entends encore la maudite sonnette. Je reste suspendu, aux aguets. Jusqu'à temps que ça passe.

LA MÈRE retourne dans la chambre. Elle fait l'amour avec le visiteur, cette visite est plus agressive.

BLANCHE
(se raconte fermement son histoire) Moi. Je suis une princesse. Puis. Un jour. I va me pousser des ailes et je pourrai faire le tour du monde comme les oies sauvages.
Puis je flotterai sur l'eau blanche.

La sonnette de la porte résonne. ROSE va chercher un autre visiteur

---

J'irai rejoindre la dame blanche au milieu du lac. Elle est belle, transparente. Elle a dit qu'elle m'attendrait. Jusqu'à la nuit des temps.

ROSE
Maman. *(ROSE est embarassée en compagnie du visiteur.)*

LA MÈRE
(sur le lit) Rostand. Pourquoi t'es jamais venu me voir?

ROSE
(plus fortement) Maman!

ROSE laisse le visiteur seul. Elle ne peut supporter les bruits venant de la chambre. Elle met ses mains sur ses oreilles, se ferme les yeux.

COLIN-MAILLARD

Impression/souvenir de ROSE.

>*BLANCHE entre à la course, elle entraîne ROSTAND vers la maison. Ils entrent et voient ROSE, seule. Le jeu de colin-maillard commence doucement, avec gaieté. ROSTAND et BLANCHE font tourner ROSE.*

BLANCHE
Regarde pas Rose.

>*Simultanément, LA MÈRE rangera les deux paires de souliers avec les autres, en exposition. Une tristesse l'habite.*

>*ROSE ne réussit pas à toucher BLANCHE et ROSTAND, ou si elle réussit, elle leur donne une autre chance. Les enfants s'amusent mais le jeu devient de plus en plus rapide et abusif envers ROSE.*

>*ROSE ne veut plus jouer, elle se défend et éclate.*

>*BLANCHE et ROSTAND, hébétés, se sauvent.*

ROSTAND réapparaît en riant et se réinstalle sur le bord de la rivière. BLANCHE le surveille à distance.

ROSE retrouve son calme. Elle est avec sa mère mourante.

ROSE
Je sens un feu en dedans de moi maman.
Dans ma tête, ma poitrine, des fois mon corps tout entier.
Il y a une lame, je la vois à l'intérieur de moi.

Pause.

T'aurais pas dû y aller à ma place maman. *(pause)* Je tiens à un fil maman.

ROSTAND
Des fois, c'est comme si y avait quelque chose de cassé en dedans de moi.
Chu broyé par en dedans, vide de nous autres.

BLANCHE disparaît.

Confidences de la Mère

De la chambre, LA MÈRE regarde ROSTAND.

LA MÈRE
Rose?

ROSE
Maman?

LA MÈRE
(s'approche tranquillement de ROSE) Rostand, i vient pas me voir.

ROSE est troublée.

———————————

ROSTAND
(s'apprêtant à entrer) Je devrais peut-être entrer. *(Il ne peut pas.)*
La mère, je l'ai cimentée dans le coeur. Pis en même temps, je l'haïs.
Chu devenu tellement petit en dedans.
Chu pas capable de bouger. Chu devenu une huître.
Ostie, j'étouffe!

———————————

LA MÈRE
Rose, pourquoi y monte pas?

ROSE
Je le sais pas.

LA MÈRE
Les choses se passent pas tout le temps comme on l'aurait voulu.

Pause.

J'aurais aimé ça qu'i vienne.
Je voulais être l'oasis.
Je suis désolée. *(ROSE s'éloigne de sa mère.)*
Je me suis asséchée assez vite.
Au plus profond de mes racines.
Je suis devenue un puits sans fond,

Dans mes entrailles, des fantômes se plaignent sans arrêt.
Je peux plus dormir Rose. Je peux plus.

Pause.

Blanche a vient des fois pis a me berce.
Je fonds.
Sa voix rauque réveille des souvenirs trop lointains, perdus.
Puis moi, je cours après. Je ne les rattrape jamais.
Puis là, Blanche elle se met à rire.
Puis ça fait mal Rose. Ça fait mal…

LA MÈRE s'est rapprochée de ROSE, elles sont tout près l'une de l'autre.

LA MORT DE BLANCHE

Souvenir de ROSTAND.

LA MÈRE et ROSE restent ensemble dans la chambre.

BLANCHE
(entre en criant, ROSTAND la suit) Rostand. Rostand, viens.

ROSTAND
Je veux pas aller là. *(pause)* Blanche, j'ai froid.

BLANCHE et ROSTAND arrivent à un endroit dangereux, sur le bord de la rivière.

BLANCHE
(en regardant au loin)
Un jour. I va me pousser des ailes. Oranges.
Puis je flotterai sur l'eau blanche.
J'irai rejoindre la dame blanche du milieu du lac.
La vois-tu Rostand? *(Elle lui prend la main pour le rassurer.)*
Elle est belle, transparente.
Entends-tu son chant?
Elle a dit qu'elle m'attendrait. Jusqu'à la nuit des temps.

ROSTAND
J'ai peur Blanche.

BLANCHE
(s'aventure plus loin, laisse la main de ROSTAND)
Rostand. Vous autres vous me verrez pas, puis vous
m'entendrez pas. Je deviendrai invisible parce que moi.
Je serai un ange tout blanc.
La vois-tu la dame blanche?

Un coup de feu venant de la maison. ROSTAND est interloqué, son attention se détourne vers la maison. Simultanément, BLANCHE perd l'équilibre, tombe à l'eau.

ROSTAND
(réalisant que BLANCHE est disparue) B l a n c h e

Rose Voit sa Mère

LA MÈRE
Rose, le jour que Blanche est morte, j'ai tout perdu.

ROSE
Moi aussi maman, j'ai tout perdu.

LA MÈRE
Les choses se passent pas comme on le voudrait des fois.
Une morte vivante. Je suis devenue une morte vivante, Rose.

Pause.

Toute ma vie, je m'étais battue pour leur échapper.

ROSE
De qui tu parles, maman?

LA MÈRE
Rose, ils m'ont rattrapée. Puis ils ont rattrappé mes enfants, tous mes
enfants.
Sauf Blanche. Peut-être.

ROSE
Maman? *(ROSE voit LA MÈRE. Elle cherche à la rassurer.)*
Les fantômes du passé sont insidieux maman
On s'enlise en pataugeant dans une boue familière.
Te souviens-tu maman? Tu disais ça.
Je me débats comme un diable dans l'eau bénite.
Moi, je riais.

ROSTAND
(sur le bord de la rivière) Je la voyais pas la dame en blanc.
Si j'avais su, j'aurais marché sur l'eau avec toi, Blanche.
Je la voyais pas la dame en blanc.
Je voulais partir aussi, mais j'avais peur.
T'es disparue, Blanche.

ROSE
Malgré tout,
tu m'as donné ça maman,
un espoir inhumain.

Mon innocence,
ma honte transpercée.
il y a si longtemps.

——————————————

ROSTAND
Je t'en ai voulu longtemps, Blanche.
J'aurais dû te prendre par la main, te dire de rester.

La sonnette de la porte résonne.

Pis après ça tout est flou dans ma tête, *(la sonnette de la porte insiste)*
y'a rien que du rouge dans ma tête.

La sonnette de la porte résonne de nouveau.

——————————————

ROSE
Je suis pas morte, maman

——————————————

ROSTAND
Rose tabarnac, si j'avais su que tu viendrais pas, je serais pas venu.

Le Viol

ROSE sort de la chambre, LA MÈRE la regarde intensément.

ROSE va répondre à la porte. LA MÈRE attend un peu, puis se lève péniblement.

ROSE ouvre la malle, prend la dernière paire de souliers. LA MÈRE n'est pas là, elle attend avec le visiteur. Il la fait rire, la complimente. Il la touche à l'épaule, elle rit. Il touche ses seins, elle est embarassée, il la touche de nouveau. Elle veut appeler sa mère, le visiteur l'en empêche.

Le visiteur l'agresse sexuellement. ROSE ne peut crier. Durant l'agression, son visage, son corps devient de plus en plus neutre. Quelque chose meurt en dedans d'elle.

ROSE se réveille et voit son agresseur, elle se sauve. Elle court éperdument.

ROSTAND
(pendant que ROSE court se cacher)
Y'a rien que du rouge dans ma tête, pis c'est plus gros que moi.

La rivière, c'était comme un aimant pour toi, Blanche.
Tu disais tout le temps qu'y avait des diamants dans l'eau
pis qu'un jour tu serais riche.
Il me semble que j'ai eu peur toute ma vie.
Je voulais tellement que Blanche revienne.

> *À l'intérieur, LA MÈRE accueille le visiteur et l'invite dans sa chambre. Cette visite est désillusionnée. Ils essaient de faire l'amour, mais LA MÈRE est épuisée, elle est arrêtée dans ses élans.*

> *ROSE entre dans la maison, elle veut appeler sa mère mais celle-ci n'est pas seule. Elle descend au cellier, elle enlève sa robe et se lave rageusement. En cachant sa robe dans le cellier, elle découvre les habits de son père.*

> *Le revolver.*

> *Elle entend les rires de sa mère. Elle est de glace en dedans d'elle-même.*

> *ROSE quitte le cellier, elle s'approche de la chambre de sa mère avec le revolver enveloppé dans le tissu rouge. Elle entre dans la chambre, s'arrête près du lit, braque le revolver et tire un coup de feu.*

> *Un coup de feu, le même que ROSTAND a entendu lorsque BLANCHE a disparu.*

> *Le visiteur tombe. Le sang jaillit. ROSE laisse tomber le revolver.*

ROSTAND
(le même cri que lorsque BLANCHE a disparu) B l a n c h e

ROSTAND court en direction de la maison.

Dans la Chambre

LA MÈRE
Rose?

> *ROSE réalise son geste, elle est bouleversée. Ébahie, elle regarde ses mains, ce sont elles les coupables. Ses mains paniquent.*

> *LA MÈRE comprend, le revolver vient du cellier. Le visiteur est mort.*

LA MÈRE
C'est moi Rose, que t'aurais dû abattre.

ROSE
Maman, j'ai peur!

LA MÈRE
Je veux disparaître.

ROSE
Maman, j'ai froid!

ROSE n'arrive pas à lui dire que ce n'est pas elle la coupable, mais lui.

LA MÈRE
Mon Dieu…. Pourquoi Rose?

ROSE court se cacher au cellier. LA MÈRE s'assoit, vidée, sur le bord du lit.

Souvenir de LA MÈRE.

ROSTAND arrive à la course dans la chambre; il reste coi, ne peut rien dire.

Silence.

La sonnette de la porte résonne. LA MÈRE sursaute. ROSTAND court à la porte. ROSE, au cellier est pétrifiée. Elle étreint les vêtements de son père.

La sonnette de la porte résonne de nouveau. LA MÈRE essuie désespérément les empreintes de ROSE sur le revolver. La sonnette insiste. ROSTAND ouvre et sort.

Les autorités envahissent la maison.

LA MÈRE réagit à leur présence. Elle a le revolver dans ses mains. Elle prend le blâme et devient l'accusée.

Elle sort de la chambre, de la maison.

Noir.

LA MÈRE MEURT

> *BLANCHE est là, opalescente. Elle joue seule, elle collectionne des pierres qu'elle place méticuleusement au bord de la rivière.*

> *ROSTAND s'assoit au bord de la rivière.*

> *ROSE trouve son chemin vers la chambre de sa mère mourante.*

ROSE
J'ai voulu oublier les effluves de mon enfance.
J'ai voulu étouffer les souvenirs, les enfouir dans un cachot.

> *Simultanément, LA MÈRE revient, fragile, elle porte son long jupon blanc. Elle s'assoit sur le lit, écoute ROSE.*

J'ai couvert ma honte d'un baume apaisant.

> *Pause.*

Mais les souvenirs déniés s'empilent. Pis à un moment donné y a pu de place, pis ça déborde. Tous mes souvenirs grossissent, me serrent la gorge. Pis je peux même pas crier.

> *LA MÈRE s'étend.*

T'aurais pas du prendre ma place maman. Des fois je me dit que ça pouvait pas être pire. Tu pensais que tu pouvais tout réparer, ben tu pouvais pas maman. C'était trop lourd maman, trop lourd pour moi.

(sentant la fin) Maudit maman…. Meurs pas, j'ai encore besoin de toi maman.

ROSTAND
(à BLANCHE) La rivière c'était comme un aimant pour toi, Blanche.

ROSE
Pourquoi c'est dans mes bras à moi que tu meurs maman?
Rostand qui reste en bas, pis toi c'est lui que tu veux voir.

ROSTAND
Tu disais tout le temps qu'y avait des diamants dans l'eau
pis qu'un jour tu serais riche.

ROSE
C'est moi maman, Rose. C'est moi qui est ici avec toi.
Je voulais que tu me pardonnes, *(pause)* l'entendre de ta bouche.
Je voulais te dire comment je regrette, je sais pas quoi au juste.
Je suis désolée.

Je voulais juste que tu m'entendes.

> *ROSE est agenouillée près de sa mère.*

> *LA MÈRE meurt.*

> *À ce moment-là, BLANCHE regarde vers la maison. Elle palpe délicatement son corps, s'assure que rien n'est brisé. Elle a un dernier regard pour ROSTAND. Puis, elle part. Pour toujours.*

ROSE
Pardon maman.

> *ROSE, ébranlée, sort de la chambre.*

> *Pendant que ROSE quitte la maison.*

LA MAISON
Ses oreilles apeurées
la douceur de son âme
où la vérité sommeille,
écorche son échine sensible.
Seule la violence est restée
La peur de la violence
possible,
humaine.

RETROUVAILLES

> *ROSE sort de la maison, arrive au bord de la rivière. Elle regarde ROSTAND un long moment. Il la voit.*

ROSTAND
(se lève) Rose?

ROSE
Rostand, elle est morte. *(silence)*
A l'aurait aimé ça te voir.

> *Un long moment.*

ROSTAND
Je pouvais pas.
J'aurais pas pu y parler.

ROSE
Moi non plus, Rostand.
Je pouvais pas.

ROSTAND et ROSE, ensemble, s'assoient. Chacun dans leur solitude.

<u>ÉPILOGUE</u>

LA MAISON
Des retrouvailles inespérées
Ils sont tous revenus
Se perdre et se retrouver
Leur histoire est gravée, ici.

Pause.

Le sang qui coule dans nos veines n'a pas d'âge.

Fin.